JACK BLACKMORE

THE UNTHRONGED
ORACLE

A STUDY OF THE POETRY OF LAURA RIDING

JACK BLACKMORE

THE UNTHRONGED ORACLE

A STUDY OF THE POETRY OF LAURA RIDING

MEREO
Cirencester

Mereo Books
1A The Wool Market Dyer Street Cirencester Gloucestershire GL7 2PR
An imprint of Memoirs Publishing www.mereobooks.com

The Unthronged Oracle: 978-1-86151-676-3

First published in Great Britain in 2016
by Mereo Books, an imprint of Memoirs Publishing

Copyright ©2016

Jack Blackmore has asserted his right under the Copyright Designs and Patents Act 1988 to be identified as the author of this work.

A CIP catalogue record for this book is available from the British Library.

This book is sold subject to the condition that it shall not by way of trade or otherwise be lent, resold, hired out or otherwise circulated without the publisher's prior consent in any form of binding or cover, other than that in which it is published and without a similar condition, including this condition being imposed on the subsequent purchaser.

The address for Memoirs Publishing Group Limited can be found at
www.memoirspublishing.com

The Memoirs Publishing Group Ltd Reg. No. 7834348

The Memoirs Publishing Group supports both The Forest Stewardship Council® (FSC®) and the PEFC® leading international forest-certification organisations. Our books carrying both the FSC label and the PEFC® and are printed on FSC®-certified paper. FSC® is the only forest-certification scheme supported by the leading environmental organisations including Greenpeace. Our paper procurement policy can be found at www.memoirspublishing.com/environment

Typeset in 12/18pt Bembo
by Wiltshire Associates Publisher Services Ltd. Printed and bound in Great Britain by Printondemand-Worldwide, Peterborough PE2 6XD

In memory of Kate
And for Jon and Naomi

Contents

Chapter 1	*The Collected Poems* of Laura Riding: preliminaries	1
Chapter 2	'Incarnations': to begin at the beginning	41
Chapter 3	'How Blind and Bright': the inward vision	53
Chapter 4	'The Signature': a bright illegibility of name	61
Chapter 5	'Chloe Or…': the story of Lilith	74
Chapter 6	'The Tiger': a Sleeping Beauty	87
Chapter 7	'The Rugged Black of Anger': the account of peace	110
Chapter 8	'One Self': the smile of death	124
Chapter 9	'An Ageless Brow': the woman in view	131
Chapter 10	'Come, Words, Away': words without music	140
Chapter 11	'Tale of Modernity': a cosmogony unveiled	157
Chapter 12	'Earth': the name of the place of human life	172
Chapter 13	'The Flowering Urn': the virgin sleep of Mother All	187
Chapter 14	'Poet: A Lying Word': a riposte to Arthur Rimbaud	199
Chapter 15	'After So Much Loss': how to live with what we know	239
Chapter 16	'Nothing So Far': beyond poetry	247
Chapter 17	Conclusions: a futility worth facing?	262

A Journey To Wabasso, Fl.32970, by Mark Jacobs	272
Appendix: cover text for Cassell's 1938 edition	299
Select Bibliography	300
Acknowledgements	304

Chapter 1

The *Collected Poems* of Laura Riding: preliminaries

Now is surely the time for a full-length study of the poems of Laura Riding. As I write this it is 78 years since the publication in 1938 of her *Collected Poems*, which, as it turned out, marked the end of her poetic career at the age of 37. That event was the culmination of more than seventeen years of the most intense engagement in the practice of poetry. As noted in the blurb on the back of the dustjacket, it was drawn from nine previous volumes; the first of these, *The Close Chaplet*, had been published only twelve years earlier, in 1926. Very many poems, published and unpublished, did not make it into *Collected Poems*, but the poems still occupy 477 pages.[1] The blurb is worth quoting at length, as it is no longer available except on the rare dust jacket of the 1938 edition. It without doubt was either written by or under the direction of the author:

> This impressive compilation […] reveals at full length a poet for whom it has long been difficult to find a label. We can now understand why her poems have defied conventional classification. We must read them in relation to one another to

appreciate the large coherence of thought behind them. Then, instead of assuming a mysterious personality at work in intellectual isolation, we recognize that here is a complete range of poetic experience controlled with sensitive wisdom.

We cannot, in fact, describe Laura Riding's poems as of such or such a type or tendency: rather, they set a new standard of poetic originality. They are undiluted: no politics or psychology, no religion or philosophical sentiment, no scholastic irrelevancies, no mystical or musical wantonness. This does not mean that they lack any of the graces that it is proper to expect in poetry: they have memorable beauty of phrase, serene humour, and a rich intricacy of movement that redeems the notion of 'pure poetry' from the curse put upon it by the aestheticians. They are, moreover, very consciously the work of a woman, introducing into poetry energies without which it is no more than 'a tradition of male monologue', not a living communication.

This deftly and intriguingly worded puff on the book's cover has not, to my knowledge, been quoted since its first appearance, unlike the heavyweight preface 'To the Reader' inside the volume. It is poignant with tender hopes for readership and recognition; its assertions of 'memorable beauty of phrase, serene humour, and a rich intricacy of movement' point as seldom elsewhere in her commentary on her poems to their positive beauty *as poems*, a beauty that this book will endeavour to illustrate along with an analysis of the poems' method and meaning. It also points directly, but with subtlety, to her ambition, as a woman, 'to introduce into poetry energies without which it is no more than "a tradition of male monologue", not a living communication', an ambition carried through into the post-poetic work, notably *The Telling*.[2]

Despite early expressions of admiration for Riding's poetry from respected contemporaries, including John Crowe Ransom, Robert Graves and W.H. Auden, published commentary, at least up until 1970, when she issued her *Selected Poems: In Five Sets* was sparse. As she wrote in the 1970 preface: 'Criticism of my work has on the whole been shy, with exceptions both beautiful and ugly, and tending towards irrelevancy' [...]³

That preface contained the first full account by Laura (Riding) Jackson (as she had then become) of her renunciation of poetry as a profession and of faith in it as an institution. She had written, she declared, referring to *The Telling*, 'that which I believe breaks the spell of poetry'.⁴ Ironically this renunciation coincided with something of an upsurge of interest in her poetry, prompted in part by the issuing of *Selected Poems*. Amongst some hostile responses there were respectful and thoughtful reviews from Roy Fuller and Michael Kirkham.⁵ In the case of Kirkham, who had published *The Poetry of Robert Graves* in 1969, this led on to essays in 1973 and 1974 evaluating her poetic method and achievement, comparing her work favourably to that of Graves.⁶ In 1979 Joyce Wexler published the first book to be written about Laura Riding, and the only book thus far to focus mainly upon the poems. Wexler communicates genuine belief in the excellence of the poems, and gives detailed attention to each phase of poetic development.⁷

Since then Jackson's own efforts, the commitment of certain editors and publishers to her work and the devoted advocacy of her poems by a few individuals led to new editions of *Collected Poems* in 1980 and 2001, the publication of her early poems, *First Awakenings*, in 1992, and Robert Nye's wide selection in 1994.⁸ There have been further expressions of admiration and praise for her poetry from eminent poets and authors including Ted Hughes, John Ashbery, Kenneth Rexroth and Paul Auster, although these have tended to be glancing if sometimes fulsome tributes. Illuminating accounts both of the experience of reading the poems, and of individual poems have been given in prefaces and introductions, and there have been a few good essays and appreciations, but nothing, since Wexler's little-noticed 1979 book, approaching an overall account.⁹

Accepting that this is indeed so, that her poems, if not ignored, have indeed been largely neglected – more so than those of any other major poet of the 20th century – why should it be so?

2

One reason is that the author herself gave short shrift to attempts to praise or comprehend her work which fell short of her exacting standards, and her spirit hovers with proprietorial eyes over this attempt, inevitably inadequate in some respects, to read a selection of her *Collected Poems*. She wrote, acutely and forbiddingly, in the introduction to the 1980 edition:

> [...] there would be many to carp, and, worse, even pretenders at understanding, false friends to the sense made with my words, condescenders for the distinction of not being fazed by them. There is but little in the records or environment of professional critical or otherwise special opinion of poets and poems to give heart to readers of my poems for exerting themselves to make close acquaintance with them.[10]

From early in her authorial career she resolutely resisted assimilation of her work into the 'storehouse of literature'.[11] *A Pamphlet Against Anthologies* by Riding and Graves made the case at book length against those editors who had been selecting and sometimes mutilating poems in order to anticipate the public's pleasure and to maximise sales, and against the pernicious influence they exerted on practising poets, Eliot and Yeats included. In her recent essay, 'Laura (Riding) Jackson: Against the Commodity of the Poem', Andrea Rexilius draws attention to and praises this stand.[12] That *A Pamphlet* was a necessary book is made clear by the examples adduced, such as Sir Arthur Quiller-Couch's unwarranted butchery, incredible to modern eyes, of what is perhaps Sir Thomas Wyatt's most famous and beautiful poem for the prestigious *Oxford Book of English Verse*.[13]

Although the anthology trade continues, often as crassly as before, the book was influential, and the authors, Riding in particular, had a shaping hand in Michael Roberts' *Faber Book of Modern Verse*, published first in 1936, one of the best anthologies of the century. She refused to give permission for her poems to be anthologized on any but her own terms, no doubt restricting her access to a wider audience.[14]

    She also advised against attempts to describe her work by relation of it to that of other authors. In a later letter to a student of her poetry she wrote:

> The difficulty that my poems make for many can be reduced by considering them as much as possible in relation to one another and as little as possible in comparative relation to other poetic work ... The clues are interior, for my poems. The exterior clues are only in the fact of poetry, of a poetic tradition, a creed plied with various fidelities and infidelities from ancient linguistic times.[15]

She even forbade the use of her own poetic material, published elsewhere than in *Collected Poems*, to help elucidate that work. She stipulated, right at the end of her life, in her preface to *First Awakenings: The Early Poems*, that

> [...] no use be made of it [that is, her early poetry] that would stimulate infusion of it into the published body of my poetic work – *Collected Poems,* 1938 and 1980, the self-determining canon of it. [...] Any critical historicizing over poetic texts that I excluded from the collected representation of my progression in the path of the poetic possibilities of such eloquence, any analysis of what I excluded from it in the form of entire poems or portions of poems, with particularistic dwelling on revisions, verbally minor, incidental or quantitatively substantial, with intent of 'research' for historical tracing of my work's development, would be especially destructive of apprehension of the on-and-on sense-clarification of itself that the whole achieved, kept on achieving, until it reached a term in the kind of eloquence to the service of which I dedicated it (dedicated my personal powers of eloquence).[16]

As with the advice given to the student quoted above, these injunctions must be heeded, if not absolutely complied with. The context makes it clear that Jackson had a particular case in mind where a book had 'maliciously mutilated' the story of her poetic career with 'ill-willed purpose not to see the work as a poetic whole'. My approach, as will be evident in what follows, is, as enjoined, to treat the *Collected Poems* as a whole; however, I have taken the risk, in some of the analysis in the essays that follow, of tracing the impact of changes made to individual poems. My purpose is, I believe, in the spirit of 'on-and-on sense-clarification' rather than 'a tearing apart of the body of [her] poetic work into poem-pieces for particularistic interpretation'.[17] Readers, as always, will judge for themselves.

Strictures such as these have helped create a polarization, or force-field, within which those who were, who are, 'with her' can comment, as it were, from the inside and usually 'shyly'. The rest are kept outside, on the assumption, based no doubt on her bitter experience, of their conscious or unconscious hostility to the poet, and to what are, by any measure, the large claims which she makes for her work. The author's own instructions can, therefore, be seen as creating one obstacle, inhibiting critical approach to and appreciation of her achievement as a poet; there are also others.

A second obstacle has been a personal hostility, amongst some influential critics or poetic 'rivals'. This may have been partly a reaction to the author's own resolutely high claims for her poems, which she made in a series of introductions to and commentaries on her own work, but the hostility will have been compounded by the often faint praise, and sometimes destructive criticism or outright dismissal, meted out to other poets and their poems, often contemporary poets with major reputations and influence, such as Yeats, Pound, Eliot and Auden, both by Riding herself (in *Contemporaries and Snobs*, in particular) and by Riding and Graves (in *A Survey of Modernist Poetry* and *A Pamphlet Against Anthologies*), and by Laura (Riding) Jackson in subsequent, post-poetic work.[18] There have been some honourable and generous exceptions among those of whom she was critical or whom she found unsympathetic – Edwin Muir and Roy Fuller come to mind – but on the whole they responded, understandably enough, by ignoring her publicly and sometimes disparaging her privately.

A third, historical, obstacle to an appreciation of her poetry has been that, in the past, lovers of poetry, 'plain readers' to use the words of *A Survey of Modernist Poetry*, almost invariably approached her poetry via an interest in the writing of Graves, who was better known, was a far more traditional poet, and had a more conventionally successful literary career. This perspective would prove unhelpful to an understanding of her poetry.[19] Following their break-up after 1940, Graves himself had an interest in misrepresenting the nature of the partnership and minimising his dependence upon Riding. As long ago as 1976 this misrepresentation was demonstrated by Jacobs and Clark, but the damaging effects upon her reputation have been lasting.[20] For all their long and at times almost incredibly productive partnership the actual poems of Graves and Riding are radically distinct.[21] Whereas there are many joint prose productions, including highly influential criticism, there is only one published joint poetic production, 'Midsummer Duet'. It is (in my view unhelpfully) included in Riding's *Collected Poems* but it is uncharacteristic.[22] In general an attentive reader would be unlikely to mistake any one poem of either author for that of the other, except perhaps where Graves 'borrowed' lines and ideas from his mentor.[23] Most obviously her poems (unlike those of Graves) do not conform to traditional expectations of what poems should be like. Whilst they use rhyme, rhythm and assonance, they have, as a rule, no *regular* schemes of rhyme or metre, no fixed syllabic system or pattern of assonance. In short an appreciation of the poetry of Graves is not likely to predispose one to an understanding of the poetry of Riding.

The difficulty has been exacerbated by the highly publicised fall-out from the break-up of the Riding-Graves partnership, which led perhaps inevitably, as in many such separations, to a polarization of friends and associates. In the wake of it there has been an understandable tendency for Riding's champions to sanctify her person and her work to the same degree that her detractors denigrate them. Both the denigration and the sanctification tend to diminish the whole. A result of the denigration (and to some extent the reaction of her champions against it) has been that literary interest in her has tended to be diverted onto often sensationalized biographical details, and these details in turn have had the effect, conscious or otherwise, of discrediting the person (or the motives or even the sanity of the person) behind the work.[24]

Fourthly, the highly-publicized renunciation of poetry by Laura (Riding) Jackson, which followed closely enough after the break-up of the partnership with Graves to seem, though wrongly, somehow to be associated with it, has meant that her poetry as Laura Riding has understandably been seen by many through the retrospective lens of that renunciation. Her first substantial account of the renunciation, in 1970, was thirty-two years after *Collected Poems*' first publication, in the preface to *Selected Poems*, in which she refers to *The Telling* saying: 'I have written that which I believe breaks the spell of poetry.'[25] This was followed by a number of other more or less detailed accounts, many of them gathered after her death in *The Failure of Poetry, the Promise of Language*.[26]

In fact she made it clear in the 1970 preface that she still judged her poems to be 'things of the first water as poetry' and that she had as a poet been 'looking to an eventual solution in poetry of the universal problem of how to make words fulfil the human being and the human being fulfil words'.[27] Unfortunately these statements have often been either regarded as invalidated by her renunciation of poetry or discounted as the suspect authorial egotism of a no longer practising poet. It is also the case that many of those who admire her post-poetic work were drawn to it by the religious, philosophical and linguistic elements, and did not come to the work through an interest in or love of poetry in general; for them her poetry represents a justifiably discarded stepping-stone on the way to greater things. In fact, a careful reading of her account of her renunciation makes it clear that her later poems are in themselves part of the post-poetic story, part – so long as they are taken with the post-poetic commentary – of the sequel:

> And just what is the sequel to my poems? I have written that which I believe breaks the spell of poetry; but I must be in no hurry as to that. I rest here as saying that this preface is part of the sequel: I do not agree to the representation of my poems unless […] I have leave to tell why there are no more — or an equivalent commentary is made on my behalf. With my poems and the commentary I point to the predicament in which poetry locks tongue, ear, the organs of feeling and intelligence, and even the sum of being, the soul; my poems are good illustrations of poetry,

> *and as such may be considered to be also part of the sequel.*[28]
> [Italics added]

Although she stopped writing poetry, she never ceased to regard herself as a poet, as is clear from Robert Nye's moving account of her, near the end of her life, which is endorsed by Mark Jacobs' own recollections of her in the 1970s.[29]

This leads us into the fifth reason, and the most serious and substantial reason, for the neglect of the poems: they are, in general, difficult, even extremely so. The author herself wrote, in the 1938 preface 'To the Reader':

> Not only am I aware of the effect of extreme difficulty that my poems have had for the majority of readers, but I offer voluntarily the statement that, *in one sense of difficulty*, more difficult poems would be hard to find.[30] [Italics added]

Whilst the point has to be made, it can be exaggerated. However unclear some of her poems may appear at first or second or even third reading, there are others that appear both limpid and attractive at first reading. 'The Wind Suffers' is an example of such a poem, anthologised on a number of occasions, the opening and concluding stanzas of which are quoted here:

> The wind suffers of blowing,
> The sea suffers of water,
> The fire suffers of burning,
> And I of a living name.
> * * *
> How for the wilful blood to run
> More salt-red and sweet-white?
> And how for me in my actualness
> To more shriek and more smile?

> By no other miracles,
> By the same knowing poison,
> By an improved anguish,
> By my further dying.

This poem makes a good starting point for a reader interested in the poems. For all its surface simplicity, which is reminiscent of the surface simplicity of Blake's finest lyrics, it tackles major and recurrent themes – what it is to be fully alive, the challenge of identity. It also introduces the paradox 'By my further dying' which occurs in various forms in other poems.

Another example is the exquisite short lyric 'Take Hands':

> Take hands.
> There is no love now.
> But there are hands.
> There is no joining now,
> But a joining has been
> Of the fastening of fingers
> And their opening.
> More than the clasp even, the kiss
> Speaks loneliness,
> How we dwell apart,
> And how love triumphs in this.[31]

The words 'love', 'death', 'beauty' and 'truth' frequent the poems. The poems explore the nature of being alive, of emotions, of mind, of thought and identity, of origins.

Further invitation to the world of the poems can be found in some of the opening lines, for example:

> With the face goes a mirror
> As with the mind a world. ('With the Face')

> Whole is by breaking and by mending.
> The body is a day of ruin,
> The mind, a moment of repair.
> A day is not a day of mind
> Until all lifetime is repaired despair. ('Autobiography of the Present')

It is these poems, these lines, these thoughts that bring this reader back repeatedly to the other poems, faintly or even less understood initially, their meanings gradually revealing themselves, like a developing negative, under the persistent and concentrated attention of the reader. For other readers it will be other poems, other lines.

The sixth and final reason for the neglect of the poems brings us back, in a way, to the obverse of the first, which was the author's refusal to conform to the expectations of the literary world and of society in general; her self-reliance and self-possession. The obverse of her refusal to conform is that a reading of her poems requires *us* to conform to *her* expectations. To quote again from her 1938 preface, where she returns to the question of 'difficulty':

> My poems would, indeed, be much more difficult than they have seemed if I did not in each assume the responsibility of education in the reasons of poetry as well as that of writing a poem. Because I am fully aware of the background of miseducation from which most readers come to poems, I begin every poem on the most elementary plane of understanding and proceed to the plane of poetic discovery (or uncovering) by steps which deflect the reader from false associations, false reasons for reading.[32]

The potential fruits of submission to the discipline of conforming to her expectations of a reader are eloquently described by Nye:

> For whatever reason, or for reasons beyond reason, as the words and their rhythms worked upon and then within me, I found in due course that here were not so much spells as acts of verbal *dis*enchantment, inspired unravellings of the world's riddle. Over the years since, I have never found these poems wanting in their account of how it is, essentially, with the result that now I might claim not just to believe them true but to know them truthful. Here is poetry as an articulation of the most exquisite consciousness, poetry as completely wakeful existence realised in words, with at the end of it the news that even poetry will not do. Here is work that reads the person reading it.[33]

This wonderfully echoes the post-poetic claim of the author to have written that which 'breaks the spell of poetry', *but in the poetry itself*, which will be demonstrated repeatedly in our account of the poems. But how many readers have the humility, the capability and the willingness to undertake the journey implicit in this statement? In her 1938 preface Riding spoke of the inertia that one must overcome to go to poetry, either as a writer or as a reader:

> Then as to readers: properly, the compulsion to read poems consists of reasons within the reader himself. There is something that he wants to do very much, and it can only be done in poetry. Yet in order to go to poetry he must overcome an extremely heavy inertia—as the poet also must. [...] To go to poetry is the most ambitious act of the mind, and the preliminary inertia one feels is the emotional measure of this ambition.[34]

To which she added, in 1980:

> There is but little in the records or environment of professional critical or otherwise special opinion of poets and poems to give heart to readers of my poems for exerting themselves to make close acquaintance with them. They must find heart for this largely in themselves.[35]

As a poet she has not, for all these reasons, had a wide circle of readers. One of John Milton's celebrated phrases comes to mind, one borrowed by the isolated and ignored poet and artist William Blake for a catalogue of his own paintings: 'Fit Audience find tho' few'.[36] The first three of the reasons listed are mainly historical and will, in course of time, gradually dissolve. The fourth, the tainting of the poetry by the viewing of it through the retrospective lens of the 'renunciation', has in part been addressed through some of the quotations and comments given above, and will in part be addressed by the next section of this introduction – and also incidentally in the course of the essays that follow on individual poems, in particular that on 'Poet: A Lying Word'. Addressing the fifth and sixth reasons will form the task of the remainder of the introduction, and of subsequent chapters.

3

Some, if not most, of the grounds of the later renunciation are entirely consistent with a fairly early account of poetry, of her view of poetry, in *Anarchism Is Not Enough* that Riding published in 1928, when still a practising and devout poet. There are several pithy pieces relating directly and specifically to poetry in the book including 'What is a Poem?' The most substantial is the section entitled 'Poetry and Music'.[37] In this she attacks and demolishes false critical analogies between poetry and music. I am unable to resist quoting the first of the six itemised contrasts between poetry and music, outrageous and offensive and comical as it is:

> All real musicians are physically misshapen as a result of platform cozening of their audience. They need never have stood upon a platform: there is a kind of ingratiating 'come, come, dear puss' in the musical brain that distorts the face and puckers up the limbs. All real poets are physically upright and even beautiful from indifference to community hearings.

Reading this today, the self-congratulatory atmosphere of the Proms is unavoidably conjured up. It gives us an insight into the savage and potentially cruel humour of Laura Riding.[38] Unfortunately the passage is so facetious that many may have failed to read further.

From the third contrast between music and poetry we get a passage foreshadowing the post-poetic account of craft in her 1970 preface:

> Rhyme and rhythm are not professional properties; they are fundamentally idiosyncratic, unavailable, unsystematizable; any formalisation of them is an attempted imitation of music by poets jealous of the public success of music.

This criticism would wipe out of consideration whole schools of poetry, and would not leave Graves unscathed. In the core essay of *Anarchism*, 'Jocasta', she breaks off from her wider analysis to expand upon her analysis of rhythm and, incidentally, to subvert accepted views of metre, of creativity, and of the very nature of poetry and prose:

> The purpose of poetry is to destroy all that prose formally represents. [...] Metre is an attempt to soften the economy and narrowness requisite in poetry; it is only likely to cause, and in the main has caused, only a more fancy, mannered prose than prose; to misrepresent the nature of restraint and limitation in poetry. The end of poetry is to leave everything as pure and bare as possible after its operation. [...]
>
> Rhythm in poetry is therefore a deadly hammer, hammer away in which each word is accented. [...] Poetry is personal, prosaic. Prose is social, dressed out in verbal amenities, poetic.[39]

To return to 'Poetry and Music', from the fourth contrast there is the following passage:

> Music is an instrument for arousing emotions. [...] Poetry is not an instrument and is not written with the intention of arousing

emotions – unless it is of a hybrid musico-poetical breed. *The end of poetry is not to create a physical condition which shall give pleasure to the mind. It appeals to an energy in which no distinction exists between physical and mental conditions.* [...] Music appeals to the intellectual disorganization and weakness of people in numbers. [...] *The end of poetry is not an after-effect, not a pleasurable memory of itself, but an immediate, constant and even unpleasant insistence on itself; indeed it has no end.* [Italics added]

This is a most serious, and challenging, criticism, from which few poems or poets are immune, including Shakespeare, as she remarked earlier in the piece:

> In this sense Beaumont and Fletcher were greater artists than Shakespeare – better musicians. Shakespeare alternated between musical surrenders to social prestige and magnificent fits of poetic remorse.

She continues her criticism in the fifth contrast:

> There is an entertaining short-story variety in music; a repellent, austere monotony in poetry. *Poetry brings all possible experience to the same degree: a degree in the consciousness beyond which the consciousness itself cannot go.* Poetry is defeat, the end which is not an end but a stopping-short because it is impossible to go further; it makes mad; it is the absolutism of dissatisfaction. [Italics added]

The reference to consciousness is crucial to what distinguishes Riding from most other poets. The reference to defeat, and to stopping-short, is exactly what Laura (Riding) Jackson later identified as the failure of poetry – here acknowledged at the height of her career as a practising poet (with the difference that she could not at this point identify the way forward). It is interesting that the reference to defeat (if not the stopping-short) echoes too the concluding sentences of her first poetic credo:

> By taking the universe apart he [the new romantic poet] will have reintegrated it with his own poetic vitality; and it is this reintegrated universe that will in turn possess him and give him rest. If this voyage reveals a futility it is a futility worth facing.[40]

The final phrase 'a futility worth facing' could make an apt if downbeat title for this current work on her poems.

Finally, the sixth contrast between music and poetry concludes:

> Music disintegrates and therefore seems active, fruitful, extensive, enlarging. Poetry isolates all loose independencies and then integrates them into one close independency which, when complete, has nothing to do but confront itself. Poetry therefore seems idle, sterile, narrow, destroying. And it is. This is what recommends it.[41]

The poetry referred to in all these passages must, of course, be primarily that of Laura Riding herself, and nobody else. As Wordsworth put it, in his preface to the *Lyrical Ballads*, with no lack of prefatory egotism on his own part:

> Every great and original writer, in proportion as he is great and original, must himself create the taste by which he is to be relished.

Riding cannot be accused of neglecting this task. On her own account she wrote, during the course of her poetic career, in order of first publication: 'A Prophecy or a Plea' (1925), *Contemporaries and Snobs* (1928), *Anarchism*

Is Not Enough (1928), the long 'Preface' to *Poems: A Joking Word* (1930), and the closely-argued preface 'To the Reader' in *Collected Poems* (1938). In addition, with Robert Graves, she wrote *A Survey of Modernist Poetry* (1927), *A Pamphlet against Anthologies* (1928) and a substantial essay, 'Poems and Poets' in *Epilogue* (1935).[42]

As noted above the crux of the criticism in 'Poetry and Music', which distinguishes her categorically (or at least consistently) from other poets and critics, is the rejection of poetry designed to have emotional impact and the promotion of poetry of consciousness. The rejection of poetry constrained by sensibility is far more radically expressed in her own writing than in the joint productions with Graves. In this context it is relevant to quote Alan Clark, a long-standing advocate of both the poems and the post-poetic work:

> Laura Riding's own early criticism, including *A Survey of Modernist Poetry*, by Laura Riding and Robert Graves (1927), provided kernels from which husky critical schools have grown: it is sad if those and other schools' scope of critical expectation has narrowed to a training in alertness for alterations in sensibility, an incapacity to recognise actual advance in consciousness.[43]

For the most part *A Survey* does indeed function as a primer for the development of poetic sensibility, for example in the penetrating and sympathetic analyses of works by e.e. cummings, John Crowe Ransom and Gerard Manley Hopkins, to say nothing of destructive criticism of many other celebrated poets past and (at that time) present. However, with the exception of the brilliant dissection of Shakespeare's Sonnet 129, about which we say a good deal more in chapters 6, 7 and 11, it stopped short of identifying actual advance in consciousness as the defining achievement of poetry.

It is possible, then, to appreciate some of the quality of Riding's poems against conventional standards, as the initial introduction to this account, makes clear. But if one is to go further, then one has to be prepared to recognise a new standard, and to be ready for the unpleasantness and destruction referred to in the passages quoted above from *Anarchism Is Not*

Enough, the unpleasantness and destruction associated with the challenge to one's assumptions and the sometimes painful growth of one's own consciousness. In this context the unlikely figure of T.S. Eliot (so often the butt of Riding's criticism) [44] comes to mind, writing of Blake in an essay in *The Sacred Wood*:

> It is merely a peculiar honesty, which, in a world too frightened to be honest, is peculiarly terrifying. It is an honesty against which the world conspires, because it is unpleasant. Blake's poetry has the unpleasantness of great poetry. Nothing that can be called morbid or abnormal or perverse, none of the things which exemplify the sickness of an epoch or a fashion, have this quality; only those things which, by some extraordinary labour of simplification, exhibit the essential sickness or strength of the human soul.[45]

The case of Blake as described by Eliot provides a parallel of sorts. In some cases it is difficult for us to accommodate great poets because they confront us with truths about ourselves, and also about themselves, and about the world, which make us uncomfortable and frightened. And this is why it is worth attempting to understand the work.

4

Riding's views on what makes a good poet are as clear, as bold and as original as her views on what makes for good poetry. In her very first published poetic credo, 'A Prophecy or a Plea', she overturned the tradition of poetry as a catharsis, as a response to experience, to living. Sardonically she summed the tradition up before dismissing it:

> Living is the inspiration, art is the expiration. As such it is critical rather than creative, a criticism of life rather than a recreation of it. Even so radical a poet as T.S. Eliot becomes, as a critic,

thoughtfully traditional. Of two artists, he says, the one who is the better critic is likely to be the better artist. In other words, life takes precedence over art which is, as of old, the recollection in tranquillity.

She proposed instead new poets:

> They will be egoists and romanticists all, but romantics with the courage of realism: they will put their hands upon the mysterious contour of life not to force meaning out of it, since unrelated to them it must be essentially meaningless to them, but press meaning upon it, outstare the stony countenance of it, make it flush with their own colors. [...]
> But these [even the better contemporary poets] nevertheless are still worshipping that old god, Experience: it is all there somewhere in life, the truth, you must only let life flow over you, inundate you, and it will leave behind with you the fine sediment of proper feeling. Here is the apotheosis of inertia. You are clay, life is a potter, it is very wonderful. [...] But who has ever learned anything from experience? We get nothing from it, we give everything to it. Development comes through self-exercise, not through being hammered upon.

She described 'the poet of the new spiritual activity' as the potter, reversing the process described above, of life as the potter:

> He is the maker of beauty, since all form originates in him, and of meaning, since he names the content. Life is create with him. [...] Confronted by a terrifying, absorbing, fascinating universe, it [the life create with him] does not cry out: 'How big, how terrifying, how fascinating!' and permit itself to be overcome by it, but answers it, since this universe, a thing apart, can be answered in no other way, atom for atom in a recreated universe of its own, a

> universe defiantly intelligible. [...] If the music will at first seem harsher than older tunes, it is because the new poet must be endowed with the ruthlessness of a pioneer. [...] He will be rude as a violator because he must advance alone, gentle as a guide, because he must get others to follow him.[46]

There is an amusing irony in this use of the masculine gender, and indeed the attribution of characteristics traditionally ascribed to men, for the new poet who in other respects may be identified closely, if not exclusively, with herself. (As I shall indicate in the essay on 'Poet: A Lying Word', the 'last-century absolutist' Rimbaud may also have been in her mind). Her essay would have made a fitting preface to her first volume of poetry, *The Close Chaplet*, in 1926, and might conceivably have increased understanding and appreciation of her work. One reason why it was not used there may be, on the evidence of *Contemporaries* and *Anarchism* (both published in 1928), that by 1926 she had already moved away from some of the language in 'A Prophecy': the use of the words 'music' and 'song' of poetry, for example, and reference to 'art' in the same breath as poetry.

One idea that remained consistent throughout her life was that good poets are 'natural', born and not constructed. This idea first occurs in her praise of Francis Thompson in 'A Prophecy':

> But if they [the new poets] are to succeed, their constitution must contain some of the elements that went to make up Frances Thompson – the magic at the start (*non murato, ma veramente nato*), the power of wonder that begets wonder, and miracle, and prophecy.[47]

The phrase in Italian comes from Vasari and means 'not built, but truly born'. The idea recurs, in relation to Rimbaud, in the first chapter of *A Survey*[48] and is repeated several times in the essay 'T.E. Hulme, the New Barbarism, & Gertrude Stein' in *Contemporaries*. Again her main target is Eliot, and his ceding of intellectual primacy to criticism, over poetry:

> As the poet, if a true poet, is one by nature and not by effort, he must be seen as writing as unconsciously (in regard to time, at any rate) as his ordinary reader lives.
>
> * * *
>
> Creative self-consciousness is a contradiction in terms; for it is clear that poets do not begin to write by effort but by nature.
>
> * * *
>
> This [blighting of the creative processes] can be well illustrated by comparing the highly organized nature of T.S. Eliot's criticism in its present stage with the gradual disintegration of his poetry since the [sic] *Waste Land*. The absolute sense of authorship has been lost and the poet finds himself counting only as he can be related to the historical period to which he accidentally belongs.[49]

There is more to be said about these ideas in the chapters on the poems.

Her approach to poetry has no allegiances with 'modernist' poets, but there are affinities with the personal radicalism, risk-taking and commitment of some of the English poets of the late 18th and early 19th century – with Shelley (evident in her early work) and with Coleridge and Blake. The affinities vary, but there is a common optimism and conviction: that one's self, one self, through the most intense scrutiny of and engagement with language and life, can take the measure of the universe:

> The Poet is not only the man who is made to solve the riddle of the Universe, but he is also the man who feels where it is not solved and which continually awakens his feelings [...] (Coleridge, Lecture on Poetry, 12 December 1811.)

5

We return in this section to the question of difficulty: what is it exactly that makes Riding's poems so difficult, as in the main they are? Her own comments on this issue do not take us very far, or perhaps we should say they do not make understanding much easier, and indeed commentaries by her on her own individual poems are sparse, and sometimes of limited value. During her poetic career there was only the lengthy but guarded and unyielding account in *A Survey* of 'The Rugged Black of Anger', a key poem.[50] In my view the opportunity was muffed, whether out of uncharacteristic reticence on the poet's part or possibly because the task had been delegated to Graves. Later she published a glancing but intriguing remark about 'The Mask' in the preface to *Selected Poems*, an essay length account of account of 'Lucrece and Nara', a strictly editorial note on 'Midsummer Duet' appended to later editions of *Collected Poems*, and helpful but brief comments on 'The Troubles of a Book' and 'The Quids' in a recording made in 1972.[51] That recording appears less guarded than many of her more formal commentaries. There is an illuminating paragraph in which she refers to the struggles and peculiarities pertaining to her poetic work 'past the half-way mark' to which we shall return in the section on the organization of *Collected Poems*. It is followed by a reference to one of her later poems, 'Disclaimer of the Person':

> Nowhere should I be taken as speaking by what are called 'symbols'. If, for instance, I say 'the sun which multiplied' or 'the moon which singled', as I do in one poem, I am endeavouring to indicate actualities of physical circumstance in which our inner crucialities of human circumstance are set. My moon may look like the old tired poetical symbol, and I like an old tired poetic romanticist, but I truly meant that the moon's being what it is where it is intervenes in our outer circumstances as a negator of the sun's fostering excessiveness in our regard, both lush and destructive—as a tempering counter-agency, relatively little but near. However foolishly mystical this may seem, nothing so far learned by scientists or experienced by astronauts disproves this.

This is a challenging passage – does she not appear to want to have her poetic cake and eat it too? To which the somewhat equivocal answer has to be: Yes!

In this context it will be helpful first to refer to Jacobs' brief but illuminating account of the last section of 'With the Face', beginning with his quotation from the poem:

> The mirror mixes with the eye.
> Soon will it be the very eye.
> Soon will the eye that was
> The very mirror be.
> Death, the final image, will shine
> Transparently not otherwise
> Than as the dark sun described
> With such faint brightnesses.

> The poem is the means of fusing inner and outer, what is with what is seen, self and image, and, earlier in the poem, mind and world. There is no difference, only sameness, between one's self and what one perceives, or, to put it another way, the universe, in its seeming largeness, is present in the human self, in its seeming smallness, and both are combined in a poem.[52]

This analysis is echoed in this book's chapter on another poem, 'One Self'. If one is to understand, to 'get into' the poems, there must be no avoiding the 'literal' meaning of them by reference to 'symbol' or 'metaphor'. What we have here is a cosmology, an ordering of the universe, in language, by one's self.

Another source of difficulty, and one for which the poet must take an often gleeful responsibility, is the use of contradiction and paradox. She frequently creates images only to undermine or detonate them within the unravelling syntax. For example, in 'The Rugged Black of Anger', the title itself sets up an expectation of some sort of outburst which both comes and goes simultaneously in the lines:

> This is the account of peace,
> Why the rugged black of anger
> Has an uncertain smile-border,

> Why crashing glass does not announce
> The monstrous petal-advance of flowers

You both have, and do not have, and in the end you do not have crashing glass and monstrous petal-advance – because here you are in the ordered world of the poet, where anarchism is not enough.

Another example is in the later, studiedly rebarbative poem 'The Signs of Knowledge', the opening stanzas of which are:

> Not by water, fire or flesh
> Does the world have that end
> Which have it must in being, having been,
> A world so privileged to begin
> And long increase of self to spin,
> And long outspinning, spinning out
> To end of thread to have—
>
> Not by water, fire or flesh,
> Not by drinking back of self,
> Not by flaming up of self,
> Not by lavish plague to lie down
> Sainted, rotted, rendered—
>
> By words the world has end,
> By words which brought
> From first articulation, wordless stir,
> To the last throbbing phrases.

All our attention is on the grotesque (albeit simultaneously negated) possibilities of a medieval Last Judgement, climaxing in the ghastly, pungent 'Sainted, rotted, rendered', before being brought to a quiet cancellation: 'By words the world has end'. 'The Signs of Knowledge' is a good example of an entire long poem that systematically 'clears the decks', with a proliferation of deliberately ugly negatives and compound neologisms, in order to leave an empty space for truth to slip into. This is dealt with at greater length in the chapter on 'Poet: A Lying Word'.

Riding delights in paradox and subversion, both at the macro level, as in her account of what a poet should be, and at the micro level of the individual poem. An example of this is given in the chapter on 'The Tiger', where we discover, hidden (well hidden) in plain view, an allusion to the tale of the Sleeping Beauty that subverts, by implication, the apparent ignorance, sadness and desolation of the heroine at the poem's ending. The subversion is serious, deadly serious, but it is also gleeful, full of playful energy. She herself repeatedly (as in the puff quoted at the beginning of this introduction) asserts her 'serene humour', her good cheer, although this feature is seldom acknowledged by commentators, irritated and frustrated as they may be by her riddling, paradoxical and contradictory poems, and by her fierce and scornful responses to most criticism. The ordering of the universe by herself is simultaneously childlike and godlike, and the humour likewise.

6

No account of the 'difficulty' posed by the poems would be complete without reference to her use of words. In her 1980 preface she quotes with evident approval two reviewers of the 1938 edition: John Holmes and the man she was later to meet and marry, Schuyler B. Jackson. The first said: 'She refreshes one's understanding of the plainest words, so providing excitement of a rare sort in poetry.' The second, she says, 'having commented that I wrote "in a language in which every word carries its full literate meaning" let the cat of future trouble out of the bag with: "For this reason language that would seem clear in Shakespeare or Mother Goose may seem obscure in Laura Riding".'[53]

This is not so simple, although our quotations from some poems (in section 2) above show how transparent her lines can appear. The difficulties are indicated in a passage in *Anarchism Is Not Enough*:

> Words have three historical levels. They may be true words, that
> is, of an intrinsic sense; they may be logical words, that is of an
> applied sense; or they may be poetical words, of a misapplied
> sense, untrue and illogical in themselves, but of supposed
> suggestive power. The most the poet can now do is to take every
> word he uses through each of these levels, giving it the combined
> depth of all three, forcing it beyond itself to a death of sense where
> it is at least safe from the perjuries either of society or poetry.[54]

As Jacobs points out, in his preface to the 2001 edition, the problem is not that of difficulty in the sense of obscurity or obfuscation but primarily that of complexity or of unfamiliarity of thought – to which I would add the apparent contradictoriness wherein the meanings of a plain word such as 'death' or 'ghost' (in a 'poetical' way, in a 'misapplied' sense) can be used to mean, or sometimes, more accurately, to include in its meaning, the reverse of, or at least something very different from the 'intrinsic' or the 'applied' sense. This approach to poetic language is consistent with the analysis and appreciation by Riding (with Graves) of the virtuous complexity of Shakespeare's Sonnet 129. In the chapters on 'The Rugged Black of Anger' and 'Tale of Modernity' we go further into what Riding (with Graves) was saying about that sonnet and relate that to both the meaning of her poems and her poetic method.

In itself, of course, there is nothing exceptional in a poet developing or uncovering meanings in words, in this way. One unobtrusive example in her own poem, 'Poet: A Lying Word', is the use of the word 'elliptic' in the fourteenth paragraph:

> This body-self, this wall, this poet-like address, is the last barrier
> long shied of in your elliptic changes

The word 'elliptic' *derives from* the Greek for falling short, deficient (as can be seen in the normal meaning of 'ellipsis' in a grammatical sense) but is normally *used* in English only to describe an oval movement as of the orbit of the planets around a centre of gravity – a centre of gravity like the poet herself in this instance. The word, with justified originality, carries both senses here, referring to readers forever orbiting and falling short of the poet. This sensitivity, this aliveness to words and their origins, prompts an unwonted comparison with John Milton, specifically the poet of *Paradise Lost*. Milton was forever enriching the meaning of his words with reference to their origins in this way.

The comparison is unwonted because Milton, by contrast with Riding's theory of poetry, is noted for his 'music', the crafting of his sound and his rhythm. Christopher Ricks, in characterising his creative procedure (in the process of exploring why Milton's metaphors are much less satisfactory than his similes) describes it in terms suggestive of 'not born but truly builded', reversing Vasari's phrase, a poet of will, not a poet by nature:

> His true poetry is created out of ancient materials, as in a foundry
> – not spun out of his own entrails, as by a spider.[55]

If we pursue the comparison for its likenesses as opposed to its contrasts, can we not see Laura Riding *both* as a poet of will (and of effort, to use her term, in contradiction) *and* as a poet by nature, one who often simultaneously spins out of her own entrails whilst creating out of ancient materials? A good example of this is in both the meaning and the process of the poem 'Incarnations' which begins with the simplest words:

> Do not deny,
> Do not deny, thing out of thing.
> Do not deny in the new vanity
> The old, original dust.

However, these plain words can only be fully understood by reference to the work that (together with Shakespeare) largely created English, namely the King James Bible (the work of a committee, but based substantially, we know

now, on the work of William Tyndale). One understanding of the 'dust' in this poem could be that it refers to the stardust resulting from the physical origins of the outward universe. But, as we argue in our essay on that poem, it is essential to include in the meaning here the 'dust' from which Adam was created, incarnated by God. Of course, Riding is engaged in her own creation, is herself the potter, and her own story will be radically different from either that of astronomy or the Bible, but an understanding of what she is about is enriched by an appreciation of that background. For her own meaning, her own religious purposes, she is obliged (and happy) to use the old original language of English created by Tyndale and King James' committee, but in doing so she 'refreshes the meaning of the plainest words'. The essential companion for a reader of the poems, other than (as she advises) the other poems in her collection, is the full Oxford English Dictionary, another product of a committee, of which she owned an edition, as noted by Jacobs in his memoir.

7

The comparison with the Milton of *Paradise Lost* provokes another suggestion, a way of viewing the *Collected Poems*. It is clear from the author's advice quoted in section 2 above that she viewed *Collected Poems* as the 'self-determining canon' of her work, and that readers should consider the poems as much as possible in relation to one another and as little as possible in comparative relation to other poetic work: 'The clues are interior for my poems'. In some respects *Collected Poems* as a whole qualifies as a single epic poem.

In the first place, perhaps serendipitously, the word 'epic' itself derives from the Greek for 'word', 'generally that which is uttered in words, speech, tale'.[56] It is hardly necessary to stress that the unbroken thread through her poetic and post-poetic career, from the poems to the dictionary project, was a belief in words and a quest to find 'how to make words fulfil the human being and the human being fulfil words.'[57] In a sense *Collected Poems* can be viewed as the forerunner in poetry of the long-gestated dictionary project which succeeded it as the focus of the author's devoted care for the remainder of her life.[58]

Linking this first point with our second is another comment from the preface to her *Selected Poems*: 'For me the essence of the adventure was in the words.' The idea of 'adventure' introduced here is also a characteristic of the epic. She refers here as elsewhere to the *story*, one which she was anxious would be curtailed in a briefer selection: 'so much curtailment of the story that the *Poems* tells makes all go too fast.'[59] *Collected Poems* is of course a 'collection', but it is an exceptionally highly organised collection, containing, in her words, 'a complete range of poetic experience':

> I am going to give you poems written for all the reasons of poetry –poems which are also a record of how, by gradual integration of the reasons of poetry, existence in poetry becomes more real than existence in time—more real because more good, more good because more true.[60]

The adventure is of the nature of a *quest*. To borrow the words of John Keats, (to which she refers approvingly in 'Addendum' to *The Telling*), 'The World is the Vale of Soul-Making' and that is a fair summary of what she was about.[61]

This brings us to the third point of likeness with epic poetry. Epic poetry, thinking of the rare successful epics such as *The Iliad*, *The Divine Comedy* or *Paradise Lost*, has to be supremely *organised* and *selective* and internally *consistent*: epic poems create, or to use Riding's word from the 1938 'Preface', they 'uncover' a world. In a way the 'collected' of the title *Collected Poems* is misleading.[62] The main body of the work is not divided up into types of poem – narrative, lyrical, reflective, sonnets, elegies – which is one accepted method of organising collections. Nor is the order strictly chronological, which is the other main way of arranging collections. Although she says in the 1938 preface that the book 'begins with her earliest poems, and its arrangement corresponds with the development of my poetic activity' the second part of that statement is more exact than the first.[63] It is, rather, divided into sections entitled 'Poems of Mythical Occasion', 'Poems of Immediate Occasion', 'Poems of Final Occasion' and 'Poems Continual'.

The organization is clearly designed to represent a progression corresponding, as she says, with the development of her poetic activity; in that sense she could have adapted her title from that of her book of stories, *A Progress of Stories*, to become *A Progress of Poems*. The main division in *Collected Poems* is around the point where 'Poems of Final Occasion begin'.[64] This is, I believe, 'the half-way mark' that Laura (Riding) Jackson was alluding to in her 1972 recording:

> Past the half-way mark, historically, in my poems, and up to the last phase, I am much preoccupied with the effort to make personally explicit the identity of myself poet and myself one moved to try to speak with voiced consciousness of the linguistic and human unities of speaking: I am restive insofar as this identity is only an implicit principle in my poetic speaking. There is also at work at the same time an effort to intensify in specificness the comprehensive reference I intended generally that my poems should have. *The two heightened impulses, working to bring within the poetic frame an explicitness and a specificness that it cannot contain and to which it cannot expand, produced within the poems themselves a struggle between compression and completeness of utterance.* I cannot briefly make the explanation of the peculiarities of this phase easier.[65] [Italics added]

The half-way mark is clear in the sequence of her published poetry, and the mark is the publication of *Poet: A Lying Word* in 1933. All but one of the poems in that, her penultimate collection, again highly organized, were selected for *Collected Poems*; three were placed towards the end of 'Immediate Occasion' the rest made up the entire 'Poems of Final Occasion' with the solitary addition of the last poem, previously published separately, 'Disclaimer of the Person'.

The nature of the break between the earlier and the later work, described so eloquently in the 1972 recording, is in the nature of a category shift. It helps explain why I (in common with others) have found it difficult to progress with my account of the poems beyond those of 'Immediate Occasion'. As the essays have progressed it became clear how the cosmology and biblical language and references that become overt in the more discursive later poems were frequently implicit, if not at all obvious, in the more compact earlier work. It is no accident, but so far as I know it has never before been remarked, that the main body of *Collected Poems*, which begins with the secret nativity of 'Forgotten Girlhood' and 'Incarnations' ends with 'Christmas 1937', with overt references to Jehovah, Jesus, the Woman and the Virgin.

The chapter on 'Tale of Modernity' gives an example of the degree of caution and care shown by this most radical poet in her delay of the unveiling of her cosmology in relation to 'the moon', even though the ideas had been in her thought early in the poems. In that poem she wrote:

> Shakespeare distinguished: earth the obscure,
> The sun the bold, the moon the hidden –
> The sun speechless, earth a muttering,
> The moon a whispering, white, smothered.

These lines begin the unveiling of elements of a cosmology: earth, sun, moon, but each with quasi-human attributes rather than astronomical ones. What are we to make of this passage? In 'Disclaimer of the Person', the last poem in 'Poems of Final Occasion', the poet wrote:

> I am not the sun which multiplied,
> I am the moon which singled. [66]

Referring to these lines Laura (Riding) Jackson said in 1972, in a passage quoted in section 5 above, but repeated here to make a new point:

> Nowhere should I be taken as speaking by what are called 'symbols'. If, for instance, I say 'the sun which multiplied' or 'the

> moon which singled' as I do in one poem *I am endeavouring to indicate actualities of physical circumstance in which our inner crucialities of human circumstance are set.* My moon may look like the old tired poetical symbol, and I like an old tired poetic romanticist, but I truly meant that the moon's being what it is where it is intervenes in our outer circumstances as a negator of the sun's fostering excessiveness in our regard, both lush and destructive—as a tempering counter-agency, relatively little but near.[67] [Italics added]

It is my impression that the poet took a calculated risk in unveiling this cosmology in 'Tale of Modernity', a risk perhaps offset initially by its attribution to 'Shakespeare'. The risk is, as the author admits, that she may be seen as an old tired poetic romanticist. She was wary of offering any point of attack to her critics.

Going back through the poems up to this point there are poems, such as 'How Blind and Bright' and 'Echoes 5' where it would have been natural to refer to the moon in contrast to the 'sun' – which appeared clearly in relation to man (as opposed to woman). Other than in the opening poem-sequence, 'Forgotten Girlhood', there are no references to the moon or Moon. There the references are smuggled in innocently under the guise of nursery rhyme, of Mother Goose, in 'All the Way Back':

> Come in, come in
> Same old pot and wooden spoon
> But it's only soup staring up at the moon.
> One, two, three,
>
> Mother and Moon and Old Trouble and me.
> How happy we'll be
> Together and all raggedy.
> I'm not a full yard,
> Old Trouble's not a full inch,

> The moon's a hole
> And mother's a pinch.[68]

Once the 'moon' has been unveiled in 'Tale of Modernity', it begins to appear regularly in the subsequent poems.[69] It is consistently set in contrast with the sun, as in the following passages; first from 'The Dilemmist' addressed to men:

> How long will the careless sun make warm
> While you go a-wintering with fancy—
> The moon adoring with sun-given eyes?

And then from 'The Reasons of Each':

> Or as to watch the sun's purposeful clouds
> Mingle with moonlight and be nothing.[70]

Particularly relevant is the following passage from the poem that precedes the title poem in *Poet: A Lying Word* (as it does also in *Collected Poems*), 'The Signs of Knowledge':

> The first sign of the two signs
> Shall be unlove of the sun.
> The second sign of the two signs
> Shall be unlife of the earth.
> And the first with the second sign locked
> Shall be undeath of the moon.[71]

But to complete the 'progress' of the poet's use of the moon we return to the poem which began the exercise, 'Disclaimer of the Person':

> I am a woman.
> I am not the sun which multiplied,

> I am the moon which singled.
> I am not the moon but a singling. I am I.[72]

So the poet is not the moon after all, but the word has perhaps been taken through each of its levels to 'a death of sense where it is at least safe from the perjuries either of society or poetry'.

8

Each of the chapters that follow is focused on a particular poem from *Collected Poems*, beginning with the full text of the poem in view. There is no consistent format, but in most instances the essays begin with an overview, including an appreciation of what might be called the more traditional poetic qualities, such as 'beauty of phrasing' and 'intricacy of movement', to quote the original blurb, and how the poems work *as poems*. The analysis then follows the poem line by line, stanza by stanza, trying to follow the author's advice by 'considering [the poems] as much as possible in relation to one another and as little as possible in comparative relation to other poetic work'.

It has though been impossible, it would be self-denying, to resist the invitation to explore connections the author herself makes, for example with Shakespeare in 'Tale of Modernity' and Blake in 'The Tiger', but there are other less explicit references, a glancing response to Emily Dickinson, for example in 'Chloe Or ...' and a more substantial response, or riposte, to Rimbaud in 'Poet: A Lying Word'. The *contrast* with other poetic work is often more relevant and illuminating than any likeness.

The author's own critical theories have been adduced where appropriate. The essay on 'The Tiger', for example, which is the first of the longer poems analysed, draws on *A Survey*'s chapter 'The Problem of Form and Subject-Matter' for its account of how parallelism and the recurrence of ideas and phrases in varying alternations can sustain a longer poem more effectively than a regular metre. The idea is applied to other poems as a simple but helpful way of appreciating the author's method of 'well-controlled irregularity'.

PRELIMINARIES

The essays on the poems have been written with a view to each standing largely on its own, so that the reader can begin at any point, singling out a poem of particular or personal interest. The notes have been set out accordingly, with references beginning afresh in each essay. However, the essays are also intended to progress, along with the poems, with the poet's words and ideas rippling out and connecting as they are uncovered, creating a cumulative impact.

NOTES

[1] Laura Riding, *First Awakenings: the Early Poems* (Manchester: Carcanet, 1992) devoted 268 pages to poems not included in *Collected Poems*. None of these had appeared in the nine published books prior to *Collected Poems*, and many of the poems in those books were also not selected for *Collected Poems*. This gives some idea of Laura Riding's intense poetic productivity.

[2] Laura (Riding) Jackson, *The Telling* (London: Athlone Press, 1972).

[3] Laura (Riding) Jackson, *Selected Poems: In Five Sets* (London: Faber 1970), 16. The best source for commentary and criticism of Riding's poetry up to 1980 is Joyce Piell Wexler's *Laura Riding: A Bibliography* (New York: Garland Publishing, 1981).

[4] Laura (Riding) Jackson, *Selected Poems*, 1970, 15.

[5] Roy Fuller, 'The White Goddess', *The Review*, 23 (1970), 3-9; Michael Kirkham, 'Laura Riding's Poems', *The Cambridge Quarterly*, 5 (Spring, 1971), 302-308.

[6] Michael Kirkham 'Robert Graves's Debt to Laura Riding', *Focus on Robert Graves*, Number 3, December 1973 (Boulder Colorado: University of Colorado Library); and it is surprising that Kirkham, who clearly had a good understanding of Riding's poetry and thought, as evidenced in his references to her poems, did not go through the door he had opened in this essay to a fuller account of Riding's poetry, although he did revise his account further in 'Laura (Riding) Jackson', *Chelsea*, 33 (September, 1974), 140-150.

[7] Joyce Piell Wexler, *Laura Riding's Pursuit of Truth* (Athens, Ohio: Ohio University Press, 1979). Wexler's account is 'an examination of her work in relation to her personal life and the literary and social environment of the modernist period', and about a hundred of the 160 pages are devoted to a study of the poems themselves.

Wexler doesn't hover 'shyly' around the edge of the work as many have. The strengths of the book are in its communication of genuine belief in the excellence of the poems; the detailed progress through the published work, giving attention to each phase (in particular the pioneering attention she devotes to *Love as Love, Death as Death, Laura and Francisca*, and 'Poems Continual'); and a detailed knowledge of the work and its context, as befits her role as bibliographer. The main weaknesses seem to me to be an over-reliance on others' accounts in respect of the biography, and the systematic interweaving of the biographical and critical elements in her own 'pursuit' of psychological explanations. These aspects would have been anathema to Laura (Riding) Jackson who broke communication with her when Wexler refused to alter her work in response to criticism.

[8] Thinking here of Sonia Raiziss, editor of *Chelsea*, of Persea Books and of Michael Schmidt's Carcanet.

[9] Robert Nye, 'Introduction', *A Selection of the Poems of Laura Riding* (Manchester: Carcanet, 1994) 1-8; Mark Jacobs, 'Preface to the Collected Poems', *The Poems of Laura Riding* (New York: Persea Books, 2001), xvii– xxviii. As to essays, good examples are: Alan J. Clark, 'Where Poetry Ends', *PN Review* no 22 (1981), 26-28, and Andrea Rexilius, 'Laura (Riding) Jackson: Against the Commodity of the Poem', made available in 2014 in the 'essays' section on the Laura (Riding) Jackson website, Nottingham Trent University. The most substantial essay to date on the poems is that by Mark Jacobs, 'Rewriting History, Literally: Laura Riding's *The Close Chaplet*', *Gravesiana* - Volume 3, Number 3, Summer 2012.

[10] Laura Riding, *Collected Poems* (Manchester: Carcanet, 1980), 12-13; reprinted in the centenary edition (New York: Persea, 2001): xliv.

[11] A phrase adapted from a passage in Laura Riding, *Anarchism Is Not Enough* (London: Cape, 1928), 18.

[12] See note 9 above.

[13] Laura Riding and Robert Graves, *A Pamphlet Against Anthologies,* first published in 1928, reprinted together with *A Survey of Modernist Poetry* (Manchester: Carcanet, 2002). The reference to Quiller-Couch and Wyatt's poem is made on pp180-181 of the reprinted edition.

[14] Not that this always prevented anthologists going ahead without her permission.

[15] From a letter to Mark Jacobs, June 21, 1973, available in the Nottingham Trent University archive.

[16] *First Awakenings* (1992) 'Author's Preface', xv.

[17] *First Awakenings*, xvi.

[18] Laura Riding, *Contemporaries and Snobs*, (London, Cape 1928); Laura Riding and Robert Graves, *A Survey of Modernist Poetry*, (London: Heinemann, 1927) and *A Pamphlet Against Anthologies*, (London: Garden City, 1928). There are examples scattered through the post-poetic work, although the comments tend to be less harsh than some of those in the earlier criticism. A sample is gathered in *Part IV*, "On Other Poets", in Laura (Riding) Jackson, *The Failure of Poetry, The Promise of Language*, edited by John Nolan, (University of Michigan, 2007), 197-212. There are also comments in Volume Two of Laura (Riding) Jackson, *The Person I Am*, edited by John Nolan and Carroll Ann Friedmann, (Nottingham: Trent Editions 2007).

[19] This approach via Graves is now perhaps less the case, when Mrs Jackson's work is becoming better known and appreciated, but then the approach to her poetry tends to be via the post-renunciatory prose, which has its own impact, as outlined in the next 'obstacle'.

[20] Mark Jacobs and Alan J. Clark, 'The Question of Bias: Some Treatments of Laura (Riding) Jackson', *Hiroshima Studies in English Language and Literature*, Vol. 21, Nos. 1 and 2, 1976; http://www.ntu.ac.uk/laura_riding/scholars/58471gp.html. (Accessed 18 August 2015.)

[21] At least one contemporary commentator was astute enough to highlight the contrasting styles of the two collaborators. The novelist Arnold Bennett, in a mixed if mainly irritated review of *Contemporaries and Snobs* on 1 March 1928 wondered sardonically: 'I should love to know what Miss Riding thinks of the admirable but sadly un-modernist poetry of her collaborator'. Quoted by Joyce Wexler in *Laura Riding: A Bibliography* (London: Garland, 1981), 119.

[22] There is an explanatory note on how the poem came about, the roles of each partner in the production, and why it was included in Riding's collection in the 2001 edition of the *Collected Poems*, 479. The poem was also eventually reprinted in *Robert Graves: Complete Poems*, edited by Beryl Graves and Dunstan Ward (Carcanet, 1999).

[23] I must draw attention here to Michael Kirkham's essay 'Robert Graves's Debt to Laura Riding', *Focus on Robert Graves*, Number 3, December 1973 (Boulder Colorado: University of Colorado Library). He concludes:

It is notable that, despite his heavy reliance on the content and style of her work, he never ceased to be a very different poet from her. The difference in their relation to a common body of thought (hers) is, it seems to me, the difference between a major and a minor poet. [...] The difference between Graves and Laura Riding illustrates, then, one distinction that exists between some minor and some major poetry. Where Graves's poetry is subjective in the sense that it reduces themes of potentially general significance to the narrow compass of a personal situation, Laura Riding's poetry expands the personal situation to include the suprapersonal.

This was courageous revisionism by Kirkham, only four years after his *The Poetry of Robert Graves* (London: University of London, The Athlone Press, 1969).

[24] You could say that, unlike Helen, in Riding's poem *Helen's Faces*, sensationalism, as well as contest and bitterness 'raged around her'. Elizabeth Friedmann's fair-minded and level-headed biography is an antidote: *A Mannered Grace* (New York: Persea, 2005).

[25] 'Preface' to *Selected Poems: In Five Sets*, 15.

[26] Edited by John Nolan, University of Michigan Press, 2007.

[27] 'Preface' to *Selected Poems* (1970): quotes from pages 16 and 15 respectively.

[28] *Selected Poems* (1970), 15-16.

[29] Robert Nye, 'Introduction', *A Selection of the Poems of Laura Riding* (Carcanet, 1994), 7.

[30] Laura Riding, *Collected Poems* (London: Cassell, 1938), xx.

[31] Other poems that appear straightforward and make an immediate impact are 'The Why of the Wind', and 'As Many Questions as Answers'.

[32] *Collected Poems*, xvii.

[33] *A Selection of the Poems of Laura Riding* (1994), 5. Because there is a line-break in the word as printed it is not clear whether or not '*dis*-enchantment' was intended to be hyphenated.

[34] *Collected Poems*, 1938, xxiii. It is at p488 in the 2001 edition of the collected poems.

[35] In the 2001 edition, xliv.

[36] Quoted in Peter Ackroyd's preface *to Paradise Lost* (Folio, 2003), x.

[37] *Anarchism Is Not Enough*, 1928. The passages from 'Poetry and Music' are all from pages 32-36

[38] This side of Riding is lost in what I have described as her 'sanctification'. Another fine example is her description of the effect of reading E.M. Forster's *A Room with a View*, which ends: 'But the truth is it affected me in the same way as would the sight of a tenderly and exquisitely ripe pimple. I longed to squeeze it and have done with it.' *Anarchism Is Not Enough*, 51.

[39] Ibid, 116-118.

[40] From 'A Prophecy or a Plea', which first appeared in *The Reviewer*, 5(2), (April 1925): 1-7 and was happily reprinted in Appendix C to *First Awakenings* (1992), 275-280. A line accidentally omitted there, as noted by Alan Clark in *Chelsea 69*, 2001, is reinstated in *The Laura (Riding) Jackson Reader* text of 'A Prophecy or a Plea', 2005, 3-8.

[41] *Anarchism*, all quotations from the section 'Poetry and Music' (32-36).

[42] To say nothing of the substantial post-poetic accounts, beginning with the 'Preface' to *Selected Poems* in 1970, and on through the 'Addendum' to *The Telling* in 1972, the 'Author's Introduction' to the 1980 edition of *Collected Poems*, to the posthumously published *The Failure of Poetry, the Promise of Language* in 2007 and *The Person I Am* in 2011.

[43] Alan J. Clark, 'Where Poetry Ends', *PN Review*, No22 (1981): 26-27.

[44] There are particularly biting criticisms in *Contemporaries*, including '… there is no sign of intellect *per se* in the [sic] *Waste Land*.' (84). However there is recognition of the poetic quality of the transitions achieved in that poem, as a sustained longer poem, in *A Survey* (23-25).

[45] From 'Blake' in T.S. Eliot, *The Sacred Wood* (London: Methuen, 1920), 88-92.

[46] In *First Awakenings*, 276-280.

[47] *First Awakenings*, 277-278.

[48] *A Survey of Modernist Poetry* (1927, reprinted by Carcanet in 2002) 14: 'Rimbaud, with all Mallarmé's science behind him and endowed with a natural poetic mind…' and 'a natural poet like Rimbaud'.

[49] *Contemporaries and Snobs* (1928) 124, 129, and 133-134.

[50] *A Survey of Modernist Poetry* (1927, reprinted by Carcanet in 2002): Chapter VI. See the essay in this book on 'The Rugged Black of Anger' for a more analytical account.

[51] 'Lucrece And Nara' in 'What, If Not A Poem, Poems?' *Denver Quarterly*, 9(2) (Summer 1974): 1-13. 'Excerpts from a Recording (1972), Explaining the Poems' is available as Appendix V in the 2001 edition of the *Collected Poems*, pp495-498. There are also brief comments on 'A Sad Boy' and 'The Quids', and reference to the essay on 'Lucrece and Nara' in a letter to Mark Jacobs dated June 21, 1973.

[52] 'Preface to the Collected Poems' in the 2001 edition of *Collected Poems*, xx-xxi.

[53] 'Preface to the Collected Poems' (2001), xliv.

[54] *Anarchism*, 12.

[55] Christopher Ricks, *Milton's Grand Style* (Clarendon Press, 1998): 57. After writing this Jacobs brought to my attention the following: 'She was the one poet of her time who spun, like Arachne, from her own vitals without any discoverable philosophical or literary deviations: and the only one who achieved an unshakeable synthesis. Unshakeable, that is, if the premise of her unique personal authority were granted, and another more startling one – that historic time had effectively come to an end.' From Robert Graves and Alan Hodge, *The Long Weekend* (London: Faber and Faber, 1940), 200.

[56] Liddell and Scott, Greek-English Lexicon, Oxford. 'Song' is very much a secondary meaning.

[57] Preface to *Selected Poems: In Five Sets*, 1970, 15.

[58] Eventually published posthumously as *Rational Meaning: a New Foundation for the Meaning of Words*, by Laura (Riding) Jackson and Schuyler B. Jackson (UP Virginia, 1997). For an example of the continuity and development of thought it is fascinating and instructive to read the poem 'Earth' alongside the 'dictionary' account of 'Earth' or 'earth' in Chapter 20 of *Rational Meaning*, 'Words and Things',(396-423).

[59] *Selected Poems*, 1970, quotations here from pages 15 and 17.

[60] 'To the Reader': xxvi-xxvii in 1938 edition of *Collected Poems*.

[61] Standardizing Keats' erratic capitalisation this quote from Keats is in Laura (Riding) Jackson, *The Telling* (Athlone, London, 1972), 180. The original is in *Letters of John Keats*, (Oxford: Oxford University Press, 1954), 266.

[62] Each of her previous selections had individual titles suggestive of or indicative of the peculiar nature of the work: *The Close Chaplet*; *Love as Love, Death as Death*; *Poems: A Joking Word*; and *Poet: A Lying Word*. I have excluded *Though Gently* and *Twenty Poems Less* as they are in the nature of experimental, works in progress and do not aim to be representative selections.

[63] The order is not strictly chronological, although in general the earlier poems are placed towards the beginning, the later towards the end.

[64] Or perhaps more aptly, but less neatly, either with 'Come Words Away' or with 'Tale of Modernity', both from *Poet: A Lying Word* but placed just before the end of 'Immediate Occasion'. In fact each of the three divisions could be said to be signalled before the break, as it were: 'Tale of Modernity' the penultimate poem of 'Immediate Occasion', 'The Rugged Black of Anger' at the end of 'Mythical Occasion', and 'Disclaimer of the Person' at the end of 'Final Occasion'.

[65] In *The Poems of Laura Riding*, the centenary edition of *Collected Poems* (2001) at Appendix V, p496.

[66] The final poem of 'Final Occasion', the only poem in that section not published previously in

the collection *Poet: A Lying Word*. 'Disclaimer of the Person' had been printed individually, in two separate parts as *The First Leaf* (in 1933) and *The Second Leaf* (in 1935). Its position in the *Collected Poems*, and the separate publication, indicate the importance given to the poem. The quotation is from page 255.

[67] In Appendix V, 496, of the 2001 edition of the collected poems.

[68] From the final section, 'All the Way Back': 7-8.

[69] It is hinted at by Graves' lines referring to Riding in 'Midsummer Duet' which follows 'Tale of Modernity':

Shall you not mock my pious ways
Finding in gloom no certain grace or troth,
And raise from moony regions of your smile
Light spirits, nimbler on the toe
Which nothing are – I no one?

[70] *Collected Poems,* 219 and 311.

[71] *Collected Poems*, 230.

[72] *Collected Poems*, 255.

Chapter 2

'Incarnations': to begin at the beginning

INCARNATIONS

Do not deny,
Do not deny, thing out of thing.
Do not deny in the new vanity
The old, original dust.

From what grave, what past of flesh and bone
Dreaming, dreaming I lie
Under the fortunate curse,
Bewitched, alive, forgetting the first stuff . . .
Death does not give a moment to remember in

Lest, like a statue's too transmuted stone,
I grain by grain recall the original dust
And, looking down a stair of memory, keep saying:
This was never I.

1

This poem is placed (one is tempted to say laid breathing in its cradle) at the beginning of Laura Riding's *Collected Poems*, after the introductory 'Forgotten Girlhood'. An earlier, slightly different, version appeared in *Poems: A Joking Word* in 1930, again near the beginning of that collection, following 'Lida' (the title of the first version of 'Forgotten Girlhood') and 'Home'. It was placed fourth in Laura (Riding) Jackson's own final selection of her poems, *Selected Poems: In Five Sets*, in 1970.

'Incarnations' lacks extrinsic 'poetic' properties. There is no metre; there is strong rhythm but this inheres entirely in the movement of the thought. Any rhyme appears incidental, unobtrusive but not unwelcome. Can we say that 'deny' in the first line rhymes with 'lie' in the sixth and 'I' in the thirteenth and final line, or that 'bone' in the fifth line rhymes with 'stone' in the tenth?[1]

Perhaps 'Incarnations' should have been placed first in *Collected Poems* as an uncompromising demonstration of intent. The language is so unadorned and fresh, and the challenges to the reader are immediate and unavoidable, whereas there is a sense in 'Forgotten Girlhood' of an authorial attempt to attract the reader into the poems by charming them, by an appeal to memory of nursery rhymes.[2] On the other hand there *are* echoes in 'Incarnations' of 'Forgotten Girlhood', in particular of the first piece, 'Into Laddery Street':

> The stove was grey, the coal was gone.
> In and out of the same room
> One went, one came.
> One turned into nothing.
> One turned into whatever
> Turns into children.

'Incarnations' is an account of being and becoming, a poetic (or human) alternative both to the biblical and to the scientific account of creation or nativity. 'Incarnation' is not a common word in Riding's poetry or prose. The term derives from medieval Christian theology and was typically used to refer to the embodiment of God in human form in Jesus, later referring more generally to a body in which a spirit or soul is incarnated, or to a person who embodies a deity or spirit in the flesh. The latter meaning is most relevant here, but the world of the Bible is frequently alluded to in the poems.

In approaching the poem one is reminded of passages from possibly Riding's most original and uncompromising prose work, *Anarchism Is Not Enough*. Here is an example, from the section entitled 'What Is A Poem?':

> What is a poem? A poem is nothing. By persistence the poem can be made something; but then it is something, not a poem. [. . .] It is not an effect (common or uncommon) of experience; it is the result of an ability to create a vacuum in experience – it is a vacuum and therefore nothing. It cannot be looked at, heard, touched or read because it is a vacuum. Since it is a vacuum it cannot be reproduced in an audience. A vacuum is unalterably and untransferably a vacuum – the only thing that can happen to it is destruction. If it were possible to reproduce it in an audience the result would be the destruction of the audience.[3]

This is a dizzying, exhilarating and dismaying passage. It should not be seen as a momentary aberration; it is consistent with the 'Preface' to *Poems: A Joking Word* (of which more later) and with several passages in the poems, examples being 'One Self', 'There Is Much At Work', and from 'Poet: A Lying Word':

> It is not a wall, it is not a poet. […] It is a written edge of time. Step not across, for then into my mouth, my eyes, you fall. Come close, stare me well through, speak as you see. But oh, infatuated drove of lives, step not across now. Into my mouth, my eyes, shall you thus fall, and be yourselves no more.[4]

Even more dauntingly for the potential critic 'What Is A Poem?' continues:

> Wherever this vacuum, the poem, occurs, there is agitation on all sides to destroy it, to convert it into something. The conversion of nothing into something is the task of criticism. Literature is the storehouse of these rescued somethings.[5]

Since first reading the poem 'Incarnations' over thirty years ago this critical mind has been agitating thus to destroy it, to convert nothing into something. It is so simple a poem, so brief, in such clear language – yet impenetrable somehow, to a direct approach.

2

In her 1972 'personal evangel', *The Telling*, Laura (Riding) Jackson gives a prose account which retrospectively illumines (and in some ways goes beyond) the poems. Of relevance to 'Incarnations' are the following passages:

> Yes, I think we remember our creation! — have the memory of it in us, to know. Through the memory of it we apprehend that there was a Before-time of being from which being passed into what would be us. [...] Souls there were not until there were bodies in which, each, diversity's extremes were brought into a union; ... another and another and another, to that rounding-in and exhaustion of diversity which is human. Thus from physicality emerge persons — ourselves. [...]
>
> But there *are* no souls, we do not *have* souls, except as we remember the Soul's before-being, in our bodily after-being.[6]

These brief quotations give, to my mind, a flavour of both what was gained and what was lost when the author renounced poetry. *The Telling* in many respects complements the poems.

Everywhere the reader recognises ideas and thoughts which cast a backward light on aspects of the poems. Furthermore she is able to speak in greater and more satisfactory detail about matters of the spirit and the soul. While retaining all her critical edge she reveals a wider sympathy and fellowship with others, particularly relevant here in her references to the prose of Coleridge, to Blake's poetic vision and to Keats' letters ('The World is the Vale of Soul-making'). She argues there:

> 'Real' poetic vision may be described as vision of spiritual meanings, in poets, operating outside poems, having only scanty representation in them. Explicit representation of it is more likely to be found outside poems, in the utterances of poets — and where found will be more substantial than what their poems yield of it.[7]

In *The Telling* the author has been able to speak more directly and effectively, as she implies here, of matters of spirit and soul, than even she could manage in her poetry. At the same time this critic misses the sheer élan and concentrated energy of the poems. The elaboration and qualification of the revelations in *The Telling* paradoxically risk, at times, on the one hand overexposure and on the other a sense of mysticism.

3

To return to 'Incarnations': the poem falls into three parts. Using the references above, the meaning of the first four lines is fairly clear: Do not deny in the new vanity the old original dust. This corresponds roughly to the point in the later account of *The Telling*, quoted above, that 'there are no souls, we do not have souls, except as we remember the Soul's before-being, in our bodily after-being.' 'Dust' is a simple word with a depth of meaning. Perhaps our first thought is of the burial service: 'Earth to earth, ashes to ashes,[8] dust to dust'; a parallel thought, perhaps, would be of the astronomical description of the stardust, from the origin of the universe, from which we ultimately derive. In this context, of incarnations, the sense is turned around from death to life, as in the original passage in Genesis:

> And the Lord God formed man of the dust of the ground, and breathed into his nostrils the breath of life; and man became a living soul.[9]

The second section of the poem, lines 4-8, sets out the context of that (potential) denial of the old original dust, or of forgetting the first stuff:

> From what grave, what past of flesh and bone
> Dreaming, dreaming I lie
> Under the fortunate curse
> Bewitched, alive, forgetting the first stuff...

The sheer excitement (and distress[10]) of being alive, 'the new vanity', leads to the forgetting of the first stuff.

The amazing continuity of the author's thought throughout her writing life is evident from the penultimate chapter of *Rational Meaning*, finally published six years after Laura (Riding) Jackson's death. It contains a sustained meditation upon the word (or, as she argues, the name) 'Earth' or 'earth' that leads in turn to a discussion of 'dust' and 'dirt':

> For Earth, which is reverenceable as the human place of being, is also, as the site of the physical engendering of human beings, a materiality out of which they have had to extract themselves: the humble fact of this is a sobering element of the dignity of being human. The dust of Earthly createdness clings to, still falls from the beautiful reality of human identity. Sense of the dirt of the formless human condition, the being something that is yet nothing, no one, of no reality of self, weighs still in the scales of human appetency, as fear's preference of body to soul, should life constitute a choice between them. [...]

And the word "dust"? Does not the subject of it, debris of earth reduced to extremely fine dispersible particles, or do not the subjects of another "dust," aggregated inert material, similarly reduced, impinge on a question of the nature of existence itself? Has not "dust" as a term specifically evocative of earth in a reduced state, or as a term of reference to a generalized state of reducedness of something from substantiality, been one of the most solemn, and mournful, of figures of depiction of the impermanence of life? If it is but a word that has no *meaning*, only a *signification*, what is to be said of the *significance* of the thing dust has in human meditation on the mortality of the bodily form of life, in which the meditating mind speaks its supra-mortal sense of the meaning of life through the meaning of words?[11]

There will be more to be said on this subject in our reading of the poem 'Earth'.

4

The final section of the poem introduces one of Riding's extraordinary images:

> Death does not give a moment to remember in
> Lest, like a statue's too transmuted stone
> I grain by grain recall the original dust
> And, looking down a stair of memory, keep saying:
> This was never I.

In the first version the first and second of these lines went, less memorably, but helpfully for our understanding of their meaning:

> Death will not give me even a moment to remember in
> Lest, like a statue's stone that will not die,
> I grain by grain [etc]

The variation from 'stone that will not die' to 'too transmuted stone' has a complementary effect, clarifying the meaning. Whilst in one way 'too transmuted' is less clear, it adds the sense of alchemy, the miracle of turning a baser material into gold. On the other hand the first version's 'that will not die' makes clearer the sense of immortality. In fact there were three stages of alchemy, of rising intensity and significance: first the transformation of base metal into gold; secondly, healing of illnesses; finally the transformation of emotional elements into spiritual, enabling a person's soul to attain unity with the divine spirit.

Initially it seems that Death (or death, the capitalisation may be simply the result of the word's place at the beginning of a line) prevents one from not denying the old original dust (a sort of double or triple negative that makes the poem seem to swallow itself). That is: Death is the enemy of the injunction of the first lines of the poem; Death would have you not remember the old original dust. Death prevents 'me' (in the first version, in the later version there is no specified person, the sense can include the reader) from unforgetting the original dust.

But why should Death do this? Because if the poet (or you or I) did recall the original dust it would (by this reading) create something both immortal ('that will not die', in the first version) and different ('too transmuted' in the later version) from the dreaming being who lies

> Under the fortunate curse,
> Bewitched, alive, forgetting the first stuff [...]

Therefore, if Death did give a moment to remember in, the poet (and the reader, in the rather more general application of the later version) would transmute so radically into something that will not die, integrating the now and the old original dust, that the poet (and the fellow-travelling reader) would

> [...] looking down a stair of memory, keep saying:
> This was never I.

This does seem at first sight puzzling. Why should the successfully integrated poet-person, in despite of Death, not denying the original dust, now say 'This was never I'? The answer is that the poet-person and the poem-person are in fact distinct. My reading is that the 'I' of the last line relates to the 'I' of lines 5-8, the bewitched, alive 'I' that forgets the first stuff. However, from the perspective of the statue's too transmuted stone the alive 'I' is incomplete, not whole. The key question, therefore, is: What exactly is the referent for 'This'?[12] Surely the answer is that 'This' is the *poem* itself? This corresponds perfectly with passages from the preface to *Poems: A Joking Word* in 1930 (the book in which the poem first appeared):

> My life reads all wrong to me because it is what would be me if I didn't feel doom. My life is me not necessarily preceding my poems. My life is feeling itself as me, my poems are feeling myself as doom. My life is me instead of doom, me postponing doom. My poems are doom instead of me, me declaring doom where I am instead of me where doom is. [...] My poems are then instead of my life. I don't mean that in my poems I escape from my life. My life by itself would be nothing but escaping, or anybody's. I mean that in my poems I escape from escaping. And my life reads all wrong to me and my poems read all right.[13]

5

Supporting, or rather complementing, this overall reading of 'Incarnations' are two of the pieces from 'Echoes'. The first has pride of place at the opening of 'Poems of Immediate Occasion':

> Since learning all in such a tremble last night—
> Not with my eyes adroit in the dark,
> But with my fingers hard with fright,
> Astretch to touch a phantom, closing on myself—
> I have been smiling. ('Echoes 1')

The second piece suggests that becoming is not a once for all process, it is continual (just as it is 'Incarnations', not 'Incarnation' in the poem in question):

> 'I shall mend it,' I say,
> Whenever something breaks,
> 'By tying the beginning to the end.' ('Echoes 11')

This is reinforced by the beautiful opening lines of 'Autobiography of the Present':

> Whole is by breaking and by mending.
> The body is a day of ruin,
> The mind, a moment of repair.
> A day is not a day of mind
> Until all lifetime is repaired despair.

At the beginning of this account of 'Incarnations' I felt moved, without quite knowing why, to use the expression 'laid breathing in its cradle' of the placing of the poem near the beginning of *Collected Poems*. It may be that this was suggested by a passage from the opening section of *Anarchism Is Not Enough* entitled 'The Myth':

> Poetry (praise be to babyhood) is essentially not of the Myth. It is all the truth it knows, that is, it knows nothing. It is the art of not living. It has no system, harmony, form, public significance or sense of duty. It is what happens when the baby crawls off the altar and is 'Resolv'd to be a very contrary fellow' – resolved not to pretend, learn to talk or versify. Whatever language it uses it makes up as it goes and immediately forgets. Every time it opens its mouth it has to start all over again. That is why it remains a baby and dies (praise be to babyhood) a baby. *In the art of not living one is not ephemerally permanent but permanently ephemeral.* [Italics added][14]

NOTES

[1] In the version in Poems: A Joking Word (London: Cape, 1930) the tenth line read 'Lest, like a statue's stone that will not die' which created a further 'rhyme' for 'deny' but at the 'cost' of no rhyme for 'bone'. Getting the words right for the thought was always the priority over 'artistic' considerations.

[2] In her introduction to the 1980 edition of Collected Poems Laura (Riding) Jackson refers to a review by Schuyler B. Jackson, whom she had not at that time met, in which he wrote: '… language that would seem clear in Shakespeare or Mother Goose may seem obscure in Laura Riding.' The reason for this seeming obscurity, he wrote, was that she wrote 'in a language in which every word carries its full literate meaning.' Collected Poems (Manchester: Carcanet, 1980), 12; reprinted in The Poems of Laura Riding (New York: Persea, 2001), xliv.

[3] Laura Riding, *Anarchism Is Not Enough*, (London: Cape, 1928) 16-17.

[4] *Collected Poems*, 235.

[5] *Anarchism,* 18.

[6] Laura (Riding) Jackson, *The Telling,* (London: Athlone, 1972) 30 (passage 28) and 31 (passage 29).

[7] Ibid, in the 'Addendum', 177-185, quotations from 180. L(R)J corrects Keats' odd capitalisation in her quote. He wrote: 'Call the world if you Please "The vale of Soul-making"': *Letters of John Keats* (OUP, 1954), 266, letter to G and G Keats, 14 Feb.—3 May 1819.

[8] 'Ashes to ashes' reminds one of the passage cited earlier, from 'Into Laddery Street':

The stove was grey, the coal was gone.

In and out of the same room

One went, one came.

One turned into nothing.

One turned into whatever

Turns into children.

[9] Genesis 2, vii. Taken from the Cambridge University Press edition of the King James Bible, 2005. In the next chapter God curses Adam for listening to his wife and eating the forbidden fruit, and gives us the source for the burial service: '[…] till thou return to the ground: for out of it wast thou taken, for dust thou art, and unto dust shalt thou return.' Genesis 3, xix.

[10] 'The most moving and at once distressing event in the life of a human being is the discovery that he is alive.' The opening sentence from 'A Prophecy or a Plea', an essay first published in April 1925 in *The Reviewer*, now available as Appendix C in Laura (Riding) Jackson, *First Awakenings* (Manchester: Carcanet, 2001), 275.

[11] Laura (Riding) Jackson and Schuyler B. Jackson, *Rational Meaning* (Virginia: UP Virginia, 1997), Chapter 20, p419; p420.

[12] A question which I owe to Alan Clark, who asked it in responding to an earlier version of the essay.

[13] Laura Riding, *Poems: A Joking Word* (London: Cape, 1930), 10.

[14] *Anarchism*, 11.

Chapter 3

'How Blind and Bright': the inward vision

HOW BLIND AND BRIGHT

Light, visibility of light,
Sun, visibility of sun.
Light, sun and seeing,
Visibility of men.

How blind is bright!
How blind is bright!

Eyes looking out for eyes
Meet only seeing, in common faith,
Visibility and brightness.

Night, invisibility of light,   10
No sun, invisibility of sun,
Eyes in eyes sheltered,
Night, night and night.

> All light, all fire, all eyes,
> Wrapt in one conference of doubt.
>
> Eyes not looking out for eyes
> Look inward and meet sight
> In common loneliness,
> Invisibility and darkness.
> How bright is blind!   20
> How bright is blind!

1

The ideas and the language of this simple, apparently artless poem function as elements integral to an understanding of more complex poems later in *Collected Poems*. Indeed, it is difficult to appreciate fully such poems as 'The Tiger', or 'Tale of Modernity' without first absorbing the meaning of 'How Blind and Bright'. It first appeared in the 1928 collection *Love as Love, Death as Death*, immediately after the poem 'Death as Death'. In that version it had two additional lines before lines 7 and 16 respectively:

> As dead, we see as dead.
>
> * * *
>
> As dead, we do not see, as dead.[1]

This introduced a paradox, familiar from a reading of poems further on in the *Collected Poems*, which, while appropriate to its context and placing in the original publication, may have been deemed unnecessary and even distracting from the poem's place in the 'story' as arranged in the poet's final collection.

The poem resembles a nursery rhyme in its simple language and its rhymes (and half-rhymes) and even a chant in its repetitions, notably the exclamations of lines 5-6 and 20-21. In form it develops mainly through simple parallelism and contrast. The first nine lines are paralleled, balanced and contrasted with the remaining twelve lines. Within that larger pattern there are particular contrasts:

> Light, visibility of light,
> Sun, visibility of sun.
> Light, sun and seeing,
> Visibility of men. (1-4)
> * * *
> Night, invisibility of light,
> No sun, invisibility of sun,
> Eyes in eyes sheltered,
> Night, night and night.
> All light, all fire, all eyes,
> Wrapt in one conference of doubt. (10-15)

Then again:

> Eyes looking out for eyes
> Meet only seeing, in common faith,
> Visibility and brightness. (7-9)
> * * *
> Eyes not looking out for eyes
> Look inward and meet sight
> In common loneliness,
> Invisibility and darkness. (16-19)

And again, with the poem's paradoxical conclusions:

> How blind is bright!
> How blind is bright! (5-6)
> * * *
> How bright is blind!
> How bright is blind! (20-21)

2

The use of 'men' at line four singles out men as opposed to women where the use of 'man' (as in 'mankind') would be more ambiguous. While 'visibility', used here four times, and 'invisibility', used three times, seem obvious words to use of light and of night, the application of the term to men, refers to men's ability to be seen in the light/sun, where one might have expected 'the vision of men', or some such stronger phrase, pointing to the sun as the source of their inspiration through their (externally focused) eyes. In fact, as it stands the line 'Visibility of men' implicitly contrasts their visibility with the relative invisibility of women. The inference is that while men may be more conspicuous (something that is historically demonstrable) there is more to women than meets the eye. The focus on visibility reminds us of an even simpler poem than 'How Blind and Bright', from the opening sequence of *Collected Poems*, 'Forgotten Girlhood'. There the first poem of the sub-section 'In Laddery Street' is 'Herself', quoted here in full:

> I am hands
> And face
> And feet
> And things inside of me
> That I can't see.
>
> What knows in me?
> Is it only something inside
> That I can't see?

The poem is about girlhood, not childhood.[2] Girls are implicitly, because of their anatomy, more likely to be curious about what's inside them that they can't see. On the other hand, in the poem which follows 'Herself' the poet writes of 'Children' generally, as opposed to 'the old ones':

Children sleep at night
Children never wake up
When morning comes
Only the old ones wake up.
Old Trouble is always awake.

Children can't see over their eyes.
Children can't hear beyond their ears.
Children can't know outside of their heads.

Children have access to something 'the old ones' have lost:

The old ones see.
The old ones hear.
The old ones know.
The old ones are old.

To return to the poem in view, the first paradoxical conclusion is unequivocal: blind is bright! The brightness of the sun blinds one to the inward vision. The second pair of contrasting, almost matching, statements (here given with added italics) is crucial:

Eyes *looking out* for eyes
Meet only seeing, in common faith,
Visibility and brightness. (7-9)
* * *
Eyes *not looking out* for eyes
Look inward and meet sight
In common loneliness,
Invisibility and darkness. (16-19)

'Seeing' in the sun is contrasted with the 'sight' of looking inward. 'Eyes looking out for eyes' create (to borrow language from *Anarchism*, and *A Survey*) a social reality, not a poetic reality (or unreality).. 'Seeing' is associated with 'common faith' – the sunlight we share and the religions based around it. 'Sight' is associated with self-reliance in the face of 'common loneliness' – the death we have in common, for example, but that each one faces alone. That is why the poem concludes in favour of the more difficult but illuminating approach of looking inward:

> How bright is blind!
> How bright is blind!

The contrast of 'seeing' with 'sight' is reminiscent of the author's distinction, as critic, between 'intelligence' and 'intellect' in the section 'Poetry and Progress' from her essay 'Poetry & the Literary Universe'.[3]

There is a much later echo and development of this thought in 'Auspice of Jewels' in which men are accused of connivance in making all of women, not just their faces, brilliantly visible:

> We are studded with wide brilliance
> As the world with towns and cities—
> The travelling look builds capitals
> Where the evasive eye may rest
> Safe from the too immediate lodgement.
>
> Obscure and bright these forms
> Which as the women of their lingering thought
> In slow translucence we have worn.[4]

I have drawn attention to the parallel between the meaning of 'How Blind and Bright' and the distinction the author makes elsewhere between social and poetic reality, but the poem itself does not deploy such language. In fact, while it is clear that the poet would include herself with the eyes that look inward there are implicitly others with her 'in common loneliness'. This is confirmed by the final lines of the middle section:

> All light, all fire, all eyes,
> Wrapt in one conference of doubt. (14-15)

A conference is the action of conversing or taking counsel on serious or important matters. The 'aloneness' experienced and expressed in poems like 'The Unthronged Oracle' was not part of a chosen role of poet as a solitary romantic, but the result of having no one else who would understand her. Her own preference seems always to have been to work in collaboration, although never, of course, at the cost of compromising her exacting standards. Men, it should be noted, are not excluded from the 'common loneliness' and the 'conference of doubt', but men are implicitly more at home with the world of the sun and the religions of the sun, whereas women are implicitly more familiar with the night, its mysteries and uncertainties:

> It is a mission for men to scare and fly
> After the siren luminary, day.
> Someone must bide, someone must guard the night.[5]

NOTES

[1] Laura Riding, *Love as Love, Death as Death* (London: Seizin, 1928), 3. The other variants are 'Eyes in eyes hidden' in respect of *CP*'s line 12, and 'Look inward for death, meet sight' for *CP*'s line 17.

[2] Interestingly the point can be missed. Thus Rexilius refers repeatedly to the poem as 'Forgotten Childhood' in her otherwise perceptive essay on Riding's poems and criticism. Andrea Rexilius, 'Laura (Riding) Jackson: Against the Commodity of the Poem', made available in 2014 in the 'essays' section on the Laura (Riding) Jackson website, Nottingham Trent University.

[3] In *Contemporaries and Snobs* (London: Cape, 1928) 79-86. The argument is not easy to follow in isolation from the context (although the example of *The Waste Land* is telling) but this excerpt gives a flavour of the thinking:

> Intelligence, the historical fallacy, is the philosophical means by which the individual makes his literal time catch up with the figurative synthetic time of the totality of matter.

> Advanced contemporary poetry is thus breathless with scholarship – the *Waste Land* [sic], a poem of four hundred and thirty- three lines, has one learned reference to every eight of these; but it is not breathless with intellect – there is no sign of intellect *per se* in the *Waste Land*. For as soon as an independent mental act needs to substantiate itself historically it ceases to be independent and ceases to be intellect. It is only rather evasively intelligent. (*Contemporaries*, 84).

[4] Laura Riding, *Collected Poems*, 277.

[5] Ibid, 'Echoes 5', 63. This is complete as given in *Collected Poems*, but comes from a long poem, 'The Lady of the Apple' in *The Close Chaplet*, (New York: Adelphi, 1926), 62.

Chapter 4

'The Signature': a bright illegibility of name[1]

THE SIGNATURE

The effort to put my essence in me
Ended in a look of beauty.
Such looks fanatically mean cruelness
Toward self; toward others, sweetness.

But ghostly is that essence
Of which I was religious.
Nor may I claim defeat
Since others find my look sweet
And marvel how triumphant
The mere experiment.

So I grow ghostly,
Though great sincerity
First held a glass up to my name.
And great sincerity claim

> For beauty the live image,
> But no deathly fame:
> The clear face spells
> A bright illegibility of name.

1

In some respects 'The Signature' is a fairly traditional poem. It does not have a regular metrical or rhyme scheme, but it begins with unobtrusive half-rhymes (me/beauty, cruelness/ sweetness) and assonance (effort, essence, ended) and finishes with a set of more emphatic rhymes – name, claim, fame and name (again).

A signature is a person's name or a distinctive mark or seal, typically used as a stamp or proof of authenticity and unique individual identity.[2] Noteworthy here, five out of the nine volumes of poems from which the *Collected Poems* was drawn were limited editions, each individual book bearing the signature of Laura Riding.[3] More figuratively, a signature work describes one as readily identifying its particular author and reminds one of the title of Chapter One of Mrs Jackson's literary memoirs, 'The Person I Am.'[4]

The theme of the poem is the tension between the achievement of a look of beauty, sweetness to others (something socially acceptable) and the achievement of (or failure to achieve) a 'legible' name, or lasting (perhaps poetic) fame. This knot of tension is set up in the opening lines and pulled tight in the climactic final couplet:

> The clear face spells
> A bright illegibility of name.

At a first reading the language of 'The Signature' could hardly be simpler, although as always with this poet there is a complexity of meaning that requires meditation on the poem itself and on its relation to other poems in the whole before a wider simplicity unfolds.

2

An immediate impression of the opening lines is of a person, a woman, as if before a mirror, making the effort to create and present her 'best' self, her essence, for others. A second impression includes the effort involved in producing a poem, ending in a look of beauty. Taking these impressions together, the word 'me' can refer to either the poet or the poem, or to both, or rather at once to the 'poem-person' as it issues from her mind and fingers.[5] But there appears to be a problem:

> Such looks [of beauty] fanatically mean cruelness[6]
> Toward self; toward others, sweetness.

A problem has been created for the self by the 'effort to put my essence in me', which has produced sweetness for others. Why is this a problem? One reason is to be found in the word 'effort'. As we noted in our introduction, for Riding the true poet 'is one by nature and not by effort'. She reinforced the point as follows:

> Creative self-consciousness is a contradiction in terms; for it is clear that poets do not begin to write by effort but by nature.[7]

A second reason for the problem created for the self is implicit in the rather oddly-placed adverb 'fanatically' ('with extreme, irrational zeal'[8]). The word derives from the Latin 'fanum' meaning a temple and was thus associated with religious frenzy, or inspiration by a deity. That connotation is reinforced by the word 'religious' in the second stanza. For Riding true inspiration could only be from within (for which a good word might be 'autochthonous', as in the 'peculiar earth' from 'As Well As Any Other') and not from any deity.

The first striking word in the poem is 'essence'. This word refers to the intrinsic nature or character of something, but it incorporates the notion of a spiritual or immaterial entity. In ancient and medieval philosophy an essence was a spiritual element additional to the four elements of the material world, as in the quintessence ('fifth essence').[9] This latter interpretation would be supported by reference to the following stanza:

> But ghostly is that essence
> Of which I was religious.
> Nor may I claim defeat
> Since others find my look sweet
> And marvel how triumphant
> The mere experiment.

The effort to put her essence in her was a successful experiment from the point of view of others, but that essence is 'ghostly'. What does 'ghostly' mean here?

Riding uses the term paradoxically and characteristically.[10] At its purest a ghost is an appearance without substance, and this is the meaning here. With this meaning, rather than the common usage of 'ghost' to indicate a supernatural apparition of a physically dead person, a ghost can be 'alive' in the usual sense, alive but incomplete, insubstantial, not whole. The *spiritual* essence has excluded the *material* elements – the 'peculiar earth' of 'As Well As Any Other', the 'old original dust' of 'Incarnations', the full material of 'in my material' of 'Prisms' – of the whole self. Hence the ghostliness, spiritual but immaterial, of the essence.

3

The first three lines of the third and final stanza read:

> So I grow ghostly,
> Though great sincerity
> First held a glass up to my name.

She grows, in consequence, ghostly, 'a shadow of what she might have been' one might say; though great sincerity (honesty, lacking dissimulation or

falsity) first held up a glass to her name. There is ambiguity here, and at least two meanings. The glass may be both a mirror (as it would be for personal beauty), and also a magnifying glass (to examine the authenticity of her writing, her signature); in both cases it involves close scrutiny. There might also be a third meaning, private and more poignant, reflecting a memory of such an occasion as the award to the young poet of the Nashville Prize in 1924, and of her being toasted, a glass being raised to her name.[11]
The final lines read:

> And great sincerity claim
> For beauty the live image,
> But no deathly fame:
> The clear face spells
> A bright illegibility of name.

At first reading one expects the second 'great sincerity' to be the subject of the sentence, in parallel with 'great sincerity first held a glass up to my name'. However, that would require the verb to be 'claims' and not 'claim'; for grammatical correctness the 'I' (from 'I grow ghostly') must be understood after 'And' or after 'sincerity', which makes the second 'great sincerity' the object of the sentence 'I claim great sincerity for beauty the live image'.

There are slight but noteworthy variants from the *Poems: A Joking Word* version of 1930. There the final lines read:

> For beauty, the actual image,
> But no actual fame:
> The clear face spells
> An illegibility of name.

The original version applies the adjective 'actual' to both 'image' and 'fame'. The final version has, by contrast, 'live image' and 'deathly fame'. 'Actual' is opposed to potential, virtual, theoretical. 'Actualness', a rare word, is used in 'The Wind Suffers':

> How for the wilful blood to run
> More salt-red and sweet-white?
> And how for me in my actualness
> To more shriek and more smile? (*Collected Poems*, 95)

In the original version she claims great sincerity for beauty, the actual image, but claims no actual fame: the clear face spells an illegibility of name. This seems rather as if the wilful blood in 'The Wind Suffers' were to run only sweet-white and not also salt-red. In the final version the contrast between 'live image' and 'deathly fame' introduces a further paradox and complicates the meaning. Firstly, if she 'grows ghostly' with the look of beauty, why is it a 'live image'? It is, as noted above, because in Riding's usage she is not referring to the apparition of a dead person (currently the common usage) but to the sweet spiritual part of a person. The paradox is further sharpened by the interpolation of 'bright' into the final line of the *Collected Poems* version. For Riding, brightness is, in the first instance, a characteristic of the sun and of the dependence of men on external visibility. This is set out in the opening lines in the fourth poem in *Collected Poems,* 'How Blind and Bright':

> Light, visibility of light,
> Sun, visibility of sun.
> Light, sun and seeing,
> Visibility of men.
>
> How blind is bright!
> How blind is bright!

In that poem the central paradox is that it is by shunning visibility, by looking inwards, that vision may be achieved:

> Eyes not looking out for eyes
> Look inward and meet sight

> In common loneliness,
> Invisibility and darkness.
>
> How bright is blind!
> How bright is blind!

Therefore, 'brightness', by neat inversion and redoubled paradox, is in a figurative sense a characteristic of 'blindness', of the truer vision that is achievable through 'a new poetic bravery that shall exchange insight for outsight and envisage life not as an influence on the soul but the soul as an influence on life'![12]

4

To return to the contrast between 'live image' and 'deathly fame': why should fame be 'deathly' (as opposed to 'actual', in the earlier version)? We might expect 'deathly' to be used in simple criticism of the superficiality and transience of 'fame', but that would not correspond with Riding's usage in other poems. There is some play with, and contrast with, the traditional idea of a poet's 'deathless fame', 'undying glory'. However, 'deathly' is not, or is not simply, a criticism of fame, but is used, as 'death' is used in the poem 'One Self' and as the words 'Death' and 'death' are used throughout her poems, in a characteristic and paradoxical fashion by Riding. In the essay on 'One Self', in commenting on the line 'Smile, death, O simultaneous mouth' we are reminded of the words of the 1930 preface 'In my poems I escape from escaping'. Here what comes to mind is the passage in Chapter VI of *A Survey of Modernist Poetry* 'The Making of the Poem', in which Shakespeare's failure to have his plays uniformly printed in his lifetime is addressed:

> But the process of externalisation must be seen to have two aspects: externalisation for the sake of a legitimate vanity in the poet, a curiosity in him about his own poems; and externalisation

as a poet's duty towards his poem. When both of these aspects are
balanced, the poem has an outward and an inward sincerity.[13]

Strange as it may seem 'deathly' indicates both the achievement of finality, of truth, and also the fact that the beauty of truth does not last, as the poet early recognised in 'Truth and Time' in the line: 'Beauty is truth but once.'[14]

So this is where the poem seems to leave us, but it leaves us on the brink of realizing a further possible meaning in the final two lines.

5

Thus far we have read the poem as promoting the pursuit of the 'signature', as the emblem of authenticity and autochthonous inspiration, over the pursuit of 'beauty', with its 'taint of complaisance'. And yet as the knot of the final couplet is pulled tighter it appears to dissolve:

> The clear face spells
> A bright illegibility of name.

One meaning of this may be that the 'clear face', representing unclouded, untroubled beauty, blinds one to the 'name', representing the signature, or personal authenticity. Another reading, however, is suggested by passages from later poems. In the opening lines of the second stanza of 'The Rugged Black of Anger', in a very different context, there is an account of the self (in this case the 'self' of anger) dissolving of its own intensity:

> Therefore and therefore all things have experience
> Of ending and of meeting,
> And of ending that much more
> As self grows faint of self dissolving
> When more is the intenser self
> That is another too, or nothing. (*Collected Poems*, 59)

And the final stanza of 'Of All the World', for example, reads:

> Of all the world, few inherit themselves,
> Few have waited, succeeded their noising,
> Not been lost among stridulous turns
> Of time-page, afar from silence's path.
> Who approach now, to speak, and of all the world?
> And what's said so late, close between them?
> The words are readable in their clear faces. (*Collected Poems*, 337)

And in the climactic final lines of the first part of 'Disclaimer of the Person' we read:

> I am my name.
> My name is not my name,
> It is the name of what I say. My name is what is said.
> I alone say.
>
> I alone am not I.
> I am my name.
> My name is not my name,
> My name is the name.
> The name is the one word only.
> The one word only is the one thing only.
> The one thing only is the word which says.
> The word which says is no word.
> The one word only is no word.
> The one word only is agreement
> Word with word finally.
> (*Collected Poems*, 255)

The achievement of sweet-white personal essence, of live, actual beauty is one goal; the achievement of an authentic personal signature written figuratively in salt-red blood is another; but neither is the ultimate goal.

Laura Riding recognised that she might be described as a mystic, but rejected the title.[15] Mysticism, by traditional definition, involves a belief either 'in the possibility of union with or absorption into God by means of contemplation and self-surrender', or 'the possibility of spiritual apprehension of knowledge inaccessible to the intellect'.[16] One could call the poems of Laura Riding 'mystical' if they were not so hard-headed, so self-possessed, so intellectual, and so scrupulously devoted to the apprehension of minute particulars. On the other hand, substitute 'The Word' for 'God', and 'self-actualization' for 'self-surrender 'in the first of the traditional definitions given above, and rephrase the alternative definition 'the apprehension of intellectual knowledge through the activity of the spirit' and one comes closer to a description of what she was about.

6

By way of a coda to this essay it is worth reflecting on the extraordinary significance of 'name' to Laura. Born Laura Reichenthal she published all her early magazine poems, as well as her first book of poems in the name of her first marriage, Laura Riding Gottschalk. She changed her name by deed poll to Laura Riding in 1927 (the background to this is given in Elizabeth Friedmann's biography)[17] and following her marriage to Schuyler B. Jackson changed it again to Laura (Riding) Jackson (containing the poetic identity). The name on her tombstone reflects a further and final evolution, to Laura Reichenthal Jackson, reincorporating the proud patronymic.

Relevant here are the opening lines from 'The Wind Suffers':

> The wind suffers of blowing,
> The sea suffers of water,
> The fire suffers of burning,

And I of a living name.
(*Collected Poems*, 95)

And the following from 'As Many Questions as Answers':

What is to be?
It is to bear a name.
What is to die?
It is to be name only.
And what is to be born?
It is to choose the enemy self
To learn impossibility from.
(*Collected Poems*, 153)

There is an apparent paradox here. This is the poet who aims at 'perfection' (as in 'only perfection matters') and at 'finality', who 'bids for an absolute rightness in her poetry' (in the words of the critic Martin Dodsworth). At the same time this is a poet, a poems-person, of protean shape-shifting change. The resolution of the apparent paradox is in the simultaneous and continuous commitment of the poet, or the poem-person, both to the ever-present 'now' and to the eternal, 'the old, original dust'. This chimes with passages 53 and 55 from Laura (Riding) Jackson's *The Telling*:

> [...] a sense of Last Things in which First Things and Last Things are one actuality ... [...]

> My subject is all ourselves, the human reality. And my subject is All, and One, the reality of All, of which we are the exponents. And my subject is Then and Now, the Then whence came our Now — the Now of complete afterness, if we but knew it. And my subject is the spirit that works between Then and Now.[18]

NOTES

[1] An early version of this essay appeared in 2011 on the Nottingham Trent University website, appended to the essay on 'One Self'.

[2] The word recurs, in 'The Last Covenant' (*CP* 265), in 'The Forgiven Past' (*CP* 344) and in the final lines of the main body of *Collected Poems*, in 'Christmas 1937':

Christmas still!

Less merry, but Jesus still the cause:
He was born—signing his name
To a tale by us to be written.

Less deathly: as the signature becomes
Our own, and crucifying hazard
Foreshortens to the death-trimmed END. (*CP*, 367)

[3] *Love as Love, Death as Death* (London: The Seizin Press, 1928); *Twenty Poems Less* (Paris: Hours Press, 1930); *Though Gently* (Majorca: The Seizin Press, 1930); *Laura and Francisca* (Majorca: The Seizin Press, 1931); *The Life of the Dead* (London: Arthur Barker, 1933).

[4] Subsequently and posthumously adopted by editors John Nolan and Caroll Ann Friedmann as the title for both volumes: Laura (Riding) Jackson, *The Person I Am* (Nottingham: Nottingham Trent University, 2011).

[5] The word poem-person is used in Laura Riding and Robert Graves, *A Survey of Modernist Poetry*, (London: Heinemann, 1927); this reference is to the reprinted version (Manchester: Carcanet, 2002), 73.

[6] Cruelness is a rare word, obsolete according to the 1971 OED, but the choice of a word with the '-ness' suffix, as opposed to the commoner and more obvious 'cruelty', is characteristic of Riding. Why choose this word? It gives the half rhyme with 'sweetness', but I believe that we can infer from other choices made by Riding that this would not be a reason for choosing the word; nor would she normally avoid a common term in preference for something unusual, as is evident throughout her work. It is a small point, but the reason I put forward is that 'cruelness' carries fewer (potentially diffuse) associations than 'cruelty' (one use of which includes harshness of smell). It is, therefore, simpler and more to the point: the quality of being cruel.

[7] Laura Riding, *Contemporaries and Snobs* (London: Cape, 1928) 124, 129. See my introduction for the wider theoretical context. One has to offset this view of 'effort' with her preface 'To the Reader', in which she speaks of 'the extremely heavy inertia' which both poet and reader must overcome in order to go to poetry. The resolution of the apparent conflict is in the 'tremendous compulsion that overcomes a tremendous inertia.' *Collected Poems*, 1938, xxiii, 2001 edition, 477. Implicitly there is a distinction between internally generated impulsion and socially generated self-conscious effort.

[8] A more straightforward but less fluid expression would be 'Such looks mean fanatical cruelness', but the actual placing leads the reader to associate the adverb, ungrammatically, with the noun

THE SIGNATURE

'looks' (and also the noun 'cruelness'), as an adjective; as well as, grammatically, with the verb 'mean'. The discomfort in the line has a queasy, onomatopoeic effect on the reader.

[9] Another meaning of 'essence' is distillation, as of perfume, which is perhaps relevant here in relation to the 'sweetness' of the look. I am reminded of an expression of my Scottish mother-in-law: 'Too sweet to be wholesome.' I think that there may also be a reaction here to Matthew Arnold's famous 'sweetness and light'.

[10] This is the first of thirty uses in *Collected Poems* of the word 'ghost' in one form or another. 'The Number', three poems after 'The Signature', uses the word three times in its nineteen lines, as it does the word '*Alive*'.

[11] An idea from Alan Clark responding to an earlier draft of this essay.

[12] From Laura Riding's 'A Prophecy or a Plea', 1925, reprinted in *First Awakenings*, 1992, 276.

[13] *A Survey of Modernist Poetry*, op. cit., quote here from the 2002 edition, Chapter 6, 73. Though not pursued further here, the passage also illuminates Riding's use of the word 'sincerity' as it occurs in this poem.

[14] Laura Riding Gottschalk, *The Close Chaplet* (New York: Adelphi, 1926), 55. The poem appears in *Collected Poems*, 73. The first two of four stanzas are much amended as 'There is Much at Work' but it has only a slight alteration to this line: 'Beauty will be truth but once.' A similar idea is the subject of 'Jewels and After'.

[15] 'And science itself, all that is less than people defining people, intellectual, dumbly prognosticating Matter. Science itself is slowing saying that Science, or Slowness, is soon over, soon-now over. The game which was no game is up, the real business is at hand. What real business? Real business is how Science says business. The business. What business? Am I a mystic? No, I am not a mystic, I am Laura. What business? Laura. How can Laura be a business? How can she not? Complete obsession. Never before, now at last. Until now, delusion of completeness, unavowed delusion. Now, complete obsession, avowed completeness, now Laura. And what of Space? Gertrude. All-together Gertrude, separate Laura. Strong all-together Gertrude, separate strong Laura. Laura alone. Gertrude everyone. Strong.' Laura Riding, 'Obsession', *Experts are Puzzled* (London: Cape, 1930)

[16] Shorter OED.

[17] Elizabeth Friedmann, *A Mannered Grace* (New York: Persea Books), 30-31. See also Alan J. Clark, 'The Names and Pseudonyms; a summary', *Chelsea 69*, 2000, 177-9.

Chapter 5

'Chloe Or…': the story of Lilith

CHLOE OR . . .

Chloe or her modern sister, Lil,
Stepping one day over the fatal sill,
Will say quietly: 'Behold the waiting equipage!'
Or whistle Hello and end an age.

For both these girls have that cold ease
Of women overwooed, half-won, hard to please.
Death is one more honour they accept
Quizzically, ladies adept

In hiding what they feel, if they feel at all.
It can scarcely have the importance of a ball,
Is less impressive than the least man
Chloe, smiling, turns pale, or Lil tweaks with her fan.

Yet they have been used so tenderly.

But the embarrassment of the suit will be
Death's not theirs. They will avoid aggression
As usual, be saved by self-possession.

Both of them, or most likely, Lil,
No less immortal, will
Refuse to see anything distressing,
Keep Death, like all the others, guessing.

1

There is a streak of tough, jaunty, sometimes satirical, humour running through Riding's early poems – 'Bill Bubble', 'The Vain Life of Voltaire', 'The Sad Boy' are examples.[1] The streak sometimes surfaces to comic effect in the middle of intensely 'serious' poems, as in 'The Tiger':

The tiger recalled man's fear
Of beast, in man-sweat they ran back,
Opened their books at the correct pages.
The chapter closed with queens and shepherdesses.
'Peace to their dim tresses,'
Chanted the pious sages.[2]

This is a miniature critique of pastoral and *The Faery Queen*, of the gentlemanly tradition of putting women on a pedestal.

'Chloe Or...' is a regularly and skilfully rhymed poem; with easy enjambement at lines 2/3, 8/9, 14/15 and 18/19 contributing to a conversational, insouciant effect. At one level Chloe and Lil resemble young women stepping out into the attractions of the Roaring Twenties, with balls, flirtations and a 'good time' – although it seems rather boring and unsatisfying.

'Chloe Or...' is one of the 'Poems of Mythical Occasion', the title of the first of the four sections of the main body of *Collected Poems*. The names of Chloe and Lil may seem modern enough but they are at the same time 'mythical', as we shall see. The alternate personae of Chloe and Lil are beautifully set up by the deceptively casual first line, and the alternating light and dark tones are sustained throughout the poem. Even a poem such as this, so apparently easy (and it is not a particularly intense or difficult poem) has its subtleties and depths, not least in the names of the personae.

'Chloe', although of course quite a common contemporary girl's name, must derive from the heroine of what has been described as the world's first novel, *Daphnis and Chloe*, set in the 2nd century AD. In that story the beautiful and innocent Chloe and Daphnis fall in love and have strong sexual feelings for each other, but their naivety and innocence postpone the consummation of their love. Both survive attempts to seduce or rape them before they get married and live happily ever after.

What of 'Lil'? Surely Lil is the 'modern' version of Lilith, an ancient figure in Jewish mythology, the Hebrew term translating as 'night creature', 'night monster'. The history of this name is highly involved and complex. The Kabbalah in one version mentions her creation as preceding that of Adam. Characteristics seen in the medieval legends about her include Lilith as the incarnation of lust, causing men to be led astray, and Lilith as a child-killing witch who strangles neonates. Other legends have her challenging God, or insisting to Adam that she be the dominant sexual partner.[3] It is no accident that one of Riding's pen-names is Lilith Outcome. Lilith also appears in an important story, 'Eve's Side of It'. In that story Lilith is described, amongst other things, as having made Eve, as being omniscient, and making Eve take her place with men in the created world 'not wanting to watch herself playing the fool all those thousands of years'.[4] Coincidentally or not, Riding's Lil makes an instructive contrast with the poor toothless victim of circumstance in Eliot's *The Waste Land* (lines 139-172).

These mythical personae alternate in the poem and in the life of the poet. Readers of Jacobs' memoir of a visit to the 77-year-old Laura (Riding) Jackson will recognise the characteristics of innocence and vulnerability coexisting with a more formidable occult power and intransigence.[5] Other writers have opted for a picture favouring one version or the other, but both aspects are essential. For all the toughness there is the innocence (and vulnerability); and vice versa. The next sections explore a little further both the toughness and the vulnerability.

2

There is the vulnerability. 'Stepping one day over the fatal sill' is a reminder of her suicide attempt of 1929 and its precursor poem 'In Nineteen Twenty-Seven', often quoted in accounts of Riding's life and poetry (but as we shall see, with significant alteration between the pre- and post-leap versions). In the *Collected Poems* of 1938 the relevant passage reads:

> Then where was I, of this time and my own
> A double ripeness and perplexity?
> Fresh year of time, desire,
> Late year of my age, renunciation—
> Ill-mated pair, debating if the window
> Is worth leaping out of, and by whom. (11-16)

In the first version of 'In Nineteen Twenty-Seven', published in the collection *Love As Love, Death As Death* in 1928 (that is, *before* the suicide attempt), the passage read:

> Then where was I, of this time and my own
> A double ripeness, a twice-dated festival?
> Fresh year of time, my youth,
> Late year of my age, renounced desire—
> Ill-mated pair, this gaudy vantage
> Looks on death, it is a window
> Not worth leaping out of. (13-19)

This is less succinct, and not as rhythmically tight, but helps clarify the meaning of the later version. At the same time the conclusion is different from that of the later versions, and the point (of the window not being worth leaping out of) is underlined a few lines later in a passage but which is deleted from later versions of the poem:

> Ill-mated any pair is, but the season
> Is a noisy one, the motor days
> Roll underneath a window
> Not worth leaping out of. (24-27)

As we know, a window was in fact leapt from, by Laura Riding in 1929, but by whom, or by which? The question is begged by an extraordinary oscillation, in otherwise almost identical later versions of that section of the poem, between 'by which' in 1930, in *Poems: A Joking Word*, 'by whom' in the first *Collected Poems* of 1938, 'by which' in her *Selected Poems* of 1970 and back to 'by whom' in the 1980 and 2001 editions of the poems. Desire and renunciation are the pair debating whether the window is worth leaping out of. In the end it is not resolved in the poem, but according to the feverish 'Preface' to *Poems: A Joking Word*, which gives, according to Elizabeth Friedmann's biography[6], a 'mythical version' of events, it is the poems and Laura Riding that went:

> Standing in that room was a quick result – I left that room, by the window of course, and poems came with me. Or rather I went with poems. I hope that you will understand about poems. They are why I am telling this, because as life it reads all wrong but as poems all right.[7]

At this point Riding was finding a fulfilment in her poems that she could not find in her 'life'. The preface, strangely as it reads, provides a convincing account of the changes that took place around the time of the suicide attempt, the renewed singleness of purpose and determination to be utterly self-reliant—self-reliance being, for her, a virtue essential to good poets, as was strongly emphasised in *Contemporaries and Snobs*. There are other poems in which the story is portrayed from different angles (see the next section). One is reminded, taking the various prose and poetic versions together, of Keats' famous comment: 'A man's life of any worth is a continual allegory [...] Shakespeare led a life of allegory; his works are the comments on it.'[8]

To return to the poem in question, in 'Chloe Or...' the innocence is implicit in the name of Chloe only, the vulnerability in the reference to potential (but apparently unfeared) fatality. The women who may 'whistle Hello and end an age' recall the poet's words as she left the window: 'Goodbye, chaps'. There is no need for definitive conclusions, but it may be Riding in the aspect of Lilith who 'most likely' went through the window in this version of the story, leaving the aspect of Chloe (her innocence, her dashed beauty) behind. By this reading it would be 'Chloe' that dies, while the aspect of Lilith, having kept Death guessing, rises again, and may in fact be immortal. On the other hand, in section 4 below, 'No less immortal' may also be read as applying more ambiguously.

3

Laura Riding was of course fortunate to survive her leap, and fortunate not to have been paralysed for life. 'Chloe Or...' refers only to keeping Death (like all the others) guessing, and exudes the stiff upper lip of England in the 1920s. Other poems, notably 'Rejoice Liars', 'Beyond', and 'Celebration of Failure', speak directly of a mortal laming, of pain, of dashed beauty. From 'Rejoice Liars' we have:

> Rejoice, the witch of truth has perished
> Of her own will—
> Falling to earth humanly
> And rising in petty pain.
>
> It was the last grandeur,

> When the witch crashed
> And had a mortal laming.

So, we think, bang goes the witch (and Lil)! Only for her to re-emerge more strongly in the poem's concluding lines:

> Away, flattery, she has lost pride.
> Away, book-love, she has a body.
> Away, body-love, she has a death
> To be born into, an end to make
> Of that eternity and grandeur
> In which a legend pines until it comes true—
> When fawning devil boasts belief
> And the witch, for her own honour,
> Takes on substance, shedding phantomness.

And again, a few pages further on in *Collected Poems* we meet 'Celebration of Failure', which is quoted in full here:

> Through pain the land of pain
> Through tender exiguity,
> Through cruel self-suspicion:
> Thus came I to this inch of wholeness.
>
> It was a promise.
> After pain, I said,
> An inch will be what never a boasted mile.
>
> And haughty judgement,
> That frowned upon a faultless plan,
> Now smiles upon this crippled execution,
> And my dashed beauty praises me.

Significantly these poems (and 'In Nineteen Twenty-Seven', and 'Beyond') are placed in the second section of *Collected Poems,* 'Poems of Immediate Occasion', with the implication of directness, with no intermediacy of mythical or fictional characters.

4

'Chloe Or...' was first published in *Poems: A Joking Word* in 1930. It may, therefore, have been written after the leap in 1929. However, its placement near the beginning of the selection (and there was normally a strongly chronological element in her sequencing) may argue for earlier drafting, even several years earlier. Backing up this argument is the line on the last page of her preface where she says 'I found many poems that were poems again in early unprinted work' which is complemented by her biographer's account of the revision undertaken for the compilation.[9] Whether revised or not, whenever it was first drafted, her selection of this poem for this book inevitably draws attention to the biographical parallel, but in a 'joking' way, in line with the title of and preface to the book. Where the poem may have been seen as too 'light' or humorous for her earlier collections it now fitted better into her spiritual biography.

By contrast with the evident anguish of 'In Nineteen Twenty-Seven' there is in 'Chloe Or...' a hardness in the women's attitude to men (and Death). If anything they have toyed with men's affections. They have been 'overwooed, half-won' but they are hard to please; they hide whatever feelings they have.[10]

'Yet they have been used so tenderly.' This is quite a surprising line. In this poem (as in others, e.g. 'The Virgin') male violence is averted, or at a distance, or quickly forgotten, although we must not overlook the 'used' which 'tenderly' qualifies. 'They will avoid aggression | As usual, be saved by self-possession.' The avoided aggression is that of men, of Death, but may also be their own. For all the insouciance and declared self-possession of this and other poems, 'The Virgin' being again an example, 'in real life' (an expression she may have rejected) love and intense relationships with men caused her, one is tempted to say, at least as much angst as they cause others.[11]

If she is troubled by men (in the poems) it is less by the horrors of male violence (although this is referred to, not very graphically, in 'The Virgin' and 'The Tiger') than by their inadequacies as lovers and as poets, most cogently and bitingly expressed in a later poem, 'The Dilemmist':

> When's man a poet then? And was he ever one?
> For if a death with the held moment stays
> That is not struck—when frantic flesh
> Runs homeward after blood fleeing
> To previous courses and reddened turns—
> That's none of him, no part forgotten,
> But of his second love a fancy
> Lying man-like in her fancied arms,
> With her own foolishness her arms filled.
>
> The man's away after the man.
>
> She understood his wooing wrong.
> He never meant her more than paper,
> Nor does his heart one icy line remember.[12]

5

Although Laura (Riding) Jackson refers to Roy Fuller as 'not friendly to my general course of thought', [13] on the evidence of his 1970 essay he was a close and, in the main, highly appreciative reader of the poems, and well understood (for example) the extent of her influence on Auden. He remarks perceptively:

> Thinking about influences on *her*, the ludicrously opposed names of Emily Dickinson and Shakespeare come to mind, the former à propos of her odd simplicities, the latter of the whole movement of her verse, and the patient and complicated delayings of her syntax […] [14]

Elsewhere (in essays on 'The Rugged Black of Anger' and 'Tale of Modernity') I shall make the connection with and the case for comparison with Shakespeare. In 'Chloe Or...' by contrast, there is a striking parallel with (and surely a reminiscence of) the well-known and anthologised poem of Dickinson:

> Because I could not stop for Death —
> He kindly stopped for me —
> The Carriage held but just ourselves —
> And Immortality.[15]

The parallels are several: the humorous tone in respect of the 'grave issues', the personalisation of abstractions, and the language. Riding's rather more elaborate 'equipage', with its connotations of outfit and equipment for a journey as well as carriage and horses, may derive from Dickinson's idea of the Carriage. In Dickinson's poem, Death stops for her; in Riding's, probably Lil will keep Death guessing. The inclusion of Immortality in the Carriage is echoed in the last stanza of 'Chloe Or.'

> Both of them, or most likely Lil,
> No less immortal, will
> Refuse to see anything distressing,
> Keep Death, like all the others, guessing.

No less immortal than who or what is a question occurring to the reader. There is deliberate ambiguity here: it may mean that Lil (and what she represents) is no less immortal than Chloe (and what she represents); may it also mean that both or one (most likely Lil) are no less immortal than Death?

Death, of course, 'Is less impressive than the least man', and is treated as just another suitor. Intriguingly, in the version of the poem published in *Poems: A Joking Word*, there is a tiny variation in that the title had four dots, 'Chloe Or....' not the three dots of the *Collected Poems* version.[16] So does it mean that in the 1930 version Chloe has come to a full-stop, while in 1938 the poet changed her mind and gave her, as well as Lil, immortality?

6

As a coda to this account of the poem, it is interesting to speculate how Laura Riding would be viewed should her leap in 1929 have proved fatal. She had, of course, already published a substantial body of poems, including two books of poetry, *The Close Chaplet* in 1926 and *Love As Love, Death As Death* in 1928. There would have been the uncollected early poems, rejected for inclusion in *The Close Chaplet* (eventually published as *First Awakenings* in 1992), and presumably also some of the poems later published in *Poems: A Joking Word* in 1930. Many of the early poems are more superficially attractive than some of the poems published in her lifetime, but of course they might never have re-emerged if there had not been a continuing interest in her work.

There would also have been the major critical works, *Contemporaries and Snobs* and *Anarchism Is Not Enough*, both by herself alone in 1928; and in addition, with Robert Graves, *A Survey of Modernist Poetry* in 1927 and *A Pamphlet Against Anthologies* in 1928. The volume of critical writings published before the suicide attempt (as compared with the published poetry) seems disproportionate, but the poetry always came first – until the famous renunciation of course.

So large a proportion of the (limited) critical attention given to her poems has been devoted to the 'Poems of Mythical Occasion' that it comes as a surprise to find that they occupy only 16% of the main body of *Collected Poems* – 56 pages, compared with the 86 pages of 'Poems of Immediate Occasion', 107 pages of 'Poems of Final Occasion', and 104 pages of 'Poems Continual'. There is no doubt that she was a prodigy, ranking alongside Rimbaud in that respect. Her poetic achievement by 1929 was enough to establish her as a major poet. As with Sylvia Plath or Dylan Thomas, an early death, and the lack of a living author's demystifying presence, might have created a mythology around her person and her work, and the sort of sustained and collective scholarship that has been lacking. Her true uniqueness as a poet may, as I believe, be most unambiguously demonstrated in her later poems, but the utterly radical beliefs underlying that later achievement had already been laid out in *Contemporaries and Snobs* and *Anarchism Is Not Enough*.

NOTES

[1] Laura Riding, *Collected Poems* (London: Cassell: 1938; reprinted by Carcanet: 1980; and Persea: 2001). 'The Vain Life of Voltaire' was originally published in book form as *Voltaire* (London: Hogarth: 1927).

[2] *Collected Poems*, 56-57.

[3] In the most substantial essay on the poems to date Jacobs points out the following midrash featuring Lilith attributed to Ben Sira dating from approximately 1000 C.E.: 'He created a woman, also from the earth, and called her Lilith. They quarrelled immediately. She said: "I will not lie below you." He said, "I will not lie below you, but above you. For you are fit to be below me." She responded: "We are both equal because we both come from the earth." Neither listened to the other. When Lilith realized what was happening, she pronounced the Ineffable name of God and flew off into the air.' Mark Jacobs, 'Rewriting History, Literally: Laura Riding's *The Close Chaplet*', *Gravesiana* - Volume 3 Number 3/Summer 2012.

[4] Laura Riding, *Progress of Stories* (New York: Persea Books, 1994) 285-292; (first edition Majorca: Seizin Press, 1935).

[5] There may be disagreement about this application of the terms 'formidable occult power' and 'intransigence' to Laura Riding. By 'occult' I mean primarily 'mysterious', 'hidden', but she herself acknowledged, albeit ironically, the impact she made on some in 'Rejoice, Liars' ('Rejoice, the witch of truth has perished'). And Jacobs's memoir, included in this book, describes how the hairs stood up on the back of his neck as he listened to her addressing Alan Clark. As to 'intransigence', in *The Person I Am* (Nottingham: Trent Editions, 2011) Volume 1, 38, she described an early example of a disagreement with her father 'to a point of matching intransigence' which led to her staying with a friend of the family for several weeks in her early high-school years. Both she and her father she describes as 'non-temporizers'. As to her formidable power, I have in mind the example of her impassioned dismantling of Graves behaviour and character in 'Robert Graves's *The White Goddess*' published as an appendix to Laura (Riding) Jackson's *The Word "Woman"* (New York: Persea Books, 1993), 205-211.

[6] 'During the years immediately following her long recovery, she wrote two versions of the event, a farcical and a mythical version. The farcical version, which she called a "self-parody" was written with George Elldge and published in 1930 as *14A*.' Elizabeth Friedmann, *A Mannered Grace* (New York: Persea Books, 2005) 138.

[7] Laura Riding, *Poems: A Joking Word* (London: Cape, 1930) 18.

[8] Letter to G and G Keats, 14 Feb-3 May 1819. *Letters of John Keats*, selected by Frederick Page (Oxford: Oxford University Press, 1954), 241.

[9] See Elizabeth Friedmann, *A Mannered Grace* (New York: Persea Books, 2005), 152-53.

[10] Compare lines from the poem *Helen's Faces*:

> But the original woman is mythical,
> Lies lonely against no heart.
> Her eyes are cold, see love far off,
> Read no desertion when love removes,
> The images out of fashion.
> Undreamed of in her many faces
> That each kept off the plunderer:
> Contest and bitterness never raged round her. (*Collected Poems*, 53)

[11] 'Despite the quickness of her mind and the usual accuracy of her intuition, there was a trustfulness—which might even be considered a naïveté—about Laura Riding in her personal relationships that was to cause her pain and disappointment throughout her life.' Elizabeth Friedmann, *A Mannered Grace*, 124.

[12] *Collected Poems*, 220. This powerful poem develops at its climax (a doubly apposite term) the theme of lust in terms reminiscent of Shakespeare's Sonnet 129.

[13] In her 1980 introduction to a new edition of *Collected Poems*, xli in the newly revised edition of 2001.

[14] Roy Fuller, 'The White Goddess, *The Review*, 23, 1970, 8.

[15] Quoted here from Ted Hughes' selection, *A Choice of Emily Dickinson's Verse* (London: Faber, 1968), 43. Riding's copy of Dickinson's complete poems is at Cornell (see note 45, p491 of Friedmann's biography).

[16] It is not a misprint. It appears with four dots on the title page also. The only other change is that in the second version an exclamation mark was inserted after 'equipage' in line 3.

Chapter 6

'The Tiger': a Sleeping Beauty

THE TIGER

The tiger in me I know late, not burning bright.
Of such women as I am, they say,
'Woman, many women in one,' winking.
Such women as I say, thinking,
'A procession of one, reiteration
Of blinking eyes and disentangled brains
Measuring their length in love.
Each yard of thought is an embrace.
To these I have charms.
Shame, century creature.'   10
To myself, hurrying, I whisper,
'The lechery of time greases their eyes.
Lust, earlier than time,
Unwinds their minds.
The green anatomy of desire
Plain as through glass
Quickens as I pass.'

Earlier than lust, not plain,
Behind a darkened face of memory,
My inner animal revives.   20
Beware, that I am tame.
 Beware philosophies
Wherein I yield.

They cage me on three sides.
The fourth is glass.
Not to be image of the beast in me,
I press the tiger forward.
I crash through.
Now we are two.
One rides.   30

And now I know the tiger late,
And now they pursue:
'A woman in a skin, mad at her heels
With pride, pretending chariot wheels—
Fleeing our learned days,
She reassumes the brute.'

The first of the pursuers found me.
With lady-ears I listened.
'Dear face, to find you here
After such tiger-hunt and pressing of   40
Thick forest, to find you here
In high house in a jungle,
To brave as any room
The tiger-cave and as in any room
Find woman in the room
With dear face shaking her dress
To wave like any picture queen...'

THE TIGER

'Dear pursuer, to find me thus
Belies no tiger. The tiger runs and rides,
But the lady is not venturous.   50
Like any picture queen she hides
And is unhappy in her room,
Covering her eyes against the latest year,
Its learning of old queens,
Its death to queens and pictures,
Its lust of century creatures,
And century creatures as one woman,
Such a woman as I,
Mirage of all green forests—
The colour of the season always   60
When hope lives of abolished pleasures.'

So to the first pursuer I prolonged
Woman's histories and shames,
And yielded as became a queen
Picture-dreaming in a room
Among silk provinces where pain
Ruined her body without stain—
So white, so out of time, so story-like.
While woman's pride escaped
In tiger stripes.   70
Hymn to the hostage queen
And her debauched provinces.
Down fell her room,
Down fell her high couches.
The first pursuer rose from his hot cloak.

'Company,' he cried, 'the tiger made magic
While you slept and I dreamt of ravages.
The queen was dust.'

And Queen, Queen, Queen,
Crowded the Captain's brain.   80
And Queen, Queen, Queen,
Spurred the whole train
With book-thoughts
And exploits of queen's armies
On gold and silver cloth.
Until they stumbled on their eyes,
Read the number of the year,
Remembered the fast tiger.

The tiger recalled man's fear
Of beast, in man-sweat they ran back,   90
Opened their books at the correct pages.
The chapter closed with queens and shepherdesses.
'Peace to their dim tresses,'
Chanted the pious sages.

And now the tiger in me I knew late.
'O pride,' I comforted, 'rest.
The mischief and the rape
Cannot come through.
We are in the time of never yet
Where bells peal backward,   100
Peal "forget, forget".'

Here am I found forgotten.
The sun is used. The men are in the book.
I, woman, have removed the window
And read in my high house in the dark,
Sitting long after reading, as before,
Waiting, as in the book, to hear the bell,
Though long since has fallen away the door,

Long since, when like a tiger I was pursued
And the first pursuer, at such and such a date,   110
Found how the tiger takes the lady
Far away where she is gentle.
In the high forest she is gentle.
She is patient in a high house.
Ah me, ah me, says every lady in the end,
Putting the tiger in its cage
Inside her lofty head.
And weeps reading her own story.
And scarcely knows she weeps,
So loud the tiger roars.   120
Or thinks to close her eyes,
Though surely she must be sleeping,
To go on without knowing weeping,
Sleeping or not knowing,
Not knowing weeping,
Not knowing sleeping.

1

This essay begins with four straightforward statements about this poem. These points, or perspectives, are summarised below.

The first point is the simple one that this is the longest, at 126 lines, of the 'Poems of Mythical Occasion', the first of the four parts of the main body of *Collected Poems*.[1] The next section considers in some depth how the poem functions technically, including how it should be read as a longer poem.

The second point is that the poem is written as a story, an adventure even, with the equivalent of a beginning, a middle and an end. None of the other longer poems from *Collected Poems* is so clearly set out in traditional story form. It is also in crucial respects a fairy tale.[2]

The third point is how personal a poem this is. Although all her poems are to some degree personal, often the ideas are foregrounded, and a poem proceeds magisterially with a set of powerful unrolling statements. Here, right at the start we get her personal, apparently angry, reaction to Blake: The tiger *in me* I know late | *Not burning bright.* 'It is not for me as it is for you', in other words. And she exposes (albeit through the mask of the story, and not in any prurient way) her most vulnerable sexual self as well as her latent strength.

The fourth point is how much this is a poem of new and challenging ideas. There is a cluster of ideas around time: 'late', 'early', 'century creature'. This cluster of ideas is linked with lechery and lust and 'the beast in me'; what it is to be a woman or a 'lady' in a world of men or by herself: vulnerable, powerful, idealised and ravaged. Linked to this is a further set of images and ideas about men's use of and dependence on 'story' and 'picture' in their approach to women. The story is itself about the nature of story and of imagery.

The following sections set out a more detailed analysis in support of each of the four statements in turn. It will become evident that as the four points, or perspectives, are developed they become interlinked and build up into a picture of the integrated complexity of the whole. As Jacobs explained, in his centennial preface to the 2001 edition of the poems:

> The 'baffling effect' of that 'difficulty' [these quotes are from the poet's original 1938 preface 'To the Reader'] is a real one, as so many readers will know. The problem is not, actually, that of 'difficulty' but that of complexity, or of unfamiliarity of thought — either or both. In their famous examination of Shakespeare's Sonnet 129 in *A Survey of Modernist Poetry*, her and Graves' point is not, as William Empson thought (*Seven Types of Ambiguity,* 1930), that the poem is an endless play of meanings and ambiguity, but that it is fourteen lines of solid integration and co-ordination, each word contributing to 'uncovering' the highly complex essence of the nature of lust as Shakespeare saw and experienced it in its general and personal setting.[3]

My intention here is to honour, so far as I am able, the complexity and integration of this poem as Riding and Graves honoured that of Shakespeare's sonnet.

2

As noted above 'The Tiger' is the longest single poem of 'Poems of Mythical Occasion'. The first published version, in *Love as Love, Death as Death*, was half as long again with several interesting if inessential sections cut from the later versions published in *Poems: A Joking Word* and *Collected Poems* (there are only minor variations between the latter two versions).[4] It is worth spending a little time on the poet's attitude toward, and approach to, longer poems.

Laura Riding produced several extraordinarily diverse longer poems. The poem originally entitled just *Voltaire* was written in 1921, and published as a book, in 1927. As Roy Fuller commented:

> One reads the poem she wrote at twenty... with amazement at its precocious cleverness, and also with admiration for its varied and original poetic texture and its individual solution of the problem of the long poem in our age. This almost unique power to dazzle one intellectually appears again and again throughout her verse.[5]

There are also the other 'prides of the workshop'[6], *Laura and Francisca* (1931) and *The Life of the Dead* (1933), both originally published in limited editions in book form. Within the main body of *Collected Poems*, employing an arbitrary category of poems over a hundred or so lines long[7], the longer poems are: 'The Tiger' (in 'Poems of Mythical Occasion'); 'Elegy in a Spider's Web', 'In Nineteen Twenty-Seven' and 'Midsummer Duet' (in 'Poems of Immediate Occasion'); 'There Follows', 'The Dilemmist', 'It Is Not Sad', 'Signs of Knowledge', 'Poet: A Lying Word', 'Benedictory' and 'Disclaimer of the Person' (in 'Poems of Final Occasion'); and 'The Last Covenant', 'Memories of Mortalities', and 'When Love Becomes Words' (in 'Poems Continual').[8]

In *A Survey of Modernist Poetry,* the second chapter is devoted to 'The

Problem of Form and Subject-Matter'. It begins with an attack on French poets (in particular) for their attempts to remedy perceived deficiencies in poetry by bringing it closer to music. The assault lacks the comic verve of the account in *Anarchism Is Not Enough*[9] but it is more specific and develops, via a penetrating analysis and comparison of longer poems of Tennyson, Eliot and Milton into a set of conclusions about poems in general:

> [...] even more strictness is to be demanded of the long poem than of the short poem. A long poem must give good reason for its length, it must account strictly for every line. Often the greater part of a long poem would be more properly put in a prose footnote. The apology of a long poem should be: 'I am really a long *short* poem.' Poe was the first modern critic to explode the dignity of the long poem of major poetry. In his *The Poetic Principle* he writes: 'That degree of excitement which would entitle a poem to be so called at all, cannot be sustained throughout a composition of any great length. After the lapse of half an hour, at the very utmost, it flags – fails – a revulsion ensues – and then the poem is, in effect, and in fact, no longer such.' Although he saw that the long poem was of necessity weak in structure, that length in itself was destructive of poetic form; by form he meant that regular form imposed on subject-matter which we have here been questioning in both the short and long poem. [...] Well-controlled irregularity instead of uncontrollable regularity makes *short* and *long* obsolete critical standards. The very purpose of this irregularity is to let the poem find its own natural size in spite of the demands put upon poetry by critics, booksellers and the general reading public.[10]

On its own, the expression 'let the poem find its own natural size' begs the question. However, some idea of what the authors mean, positively, by 'well-controlled irregularity' can be gleaned from passages earlier in the chapter where they quote a poem by Hart Crane to show how an impression of

THE TIGER

regularity can come from 'a careful alternation of images, from a regularity of design more fundamental than mere verse regularity' and a passage from the authorized version of the Bible to show how the effect of regularity is achieved 'by the recurrence of ideas in varying alternations to show the movement of the poem'. In the passages from both Hart Crane and the Bible they detect 'parallelisms' by which later lines give added complexity or ironic contrast to earlier lines. They continue:

> Poetry so treated is nothing more than a single theme subjected
> to as many variations as its first or simplest statement will allow,
> even to the point where it ironically contradicts itself. There is in
> it no room for, and no reason for, a separate element of form.[11]

How does this approach help us with 'The Tiger'? In the first place we note that the poem's opening statement: 'The tiger in me I know late, not burning bright' is paralleled at line 31 (which begins the second part of the story): 'And now I know the tiger late' and at line 95 (which begins the last part of the story): 'And now the tiger in me I knew late'. Similarly the colour green, in 'The green anatomy of desire' (line 15) is picked up in 'Mirage of all green forests' (line 59) which also picks up 'Thick forest' (line 40) and in turn looks forward to 'In the high forest she is gentle' (line 113).

This of course, by itself, is a mechanical and simplistic approach, but it can be expanded and developed into a greater complexity. For example, the ideas of the 'cage' and of the tiger as 'the image of the beast in me' are initiated at line 24 in staccato sentences and with striking imagery:

> They cage me on three sides.
> The fourth is glass.
> Not to be image of the beast in me,
> I press the tiger forward.
> I crash through.
> Now we are two.
> One rides.[12]

These images are paralleled in the more languid and contrasting lines 104-108 and 115-117, from the concluding section of the poem:

> I, woman, have removed the window
> And read in my high house in the dark,
> Sitting long after reading, as before,
> Waiting as in the book, to hear the bell,
> Though long since has fallen away the door,
> * * *
> Ah me, ah me, says every lady in the end,
> Putting the tiger in its cage
> Inside her lofty head.

In the first of the two quotations, the window takes up the image of the glass from line 25 and the door that has fallen away echoes the cage of line 25; both are more peaceful, or gentle (but unhappy) as befits the apparent tone of the conclusion of the poem.

Again, the latter passages pick up on the ideas of learning and books first referred to at 22-23: 'Beware philosophies/Wherein I yield' and 35-36: 'Fleeing our learned days she reassumes the brute' and they are developed further in the comic passage 89-94:

> The tiger recalled man's fear
> Of beast, in man-sweat they ran back,
> Opened their books at the correct pages.
> The chapter closed with queens and shepherdesses.
> 'Peace to their dim tresses,'
> Chanted the pious sages.

The men in the poem have got their ideas about women from books and from pictures. They run back to their books for reassurance that the women or 'ladies' are not dangerous, can be patronized.

Towards the end of the poem:

> Ah me, ah me, says every lady in the end,
> Putting the tiger in its cage
> Inside her lofty head.
> And weeps reading her own story.
> And scarcely knows she weeps
> So loud the tiger roars. (115-120)

This attention to parallelisms within the poem as it unfolds is a method of paying attention to what the poet is saying, as opposed to what you as the reader intend to read.

Turning from imagery to what might be termed the prosody, or technique of versification, we would not expect – after the accounts from *A Survey* and *Anarchism Is Not Enough* noted above – a regular rhyme scheme or metre.[13] We do get, however, as in so many of her poems, unaffected and 'natural' seeming line-end rhymes throughout the course of the poem – at 3-4, 16-17, 33-34, 66-67, 80 and 82, 91-95, 99 and 101, 106 and 108, 122-123, 125-126. In addition there are assonances and weak rhymes, but none of it draws much attention to itself; it is unsystematic. It is worth pointing out (highlighted in my italics in the following) just some of the internal rhymes/assonances that help sustain the momentum of the poem throughout:

> Lust, earlier than *time*,
> *Unwinds* their *minds*. (14-15)

> To *brave* as any room
> The tiger-*cave* and as in any room
> Find woman in the room
> With dear face shaking her dress
> To *wave* like any picture queen . . . (43-47)

> Until they *stumbled* on their eyes,
> Read the *number* of the year,
> *Remembered* the fast tiger. (86-8)
> And scarcely *knows* she weeps
> So loud the tiger roars.
> Or thinks to *close* her eyes. (109-111)

There is no regular metre, with lines that resemble iambic pentameter alternating with much shorter two-beat lines. On the other hand, there is a living pulse to the verse based on the succession of clear statements, giving what Clark describes as 'that cumulative power of statement'; these statements alternate between the emphatically staccato, as in lines 24-30, 37-38, 102-103 and others unwinding more gradually, as at 51-61, 62-70, 104-112.[14]

The use of parallelism, the unsystematic but recurrent and effective use of rhyme and assonance, the living pulse of statement; these are sources of poetic strength. There is also the 'memorable beauty of phrase' referred to in her blurb on the dust jacket for the first edition of *Collected Poems*. Examples in this poem include:

> The green anatomy of desire
> Plain as through glass
> Quickens as I pass. (15-17)

> Not to be image of the beast in me,
> I press the tiger forward.
> I crash through.
> Now we are two.
> One rides. (26-30)

> Such a woman as I,
> Mirage of all green forests—
> The colour of the season always
> When hope lives of abolished pleasures. (58-61)

> While woman's pride escaped
> In tiger stripes. (69-70)

> 'O pride,' I comforted, 'rest.
> The mischief and the rape
> Cannot come through.
> We are in the time of never yet
> Where bells peal backward,
> Peal "forget, forget".' (96-101)

None of these passages sacrifices meaning for music, but in all there is economy, concision and impact.

3

The second point was that the poem has a traditional structure as a story, an adventure story. To sketch it out roughly, in part one (lines 1-30) the scene is set: the poet, a woman, is surrounded by men, lechery, and lust; she (and the tiger in her) escape. Part two is the pursuit, the listening with 'lady ears', the implied seduction and the yielding as queen, the escape of pride in tiger stripes (lines 31-70). The third part is the commotion of the men and their bookish reaction (lines 71-94). The final part (lines 94-126) describes the lady reminiscing and reflecting in the freedom but also the loneliness of her survival.

This story-like structure is appropriate to its position as the penultimate and crowning 'poem of mythical occasion'.[15] It also has elements of fairy tale: transformations of human into beast and back again, appearances not being what they seem, references to magic, to armies, queens and shepherdesses, and somewhat detached and unsettling references to violence.

Buried in plain view within the story, at its end, there is a highly significant allusion, I believe, to the story of *Sleeping Beauty*. In the second part of the story, the pursuit, the 'lady' explains why she has awaited the pursuers:

'Dear pursuer, to find me thus
Belies no tiger.
The tiger runs and rides, [...]
But the lady is not venturous,
Like any picture queen she hides
And is unhappy in her room,
Covering her eyes against the latest year,
Its learning of old queens,
Its death to queens and pictures,
Its lust of century creatures,
And century creatures as one woman,
Such a woman as I,
Mirage of all green forests—
The colour of the season always
When hope lives of abolished pleasures.' (Lines 48-61)

In the traditional fairy story (and also, to look forward a moment, in Blake's 'The Little Girl Found', one of this poem's antecedents) the innocent girl is sexually awakened, or the poor girl becomes a princess – or both. In this poem the hope of 'abolished pleasures' symbolised by the 'mirage of green forests' is to put it mildly unfulfilled. The 'lady' yields but experiences pain (line 66) and by inference 'mischief and rape' (line 97). In the earliest known version of *Sleeping Beauty*, in *Perceforest,* the sleeping girl is actually raped whilst asleep and only wakes after giving birth to twins. This may have prompted the lines 'The mischief and the rape | Cannot come through.' Another fairy tale, *The Glass Coffin*, in which a maiden is freed from a glass chest, may have suggested the imagery of the cage with a fourth side of glass in lines 24-30.

In the high forest she is gentle.
She is patient in a high house.
Ah me, ah me, says every lady in the end,

> Putting the tiger in its cage
> Inside her lofty head.
> And weeps reading her own story.
> And scarcely knows she weeps,
> So loud the tiger roars.
> *Or thinks to close her eyes,*
> *Though surely she must be sleeping,*
> To go on without knowing weeping,
> Sleeping or not knowing,
> Not knowing weeping,
> Not knowing sleeping. (Lines 113-126, italics added)

The clue is in the unexpected line 'Or thinks to close her eyes'. Why would she close her eyes? Again we have a characteristic paradox of Riding's poems. She would close her eyes in order to wake up, inverting the traditional story of the Sleeping Beauty – who has to be awoken by the kiss of the prince! She would close her eyes to look inward, as in the deceptively simple poem 'How Blind and Bright':

> Eyes not looking out for eyes
> Look inward and meet sight
> In common loneliness,
> Invisibility and darkness.
>
> How bright is blind!
> How bright is blind!

Or, as in the opening fragment of 'Poems of Immediate Occasion', 'Echoes 1':

> Since learning all in such a tremble last night—
> Not with my eyes adroit in the dark,
> But with my fingers hard with fright,

> Astretch to touch a phantom, closing on myself—
> I have been smiling.

Therefore the concluding lines of 'The Tiger', which seem at first and second reading to be pessimistic and fatalistic, contain hope – not of 'abolished pleasures' but of awakening to herself, the awakening (and the reference to the traditional story) being implicit in the line 'Though surely she must be sleeping'.

This belies the apparent gentleness and resignation at the end of the 'story'. Or rather the end of the story contains another story altogether. We are left with 'the tiger back in its cage | Inside her lofty head', ready to be integrated into the woman knowing it 'late'. The lady's weeping is all but drowned out by the roar of the tiger in the lines immediately preceding 'Or thinks to close her eyes':

> And weeps reading her own story.
> And scarcely knows she weeps,
> So loud the tiger roars.

As a modernist story the poem also reflects upon the role story itself plays in creating the context for the action described. Our fifth section, on the ideas set out in the poem, reflects on this aspect further. Here it is worth noting how (as in other poems, examples being 'One Self', 'Incarnations' and 'The Rugged Black of Anger') the poem ultimately appears to detonate itself, to swallow itself, or turn itself upside down. In this case all the 'lady' has to do is to close her eyes and to wake up for the whole story to disappear, or to be transfigured.

4

The third point was how personal a poem this is. The poem has at least two important literary antecedents. Firstly, there are the famous lines of Shakespeare that provide the idea of the tiger within a woman:

THE TIGER

> O tiger's heart wrapped in a woman's hide
> How couldst thou drain the life-blood of the child
> To bid the father wipe his eyes withal,
> And yet be seen to bear a woman's face?
> Women are soft, mild, pitiful, and flexible—
> Thou stern, obdurate, flinty, rough, remorseless.[16]

Riding's tiger could be seen as an inversion of this pious travesty of womanhood.

Secondly, and more substantially, there is the precedent of William Blake's 'The Tyger'. This is signalled in the poem's opening line, which is in direct contrast to Blake's: 'Tyger Tyger, burning bright, In the forests of the night'. Blake's 'Tyger' is a covert challenge to the existence of God. He poses the tiger as a force to be reckoned with, equal to God in the universal law of nature: 'What immortal hand or eye | Dare frame thy fearful symmetry', etc. But Blake's tiger is also Blake himself, his extraordinary imagination ('the forests of the night'); his seizure of power. He himself is a force of nature to be reckoned with.

Here, as noted in the opening section of this chapter, right at the start of her poem we get Laura Riding's personal, apparently angry reaction to William Blake. This poet's, this woman's experience is different, as is made immediately clear: 'The tiger *in me* I know late | *Not burning bright*.' Equally relevant to 'The Tiger' are Blake's long ballad-style poems 'The Little Girl Lost', 'The Little Girl Found' from *Songs of Innocence*. The little girl is called 'Lyca' (a name echoed in that of 'Lida', of Riding's ''Forgotten Girlhood', surely?). Blake's poems are about sexuality, about how innocence deals with, transmutes, experience. (Remember, by contrast, Riding's 'But who has ever learned anything from experience? We get nothing from it, we give everything to it.')[17] There are echoes in Riding's 'The Tiger' of the oft repeated sleeping/weeping lines in the Blake poems, for example: 'How can Lyca sleep | If her mother weep'; 'Weep not for the maid | In the palace deep | Lyca lies asleep'; 'And saw their sleeping child | Among tygers wild.' The woman's experiences, as related in 'The Tiger', are less fulfilling:

> So to the first pursuer I prolonged
> Woman's histories and shames
> And yielded as became a queen
> Picture-dreaming in a room
> Among silk provinces where pain
> Ruined her body without stain—
> So white, so out of time, so story-like
> While woman's pride escaped
> In tiger stripes. (Lines 62-70)

At this remove it may be permissible to note a possible reference to the relationship with Robert Graves:

> And Queen, Queen, Queen
> Crowded the Captain's brain.
> And Queen, Queen, Queen,
> Spurred the whole train
> With book-thoughts. (Lines 79-83)

'Captain' is not an infrequent title for a hero or villain of a narrative ('Captain Carpenter', in John Crowe Ransom's poem, for example), and it is not necessary to the poem for us to identify this particular Captain with Captain Robert Von Ranke Graves of the Royal Welch Fusiliers, but if she had wished to avoid the identification the poet could have chosen some other designation, such as 'Prince', or 'Hero'.

The Captain is the 'first pursuer', noted in an aside in the first version of the poem in 1928 as 'the wisest' of the pursuers. This aside is excised from subsequent versions, reflecting perhaps the cooling of the personal relationship of Riding and Graves. This suggestion is reinforced by other alterations between poems in *Love as Love, Death as Death* and their later versions. In particular there is an extraordinary passage in the poem 'Love as Love':

> Your face is death asleep
> And my praise wakeful on it.

But wake not, death,
And wake not, guarded face.

So you are womanly and I can kiss
All manliness away
That might awaken harshly
And seize me without praise
In eyes lusting but to bury me
In eternal blindness, and deeply.[18]

This passage, so personal, perhaps not surprisingly was excised from later versions of the poem.[19]

To return to Blake: he was emphatically not a 'gentleman', either in his social standing or his approach to women. He championed free expression of sexuality 'The lineaments of Gratified Desire' for both men and women alike.[20] His own mythologizing was not of the queens and shepherdesses variety. A 'gentleman's' behaviour is determined and restricted (insofar as he is a gentleman) by his social position. The same goes for the gentleman's counterpart, the 'lady'. The woman is different, which point takes us to the final section of this account.

5

The fourth point is how much this is a poem of new and challenging ideas. Right at the beginning the reader is faced with a bewildering cluster of ideas around time. This cluster of ideas is linked with lust and lechery and 'the beast in me'; what it is to be a woman, or a 'lady' in a world of men or by herself: vulnerable, powerful, idealised and ravaged.

The poet knows the tiger 'late' (1, and again at 31, 95). She is a 'century creature' (10, paralleled at 56 and 57). The poem continues:

To myself, hurrying, I whisper,
'The lechery of time greases their eyes.

> Lust, earlier than time,
> Unwinds their minds.
> The green anatomy of desire
> Plain as through glass
> Quickens as I pass.'
>
> Earlier than lust, not plain,
> Behind a darkened face of memory,
> My inner animal revives. (11-20)

Bafflement in a reader coming across these thoughts without preparation (and at the time of the poem's first publication there was not much of that, unless one had first read and understood *Anarchism Is Not Enough* or *Contemporaries and Snobs*) would be understandable. Riding believed that we are at the end of history, when time itself is over, finished. History is dead. This, the twentieth century, is the new time, the 'modernist' time, post the Victorian modern age – and all is possible for the 'century creature'. The ideas are implicit in some other poems (as in 'World's End') and explicit in later prose work, particularly in the essays in *Epilogue*.[21]

An orderly reading would place 'the lechery of time' as the most recent phenomenon, then 'lust, earlier than time' (and presumably deeper); then earlier still, not plain, (and deeper still), 'my inner animal', identified here as the tiger. However while the tiger is the *earliest* of the phenomena described it is the tiger in her, known *late* by the poet, that is pressed through into the present now. As she put it in 'Incarnations':

> Do not deny in the new vanity
> The old, original dust. (3-4)

This helps explain an apparent oddity of expression in a complex passage of 'The Tiger':

'Company,' he cried, 'the tiger made magic

> While you slept and I dreamt of ravages.
> The queen was dust.' (76-78)

The tiger has the effect of tying the beginning to the end, as in 'Echoes 11', and in a different context, the later poem 'Doom in Bloom':

> Now flower the oldest seeds.
> The secret of the root no more
> Keeps jealous distance from the air. (1-3)

In the first parts of the poem the tiger is not integrated with the poet:

> Not to be image of the beast in me,
> I press the tiger forward.
> I crash through.
> Now we are two.
> One rides. (26-30)

> While woman's pride escaped
> In tiger stripes. (69-70)

In the end:

> Ah me, ah me, says every lady in the end,
> Putting the tiger in its cage
> Inside her lofty head. (115-117)

But the passage goes on to its covert resolution, as described in section 3 above:

> And weeps reading her own story.
> And scarcely knows she weeps,
> So loud the tiger roars.

> Or thinks to close her eyes,
> Though surely she must be sleeping,
> To go on without knowing weeping,
> Sleeping or not knowing,
> Not knowing weeping,
> Not knowing sleeping. (118-126)

If only she would close her eyes, go back to sleep, and thus wake up to the source of her strength!

NOTES

[1] The opening poem-sequence 'Forgotten Girlhood' is longer but made up of several discrete poems.

[2] There are shorter poems in Poems of Mythical Occasion' which have fairy story elements, a good example being 'The Sad Boy'.

[3] *The Poems of Laura Riding* (Persea, 2001) xxvii-xxviii. This is the revised 'centennial' edition of Laura Riding, *Collected Poems* (Cassell, 1938, and Carcanet, 1980).

[4] Laura Riding, *Love as Love, Death as Death* (London: Seizin, 1928) 9-15 (not 19, as misprinted on contents page); *Poems: A Joking Word* (London: Cape, 1930) 101-105; *Collected Poems* (London: Cassell, 1938) 54-58.

[5] Fuller, Roy, 'The White Goddess', *The Review*, Number 23 (1970), 5. However, he goes on in less sympathetic vein: 'But the intellect, as has been seen, had to work with emotions of equal intensity, and I think the final verdict must be that the partnership was infrequently in balance.' He also finds Riding's own *Anarchism Is Not Enough* and *Contemporaries and Snobs* exasperatingly unsatisfactory and compares them adversely with the Riding/Graves collaborations. We shall return to this categorical separation of intellectual and emotional functions in other essays. It lies at the heart of the difficulty that critics and readers have experienced with Riding's work.

[6] As she refers to them in the 1938 introduction.

[7] It is an arbitrary cut off. There are many more poems of 60-100 lines, particularly in 'Poems of Final Occasion' and 'Poems Continual'.

[8] There is no doubt that while she continued to produce wonderfully succinct and elegant shorter poems right up to the end of *Collected Poems* (for example: 'Be Grave Woman', 'Divestment of Beauty', 'Doom In Bloom', 'Nothing So Far') the tendency was the production of longer and in some respects less 'poetic' poems. There is a particular concentration of longer poems in the latter part of 'Final Occasion', when her poetry reached its greatest intensity, and she her poetic climax.

[9] 'Poetry and Music' in Laura Riding, *Anarchism Is Not Enough* (London: Cape, 1928) 32-36. See the 'Introduction' for a full account.

[10] *A Survey of Modernist Poetry*, 27-28. This account could be said to derive from Coleridge's theory of organic form.

[11] Ibid, 23.

[12] The initial imagery of the cage with a fourth side of glass is reminiscent of a fairy tale of *The Glass Coffin*. Note too how this imagery is echoed, and negated, in the poem which follows 'The Tiger' in all three collections cited in note 4 above, 'The Rugged Black of Anger':

> This is the account of peace,
> Why the rugged black of anger
> Has an uncertain smile-border,
> Why crashing glass does not announce
> The monstrous petal-advance of flowers (19-24)

[13] In the core essay of *Anarchism*, 'Jocasta', she overturns accepted views of metre, of creativity, and of the very nature of poetry and prose, as noted in the introductory chapter.

[14] Clark, Alan J, 'Where Poetry Ends', *PN Review,* no. 22 (1981): 26-28. The quotation is from p27. Clark also notes the effective use of parallelism by Riding in her poems.

[15] The final poem of 'Mythical Occasion' is 'The Rugged Black of Anger' which, we argue in a separate essay, initiates the 'Poems of Immediate Occasion'. It is no accident that, as indicated (in note 12 above) in all three of the collections in which both poems appear 'The Tiger' immediately precedes 'Rugged Black'.

[16] 3 Henry VI; Act I, iv, 138-143.

[17] In 'A Prophecy or a Plea' (1925), reprinted in Laura Riding, *First Awakenings* (Manchester: Carcanet, 1992), 279.

[18] In *Love as Love, Death as Death* (56), part VI of the poem. *Love as Love, Death as Death* was a very limited edition – only 175 signed copies issued.

[19] Entitled 'Love as Love' in *Poems: A Joking Word*; 'Rhythms of Love' in *Collected Poems*.

[20] From 'The Question Answerd'.

[21] For example 'Preliminaries' at the beginning of each of the three *Epilogue* volumes: 'Now time has reached the flurrying curtain-call/That wakens thought from historied reverie' (blank page, vi).

Chapter 7

'The Rugged Black of Anger': the account of peace

THE RUGGED BLACK OF ANGER

The rugged black of anger
Has an uncertain smile-border.
The transition from one kind to another
May be love between neighbour and neighbour
Or natural death; or discontinuance
Because, so small is space,
The extent of kind must be expressed otherwise;
Or loss of kind when proof of no uniqueness
Confutes the broadening edge and discourages.

Therefore and therefore all things have experience   10
Of ending and of meeting,
And of ending that much more
As self grows faint of self dissolving
When more is the intenser self
That is another too, or nothing.
And therefore smiles come of least smiling—

The gift of nature to necessity
When relenting grows involuntary.

This is the account of peace,
Why the rugged black of anger   20
Has an uncertain smile-border,
Why crashing glass does not announce
The monstrous petal-advance of flowers,
Why singleness of heart endures
The mind coupled with other creatures.
Room for no more than love in such dim passages
Where between kinds lie only
Their own uncertain edges.

This such precise division of space
Leaves nothing for walls, nothing but   30
Weakening of place, gentleness.
The blacker anger, blacker the less
As anger greater, angrier grows;
And least where most,
Where anger and anger meet as two
And share one smile-border
To remain so.

1

Readers of Riding's poems are familiar with the sense that hers is original and challenging work. Even if one comes to the poem with that expectation, 'The Rugged Black of Anger' seems almost without precedent in its combination of analytical dissection and controlled emotional intensity. It is like heart surgery on language. It seems at first reading both clear and opaque. The first two lines seem unexceptional, almost commonplace:

> The rugged black of anger

Has an uncertain smile-border.

The first interesting word here is 'rugged', with its connotations of rugged individualism and severe, frowning features. From other remarks Riding makes about her character, one can recognise the poet-person in these lines.[1]

The following seven lines take us abruptly into new territory. They move from the particular (the case of anger, rugged black and its smile-border) into a general statement of how things end and meet:

> The transition from one kind to another
> May be love between neighbour and neighbour;
> Or natural death; or discontinuance
> Because, so small is space,
> The extent of kind must be expressed otherwise;
> Or loss of kind when proof of no uniqueness
> Confutes the broadening edge and discourages.

This reads like an exegesis or a taxonomy, of the various ways things relate to each other, as the following lines confirm, summing up (before moving on again):

> Therefore and therefore all things have experience
> Of ending and of meeting […]

In a way the poem can be read as an example of fulfilment of the promise made in Riding's manifesto poem, 'As Well As Any Other':

> For in peculiar earth alone can I
> Construe the word and let the meaning lie
> That rarely may be found.

In 'The Rugged Black of Anger', the first two lines are in a sense the 'peculiar earth', the intense, and 'owned', experience of an emotion (and its border), through which arises the seemingly dispassionate, didactic even, analysis which follows. The poem can be adduced as a telling counter-example to the criticism of Roy Fuller, in his otherwise largely sympathetic review of her *Selected Poems*:

> This almost unique power to dazzle one intellectually appears again and again throughout her verse. But the intellect, as has been seen, had to work with emotions of equal intensity, and I think the final verdict must be that the partnership was infrequently in balance.[2]

2

The question arises: why are anger and its 'smile-border' the subject(s) for the poem, as opposed to some other emotion or concept? In *Collected Poems* the poem is placed at the end of 'Poems of Mythical Occasion', the following section being 'Poems of Immediate Occasion'. The preceding three poems, 'Helen's Burning', 'Helen's Faces', and 'The Tiger', are explicitly concerned with the fate and identity of woman. The first two of these poems refer to the mythical Helen of Troy; the third tells a story using the figure of the tiger. 'The Rugged Black of Anger' is direct, unmediated by story or reference to myth; but while its conclusions are general they are grounded in, arise out of, consideration of the particular, the person: the rugged black of anger (and its smile-border). It is my impression that this particular emotion or rather these particular emotions (the smile-border being as relevant as the anger) were experienced in considering woman's fate and identity.

'The Rugged Black of Anger' was also placed directly after 'The Tiger' in *Poems: A Joking Word* in 1930. That superb poem begins, as we have seen, with, for Riding, an exceptionally direct reference to another poem, namely one of William Blake's *Songs of Experience*, 'The Tyger'.

In *A Survey of Modernist Poetry*, Riding and Graves afford an almost unique degree of respect to Blake, comparing him most favourably with the

Romantics in a lengthy aside:

> Blake was also a radical: one of the few Englishmen who dared walk about in London wearing a cap of Liberty. But he is a very rare instance of a poet who could afford not to affect a class-technique: for he was on intimate terms with the angels and wrote like an angel rather than like a gentleman. […] *If a man has complete identity with his convictions, then he is tough about them, he is not sentimental* […] The Romantic Revivalists were all spoiled as revolutionaries by their gentility. Blake was in no sense a Romantic Revivalist. *He was a seer, or a poet. He despised the gentry in religion, literature and painting equally. That is why there is little or nothing of Blake's mature work that could be confused with that of any contemporary or previous writer. He did not forfeit his personality by submitting to any conventional medium; and he did not complain of the neglect of his poems by the greater reading public.*[3] (Italics added)

I am not sure that Blake was quite so uncomplaining, but the portrait otherwise is compelling, and begs comparison with the present poet. Her later comments on Blake are more qualified, but they are interesting for the contrast they elicit between her own later poetry (and post-poetic work) and Blake's later poetic work. In 'Addendum' to *The Telling* she wrote:

> He locked up his poetic vision within a siege-enclosure to keep it from the temptations of spiritual curiosity: it was tamed to know nothing beyond the myth-structure, the private cosmogony, he created for its occupancy. Keen was his poetic sight for all within this narrowly personal spirituality. Poetic vision was here held in duress to serve as a private religious vision inaccessible to outer questioning, influence, assault.[4]

Whereas Blake's later work, his billowing 'prophetic books' turned inward, became impenetrably symbolic and banal by turns, Riding's impulse, as we shall see in essays on the later poems, 'Tale of Modernity' in particular, was gradually to uncover her cosmogony (or cosmology, as we refer to it), to make it more accessible.[5] This eventually led her out of poetry, but her later poems bear witness to her attempts as a practising poet to share her spirituality and religious vision.

There is an almost equally famous, and perhaps more relevant, quotation from Blake from *The Marriage of Heaven and Hell*: 'The tygers of wrath are wiser than the horses of instruction.'[6]

Blake's statements are often paradoxical, but he proceeds, as he says, by contraries; his work becomes increasingly mythological and impenetrable. Riding too is frequently paradoxical, but her work becomes more analytical and less mythological. She has more intellectual resources, in particular in her access to and faith in language. For Riding, forces of nature have to be recognised but also construed. There is a tiger of wrath, but there is also a horse of instruction at work in 'The Rugged Black of Anger'. And there is, one could argue, the wisdom of both.

3

A key word in the opening section of the poem is the plain word 'kind'. The use of 'kind' here can be illuminated by reference to the opening passage of *Contemporaries and Snobs*, from the section entitled 'Shame of the Person'[7]:

> There is a sense of life so real that it becomes the sense of something more real than life. Spatial and temporal sequences can only partially express it. It introduces a principle of selection into the undifferentiating quantitative appetite and *thus changes accidental emotional forms into deliberate intellectual forms; animal experiences related by time and space into human experiences related in infinite degrees of kind.* It is the meaning at work in what has no meaning; it is at its clearest, poetry. (1928, page 9, my italics)

That the author was both proud of 'The Rugged Black of Anger' and conscious of the difficulty readers might experience is evident from the fact that an analysis of the first eighteen lines (of an early version of the poem, quoted without attribution to Riding) is given in Chapter 6 of *A Survey of Modernist Poetry*. In this chapter, entitled 'The Making of the Poem', the authors attack the idea that a poem can or should be an expression of ideas that could be otherwise described in prose:

> Now, to tell what a poem is all about in 'so many words' is to reduce the poem to so many words, to leave out all that the reader cannot at the moment understand in order to give him the satisfaction of feeling that he is understanding it. If it were possible to give the complete force of a poem in a prose summary, then there would be no excuse for writing the poem: the 'so many words' are, to the last punctuation-mark, the poem itself.
>
> * * *
>
> What are we to do, then, since the poem really seems to mean what it says? All we can do is to let it interpret itself, without introducing any new associations or, if possible, any new words.[8]

The illustration they give is as follows:

> The rugged black of anger
> Has an uncertain smile-border.
> The transition from one kind to another,
> As from anger, rugged black,
> To what lies across its smile-border,
> May be love between neighbour and neighbour
> (Love between neighbouring kind and kind);
> Or natural death (death of one,
> Though not of the other); or discontinuance
> (Discontinuance of kind,
> As anger no more anger)

> Because so small is space
> (So small the space for kind and kind and kind),
> The extent of kind must be expressed otherwise
> (The extent of kind beyond its border
> Is end of kind, because space is so small
> There is not room enough for all
> Kinds: anger *angrier* has to be
> So by an uncertain smile-border);[9]

Anger may change into something else in four carefully described ways, but it is noteworthy that the most expansive exposition is given to the third alternative, of

> […] discontinuance
> Because, so small is space,
> The extent of kind must be expressed otherwise;

In this case *angrier* anger has to be expressed by an uncertain smile-border.

> And therefore smiles come of least smiling—
> The gift of nature to necessity
> When relenting grows involuntary.

4

This explication, this literal unfolding of the poem in its own terms, may not, however, appear particularly satisfying, especially when compared with *A Survey's* exciting and ground-breaking analysis of Shakespeare's Sonnet 129. *A Survey's* analysis of 'The Rugged Black of Anger' has not, to my knowledge, been taken up by subsequent critics of Riding's poetry, whereas the analysis of the sonnet has stimulated a whole school of criticism.[10] The choice of the particular sonnet by Shakespeare is interesting and relevant. Its subject is lust, and the language used is exceptionally direct and sexually explicit.

Elsewhere Riding wrote, approvingly: 'Shakespeare knew Lust by day, | With raw unsleeping eye.'[11] A similarity between lust (in Shakespeare's time) and anger (in Riding's) is that they were troubling and perceived as socially dangerous emotions. In other poets the emotions are sublimated or demonised. By contrast Shakespeare and Riding enact and articulate a full experience of the emotions through language. They take them up to and beyond their limits. The poems accommodate lust and anger as humanly essential emotions that do not have to be destructive.

To return to *A Survey*:

> Lust in the extreme goes beyond both bliss and woe; it goes beyond reality. It is no longer lust *Had, having and in quest*, it is lust face to face with *love*.[12]

It is interesting that at this point the authors of *A Survey* depart somewhat from the 'rule' adopted in respect of their analysis of the Riding poem of 'letting the poem interpret itself without introducing any new associations or, if possible, any new words.' The idea that lust in the extreme goes 'beyond reality' and is 'face to face with love' goes beyond the words of the sonnet – which does not include the word 'love'. Whilst it might be argued that it is implicit in Shakespeare the idea is very much, I think, Riding's own, and is consistent with the concluding lines of her poem:

> The blacker anger, blacker the less
> As anger greater, angrier grows;
> And least where most,
> Where anger and anger meet as two
> And share one smile-border
> To remain so.

As lust in the extreme is face to face with *love* in Shakespeare's sonnet, so anger in the extreme is face to face with smiling, with *peace* in Riding's poem.[13]

5

Riding's poem is in some respects complemented, and some of the ideas expanded, by a wonderful later essay from *Epilogue* entitled 'In Defence of Anger':

> Anger is precious because it is an immediate, undeniable clue to what our minds (so much more cautious in rejection and resistance than our bodies) will not tolerate. It is precious because it is momentary: it is a momentary act of disassociation which makes a basic review of an association possible – compels a basic review. Anger has, properly, a constructive sequel of clarification.
>
> * * *
>
> Anger combines judgement and emotion in a single impulse. [...] Anger cannot be ignored; it challenges the whole surrounding situation and demands an intelligent positive attention.
>
> * * *
>
> Life consists essentially of the difficult occasions. [...] By difficult occasions I mean those in which we rely on judgement rather than on social habit, those in which we must behave originally and which are the integers of our consciousness, as the easy occasions are mere fractions.
>
> * * *
>
> Anger is a precious emotion, but it is also a generous one, as judgement is a generous faculty. The person who possesses the faculty of judgement possesses it exactly because his field of potential satisfaction is extensive and not niggardly: extent necessitates judgement as a large place necessitates government, and a very small place does not. The field of anger is as extensive as the field of potential satisfaction; it is indeed the same field.
>
> * * *
>
> I myself am always grateful to the anger-provoking situation, for the clarity it produces – whether it is my anger or someone else's.

> My only complaint, in relation to anger, would be that there is not enough of it. It is a remarkably infrequent occurrence, considering the frequency of exhortations against anger. I love seeing a person in anger as I love hearing a person think: we do not often so honour one another.[14]

These snippets give only a flavour of the sustained and cogent account which makes essential reading for anyone wishing to understand the author and her work.[15]

6

Exploring the links between the language and ideas of the poem and those of her prose has been diverting – in both senses. We have anticipated and potentially dulled somewhat the impact of the great climax to the poem:

> This is the account of peace,
> Why the rugged black of anger
> Has an uncertain smile-border,
> Why crashing glass does not announce
> The monstrous petal-advance of flowers,
> Why singleness of heart endures
> The mind coupled with other creatures.

This is powerful and unprecedented imagery. We are familiar with 'the monstrous anger of the guns.'[16] The world could not exist if anger expanded indefinitely in the destructive manner of war. The concept of flowers engaged in 'monstrous petal-advance' is startling, but of course monstrous is what flowers are not, they expand in order to be themselves. 'Flowers' in Riding's decidedly un-naturalistic poetics are typically associated with personhood, particularly womanhood.[17] Beneath the apparently impersonal and ungendered surface of the poem can we not detect also a humorous reminiscence of the misogynistic phrase 'monstrous regiment of women' in these lines? The poem is as much about woman as is 'The Tiger', but about a woman in control. Healthy anger, answered healthily, produces progress, advance in consciousness, not destruction.

The lines create the image of crashing glass and monstrous petal-advance only to negate it with 'not'. This contrasts with and at the same time develops the imagery in 'The Tiger':

> They cage me on three sides.
> The fourth is glass.
> Not to be image of the beast in me,
> I press the tiger forward.
> I crash through.
> Now we are two.
> One rides.
> ('The Tiger', 24-30)

7

'The Rugged Black of Anger' represents a new type of poem, which is a reason why it was chosen for analysis (a rather shy analysis) in *A Survey*. In the *Collected Poems* it is set at the end of 'Poems of Mythical Occasion' and is the doorway into 'Poems of Immediate Occasion', exemplifying the more direct approach. At the same time it demonstrates poetic power and striking imagery, albeit (characteristically) the most striking imagery is effectively dissolved as it is created.

NOTES

[1] In the poems too: 'This resolve: with trouble's brow' from 'An Ageless Brow'; or 'After Smiling', or 'Because I Sit Here So'.

[2] Roy Fuller, 'The White Goddess', *The Review*, Number 23 (1970), 5.

[3] Laura Riding and Robert Graves, A *Survey of Modernist Poetry* (London: Heinemann,1927; Manchester: Carcanet 2002) 96 in 2002 Carcanet edition.

[4] Laura (Riding) Jackson, *The Telling* (London: Athlone, 1972), 181. In her introduction to the 1980 edition of *Collected Poems* she is more disparaging, referring (in adverse comparison, in this respect, with Matthew Arnold to): 'the religiose megalomania that made Blake—for instance—a politician of paradise answering to his personal sense of moral superiority.' (Quoted here from pxxxvii of the centennial edition).

[5] For a while in Mallorca, between 1932 and 1934, Jacob Bronowski, later to win fame as the author of *The Ascent of Man*, worked closely with Laura Riding on *Epilogue*. As noted by Elizabeth Friedmann in her biography *A Mannered Grace* (New York: Persea, 2005), 228-30, it seems unlikely that he owed nothing to Laura Riding in respect of his influential work *William Blake: The Man Without a Mask* (London: Secker and Warburg, 1944) later revised as *William Blake and the Age of Revolution* (London: Routledge and Kegan Paul, 1972), although he made no mention of her. He gives a persuasive account of the prophetic books, how and why they differ from and in the main lack the brilliance of the poetry.

[6] William Blake, *The Marriage of Heaven and Hell*, ('Proverbs of Hell', number 44). Wrath is 'intense anger or indignation' (OED); it could lie on the other side of the smile-border of 'the rugged black of anger'.

[7] It is impossible to resist going beyond the immediate scope of this account with a reference to Laura Riding's introduction to Homiletic Studies (which include the essay 'In Defence of Anger' referred to later). This succinctly attacks the disintegration by psychology of the 'natural person', and attempts to reinstate the notion of character. To quote but one resonant remark: 'Our persons have grown ghostly under the influence of psychological analysis, which composes a common, public person out of the old privately vested qualities.' In Laura Riding and Robert Graves, *Essays from 'Epilogue' 1935-1937*, (Manchester: Carcanet 2002), 79. Incidentally, this remark helps us to understand the uses of the term 'ghostly' in several of the poems.

[8] *A Survey of Modernist Poetry* (Manchester: Carcanet 2002), 67, 71.

[9] Ibid.

[10] The explication of 'Rugged Black' is followed by an attack on the 'laziness of the plain reader', who is not prepared to slow down his reading. 'Increasing the time-length of reading is one way of getting out of the prose and into the poetic state of mind, of developing a capacity for minuteness, for seeing all there is to see at a given point and for taking it all with one as one goes along. We have forgotten, however, that the plain reader, while he does not object to the poetic state of mind in the poet, has a fear of cultivating it in himself.' *A Survey*, 72.

[11] 'Tale of Modernity', *Collected Poems*, 142. Our essay on this complex poem develops the account of *A Survey's* analysis of the Shakespeare sonnet.

[12] *A Survey*, 2002, 35.

[13] Compare again Blake's 'A Poison Tree': 'I was angry with my friend: I told my wrath my wrath did end.'

[14] *Essays from 'Epilogue' 1935-1937*, 87-99; quotations are from 88, 90, 92, 95, 96.

[15] The account of anger in the essay, written several years after 'Rugged Black' is not entirely consistent with the poem. For example: 'We cannot say of a person that he has let himself get

too angry: there are no degrees in anger, as there are no degrees in judgement.' (p97). In the poem, by contrast: 'The blacker anger, blacker the less| As anger greater, angrier grows'. The essay presents an ideal view of anger, and distinguishes brilliantly the beneficial form from other forms of what are commonly regarded as forms of anger such as petulance, the fury of hate, and war.

This later account foreshadows (for this writer), for all its brilliance, difficulties later encountered in the ambitious but not fully achieved dictionary project. Laura Riding was first and foremost a poet. What does a poet do when his work as poet is completed (as with the publication of *Collected Poems* her work as a poet had been)?

[16] From Wilfred Owen's 'Anthem for Doomed Youth' of course. One is reminded that the whole of Riding's poetic work was written and published between the end of the Great War and the beginning of the Second World War. She was, as were so many, concerned with how peace could be achieved and sustained, and ventured into the public realm with *The World and Ourselves*, the final volume of *Epilogue* published in 1938.

[17] For example in 'Postponement of Self', 'The Flowering Urn', and 'The Nightmare'.

Chapter 8

'One Self': the smile of death [1]

ONE SELF

Under apparel, apparel lies
The recurring body:
O multiple innocence, O fleshfold dress.

One self, one manyness,
Is first confusion, then simplicity.
Smile, death, O simultaneous mouth.
Cease, inner and outer,
Continuous flight and overtaking.

1

During the period of their creation Riding was moved to present her poems as being 'instead of my life'. This is one statement in the startling preface to *Poems: A Joking Word* published in 1930, referred to earlier in the essay on 'Incarnations'. As with any of her work this preface has to be read as a whole, but the following paragraphs are relevant, beginning with the opening paragraph:

> Before anything has got to be, it has got to be preceded by something that has not got to be. These poems have got to be. Or rather, when they weren't they had got to be. Or rather, I had got not to feel myself and think doom but to think myself and feel doom.[2]
>
> My poems then are instead of my life. I don't mean that in my poems I escape from my life. My life itself would be nothing but escaping, or anybody's. I mean that in my poems I escape from escaping. And my life reads all wrong to me and my poems read all right. And by doom I don't mean the destruction of me. I mean making me into doom – not my doom but doom. Made into doom I feel made. I also feel making. I feel like doom and doom feels like me.[3]

As in some of her other prose work of this period, there is an intense playfulness-in-earnest about this preface. 'Doom' is a highly charged term: as well as the sense 'fated ending to a person's life', it contains the Old English sense of judicial decision and the Middle English sense of personal opinion judgement and the Last Judgement.[4] Riding sought to achieve that finality in her poems, to be not just creative but creator.

2

Earlier versions of 'One Self' appeared as 'One Sense' in Riding's first selection of poems, *The Close Chaplet* in 1926 and again, revised, in *Poems: A Joking Word* in 1930. Revised again, the final version appeared in *Collected Poems* in 1938 and was unaltered in later editions, including her 1970 *Selected Poems: In Five Sets*. More than any poet in recent times, Riding conceived of her *Collected Poems* as a whole work, a universe.[5] She improved many of her poems through a number of published versions.

There are some striking features of these improvements.

Firstly there is increased precision, often with the introduction of exact, almost technical, terminology. In 'The Rugged Black of Anger', for example, she altered the ninth line from 'Strikes the broadening edge and discourages' to 'Confutes [*proves false*] the broadening edge and discourages'. In 'Incarnations' the 1930 version 'Lest, like a statue's stone that will not die' becomes 'Lest like a statue's too transmuted [*changed into another form or substance, as in alchemy*] stone' in the 1938 edition. In her 'manifesto' poem 'As Well as Any Other', which opened *The Close Chaplet* in 1926 edition, the clinching final lines in the original read:

> For in *untraveled soil* alone can I
> *Unearth the gem or* let the *mystery* lie
> That *never must* be found. (Italics added)

In the 1930 (and subsequent) version the lines read:

> For in *peculiar earth* alone can I
> *Construe the word and* let the *meaning* lie
> That *rarely* may be found. (Italics added)

These are substantial changes. As Robert Nye observed, 'construe' is a very sharp word to find at the heart of a song. 'It pricks the mind into remembrance that meaning is all, and that for this poet nothing but heart-felt meaning finally matters.'[6] In a long and hostile review of Riding's achievement, Marjorie Perloff selects this poem, and Nye's praise of it, for particularly scathing treatment. She says, surprisingly, of the changes made between 1926 and 1938: 'What I find astonishing about the revision is how little difference it makes.'[7] But the poet has substantially changed the words and the sense in the final version. From a mystery that never must be found to a meaning that rarely may be found – the language is cooler; the increased confidence in her powers is clear. The introduction of 'peculiar' is telling. The meanings include: 'that is one's own private property', 'of separate or distinct constitution or existence', and 'distinguished in nature, character or attributes from others'.

While not ruling out companionship, she is conscious of going it alone, and of doing so within her own resources.

The second feature of the improvements is the unique ruthlessness she displays in discarding parts of lines, or several lines, or whole sections of poems. At the same time the fragments or sections that remain are re-presented sometimes out of the context of the original poem but contributing to a new collection, a whole 'poems'. As she said in her 1930 preface:

> I have left out here any poems in already printed work that I came round to strange doom in – any poems where poems couldn't be said to be a joking word. I found many poems that were poems again in early unprinted work. Wherever anywhere I found poems again but also a strangeness as of poems once, I cut away the strange part and the familiar part became more familiar. And there are the poems now, no less poems now, no less poems again if again is, as I have reason to believe, now. [8]

Usually the result is improved overall coherence, but the process can occasionally be confusing.

Poems: A Joking Word has five sections or 'poems' entitled 'Fragments', not counting 'Fragments from Alastor'. Strangest is number 3 of the first group of 'Fragments' on page 43, where parts of lines appear like bits of papyrus out of the Alexandrian desert with most of the text missing.[9]

3

In the poem 'One Sense', in the 1926 *Close Chaplet* version, there are three lines, given here in italics, between lines 2 and 6, which were removed from subsequent versions:

> Under apparel, apparel lies
> The recurring body.
> *Night to uncover the surprise*
> *Of nakedness is deep flesh,*

> *Is abyss and body under body*:
> O multiple innocence,
> O fleshfold dress.

The three lines are much more explicitly sensual than the revised version. Removing them (as was done for the 1930 version and thereafter) definitely concentrates meaning and gives more delicacy of movement than the earlier version.

There is an opening doubleness of meaning: under apparel lies apparel, under apparel lies the recurring body. The word 'apparel' is the first of several interesting words in the poem. It connotes appearance as well as dress, as is clinched in the wonderful expression 'fleshfold dress' which conjures up a living sculpture, 'fleshfold' being a creation of Laura Riding's. The idea of a living sculpture may also remind us of the 'statue's too transmuted stone' in 'Incarnations'. 'Recurring' is also a rich term: it connotes reappearance, suggesting persistence through a number of incarnations, which likewise leads one back to the poem of that name. Perhaps the most striking expression in this section of the poem is 'O multiple innocence'. There is a reminiscence of the optimistic 'uncovering of the lovelies' described in 'The Mask'. Paradise is not lost, there is no Fall. Each day, each moment, begins afresh.

The 1926 poem also has a middle section, excised in later versions.[10] The final section of the poem was revised in 1930 and improved again in 1938. The 1930 poem reads:

> One sense, one mutualness,
> Is first confusion, and then peace.
> Smile, death, O simultaneous mouth.
> Be clear, identical brow, O death.
> Cease, inner and outer,
> Continuous flight and overtaking.

This becomes, in 1938:
> One self, one manyness

> Is first confusion, then simplicity.
> Smile, death, O simultaneous mouth.
> Cease, inner and outer,
> Continuous flight and overtaking.

Again this is more concise, and the rhythm is tighter. What is being described here is like a metamorphosis. 'Death' is used in a characteristic and paradoxical fashion by Riding. We are reminded of the words of the 1930 preface 'In my poems I escape from escaping.' This poem/the self ends its life in achieving its 'final' and unchanging form; at the same time there is a wonderful sense of movement being both stilled and enacted by the resolution of the poem's meaning and rhythm.

What are we to make of the change of the title, and of a crucial word in the poem itself – from 'One Sense' to 'One Self'? The word 'sense' incorporates a cluster of meanings: meaning, perception, feeling and soundness of judgement. The key difference between the 1930 and 1938 versions of the poem lies in the change from 'mutualness' to 'manyness', both rare words. 'Mutualness' brings into the poem involvement of at least one other, as in love. Supporting this interpretation one could adduce the following lines from 'Lucrece and Nara':

> Astonished stood Lucrece and Nara
> Face flat to face, *one sense* and smoothness... (My italics)

In the 1970 selection Laura (Riding) Jackson placed 'One Self' immediately after 'Lucrece and Nara'.

The self, on the other hand, can be 'any of various conflicting identities conceived as existing within a single person' and the 'true or intrinsic identity'.[11] The move from 'sense' to 'self' involves the whole person, but the person alone. My reading would link the poem back to 'The Quids' (the manyness of the Quids contained within the Monoton) and forward to 'Nothing So Far':

Yet here, all that remains

> When each has been the universe:
> No universe but each, or nothing.
> Here is the future swell curved round
> To all that was. (9-13).

NOTES

[1] An earlier version of this essay was presented as a paper to The Laura (Riding) Jackson Conference at Cornell University in 2010, and appears on Nottingham Trent University's Laura (Riding) Jackson website.

[2] Laura Riding, *Poems: A Joking Word*, (London: Cape, 1930) 9.

[3] Ibid, 10-11.

[4] OED.

[5] This is also true to a greater or lesser extent of her four earlier collections, *The Close Chaplet* (New York: Adelphi, 1926); *Love as Love, Death as Death* (London: The Seizin Press, 1928); *Poems: A Joking Word* (1930); and *Poet: A Lying Word* (London: Arthur Barker, 1933). The arrangement is less marked, perhaps, in *Love as Love, Death as Death* than it is in the other collections.

[6] Robert Nye, *A Selection of the Poems of Laura Riding* (Manchester: Carcanet, 1994), 3.

[7] Marjorie Perloff, 'The Witch of Truth', *Parnassus*, 23, Mo 1, (1998), 334-53, a review occasioned by the publication (separately) of *Rational Meaning* and Nye's selection (see note 6).

[8] *Poems: A Joking Word*, 1930, 22

[9] This process of refinement, of creating a whole of a new arrangement of parts, continued with Laura (Riding) Jackson's 1970 edition *Selected Poems: in Five Sets*. The redaction there of 'Benedictory' is decidedly odd: 54 quatrains in *Collected Poems* reduced to 14 disjointed quatrains in *Selected Poems*. It is impossible to envisage anyone making sense of the truncated version on its own.

[10] Over the membrous edifice

The robe is outer,

But outer as a heart in blood remiss

To be white atmosphere,

The pulse of a transparency: O secret rustling,

O plain murmur in dark vein.

[11] OED.

Chapter 9

'An Ageless Brow': the woman in view

AN AGELESS BROW

This resolve: with trouble's brow
To forswear trouble and keep
A surface innocence and sleep
To smooth the mirror
With never, never,
And now, now.

The image, not yet in recognition, had grace
To be lasting in death's time, to postpone the face
Until the face had gone.
Her regiments sprang up here and fell of peace,   10
Her banners dropped like birds that had never flown.

And her arrested hand, clasping its open palm,
Pressed on from finger to finger
The stroke withheld from trouble
Till it be only ageless brow,

A renunciatory double
Of itself, a resolve of calm,
Of never, never, and now, now.

1

This is the fourth of 'Poems of Immediate Occasion' and follows 'One Self', subject of the preceding essay. Where the theme of that poem could be summed up as 'simplicity out of confusion', this one has the theme of 'peace in the face of trouble'. An original version appeared under the title 'Her Ageless Brow' in Riding's first book in 1926, *The Close Chaplet*. It had ten more lines and four stanzas rather than three. The reduced and amended version of *Poems: A Joking Word* in 1930 was reproduced unaltered, as here, in *Collected Poems* and subsequently in *Selected Poems: In Five Sets*.

The poem has no rhyme scheme, but it does have the kind of irregular, unobtrusive rhyming (brow/now, keep/sleep, grace/face, palm/calm, trouble/double) and half-rhyming (mirror/never, face/peace, gone/flown) familiar from other poems. There is no metrical form, and no regularity about the rhythm, but it plainly flows effectively with the thought, moving smoothly and relatively swiftly in the first stanza before slowing almost to a halt at the beginning and the end of the second, and then picking up pace in the third before slowing in the final two lines. There is some repetition of phrase ('never, never and now, now') and of the 'brow/now' rhyme, and some development by parallelism as in 'with trouble's brow | To forswear trouble' and 'The stroke withheld from trouble | Till it be only ageless brow'.

In an important way this poem is the sister poem to 'The Rugged Black of Anger', the final poem of 'Mythical Occasion' which was also an account of peace, of peace emerging through the far side of intense anger:

This is the account of peace,
Why the rugged black of anger
Has an uncertain smile-border,
Why crashing glass does not announce
The monstrous petal-advance of flowers

This poem is another account of 'peace', of peace created by a woman in the face of trouble, or more drastically, mankind's proclivity to war. There is an echo of the more light-hearted 'Chloe Or...' where the two young women 'will avoid aggression | As usual, be saved by self-possession.' It is an account that is more *immediately* a self-portrait than either 'Chloe Or...' which is mythological, or the outwardly impersonal, generalized analysis of 'The Rugged Black of Anger'.

2

In the first stanza we initially understand the poet to be speaking to and from within herself, in the first person – although on reflection she may equally be addressing other women. 'This resolve' may at first reading be taken as a noun, but it is stronger when 'resolve' is read as an imperative verb. Why, though, not simply 'decide', or 'determine'? As well as the obvious sense here of taking a firm decision, 'resolve' contains the senses of dissolving, reducing into constituent parts or changing into a simpler form, sorting out a problem, or making something clearer or more distinct, senses which carry through to the rest of the stanza and the first three lines of the next.

'Trouble's brow' recalls the stern rugged black of anger, a frown of perplexity, and perhaps of Hamlet's 'taking arms against a sea of troubles'; but she resolves to 'forswear trouble and keep | A surface innocence and sleep'. This reminds us of the repeated motif of 'trouble', 'Old Trouble' throughout the poems that make up the sequence 'Forgotten Girlhood'.[1] The lack of punctuation in the first four lines, where one might have expected commas after 'trouble' in line two and 'sleep' in line three is noteworthy; it gives an onomatopoeic sense of a dissolving set of reflections, appropriate to 'smoothing the mirror'.

There are reminders of other poems: the surface innocence (in the face of Death and men) of Chloe, the self-possession of both her and Lil; the self-possession reasserted after the possession, the violence and the passion in 'The Virgin'; and the lines 'The mischief and the rape | cannot come through' from 'The Tiger'. The surface innocence and sleep also recall the allusion in

'The Tiger' to the Sleeping Beauty. However, in this poem the trouble is a more general perplexity and disturbance of the mind in the world, a disturbance reflected in the face. In 'Pride of Head' she wrote, at the end of the first stanza:

> My head is at the top of me
> Where I live mostly and most of the time,
> Where my face turns an inner look
> On what's outside of me
> And meets the challenge of other things
> Haughtily, by being what it is.

And in 'With the Face'

> With the face goes a mirror
> As with the mind a world. […]
>
> The mirror mixes with the eye.
> Soon will it be the very eye.
> Soon the eye that was
> The very mirror be.

She resolves to 'smooth the mirror' with what seems a simple lullaby to soothe a troubled child: 'never, never' is what an adult might say to bring a child awakening from a troubling dream back to reality; 'now, now' both a reassurance ('there, there') and a hushing ('that's enough'). By the time we reach the second iteration of 'never, never and now, now', as a refrain, at the end of the poem it is clear that more is meant.

3

Readers of her poems, if they are to understand them, have to expect and to allow their reading minds to be baulked by rhythmic irregularities, and arrested by the striking use of language and of imagery, as here, in the second stanza:

> The image, not yet in recognition, had grace
> To be lasting in death's time, to postpone the face
> Until the face had gone.
> Her regiments sprang up here and fell of peace,
> Her banners dropped like birds that had never flown.

This slows the reader (like the poet's time) to a halt. The first three lines, in particular, are initially baffling. Why is the image 'not yet in recognition'? What does it mean to have 'grace to be lasting in death's time'? What or whose image is it that postponed the face until the face had gone? And why had the face gone?

This second stanza brings woman, as universal woman, into the picture. The past tense of the first three lines takes us back to before the present time of the first stanza, before the resolution is made by the particular woman Laura Riding; it is a brief history of time leading up to that singular resolution. The 'image', woman's image, had grace to be lasting throughout time ('death's time', about which more later). Whilst an image may be a reflection or likeness, referring back to the mirror in line four, it is also, in modern parlance, the way in which the character of someone is perceived externally, by the public, often, as here, by implicit contrast with an unseen 'reality'. The image, then, may not yet have been 'recognized for what it is, or 'brought into clear focus' – or 'resolved', as when a photograph is developed. 'Not yet in recognition' also has the sense of not yet acknowledged as true, as sovereign, as in a people's recognition of a monarch, or a religion, or, as here, of the nature of woman.

The image, and 'grace', calls to mind the religious icons of the Virgin Mary, the suffering innocence of the female saints, and of the wives and mothers of mythical and historical heroes. No true face emerged until after, in the twentieth century, the distinctive face of woman had almost gone altogether, with the superficial erosion of differences between men and women. Now this particular woman steps forward, with characteristic courage.

Her regiments sprang up 'here', at the very point of the image having postponed the face until the face had gone. Although, as in 'The Rugged Black of Anger', this is an account of peace, it is obviously not an account of weakness; rather, it is the story of strength recognized and power withheld. There is more than a touch of the author's self-proclaimed 'serene humour' in the word 'regiments', which calls to mind the woman-fearing expression 'monstrous regiments of women', and in turn adds a humorous nuance to the 'monstrous petal-advance of flowers' in 'The Rugged Black of Anger'.[2] She might have declared war on man for his failings but instead she forswears trouble; a different resolution is needed.

4

> And her arrested hand, clasping its open palm,
> Pressed on from finger to finger
> The stroke withheld from trouble
> Till it be only ageless brow,
> A renunciatory double
> Of itself, a resolve of calm,
> Of never, never, and now, now.

The final stanza of the first version of the poem, 'Her Ageless Brow' in *The Close Chaplet* has more detail:

> *One memory remained, slower than glass,*
> *Most forgettable, forgotten,*
> *Made the face stay, be sooner:*
> In her complete hand, clasping its open palm,
> The broad forehead from finger to finger,
> The stroke withheld from trouble
> *While trouble found its brow,*

> *Saw first the previous double*
> Of itself, this resolve of calm,
> Of never, never, and now, now. (Italics added)

The italicized passages help us to understand the later, more succinct version of the poem.[3] They describe her recovery of the forgotten memory of our origin, the bringing forward of that into her present face; this has enabled 'trouble' to face itself and to acquire the resolve of calm.[4]

As a poet, she is delivering her judgement. She is not prophesying 'the end is nigh' but saying this must be the end. Time is brought to a stop in her ageless, immortal brow, hence the deeper meaning of 'never, never and now, now'. History is dismissed, all is immediate. As a poet, she must step forward and deliver the judgement. 'Her' here, is identical with (as she would capitalize it later) Truth, as of a voice striking across the world.

If time and history has come to its end, as Riding was consistently to argue for the rest of her life, then there is a naturalness that it should come about by, or through, the opposite to man, which (as told in the *Epilogue* essay 'The Idea Of God') is woman.

5

In the first section it was said that this poem is another account of peace. But the peace is increasingly hard-won, one is tempted to say, hard-fought. Here we have the implicit threat of 'The stroke withheld from trouble'; as *Collected Poems* progress sustaining a 'surface innocence and sleep' becomes still more of an effort. She becomes more openly challenging, more uncomfortable for men, as in the final stanzas of 'After Smiling':

> It was a war then rumoured,
> Scarcely declared, battleless,
> A guest as hostage fancied,
> I moved the soldier-lusts in you:
> Thus did you honour me.

But never have we fought,
Never till now, I departed
And the peace-troth raised.
I departed, since of soul-age
You now, grown to greed immortal
Of contradiction, to be the else
You made kinged state against,
To be more world, kinghood of not-you.

Now not to smile again:
Be greeted here, having come
Like Rome to sit you down
Upon eternal Rome. Eternity
In my look, celebration
Loud in yours, we'll partner glory
And visit empire on each other
Disputedly, of which, long death, decide![5]

This turbulence, masked as it is, mostly, by the resolve to maintain 'a surface innocence' and 'serene humour', breaks eloquently forth, albeit under magnificent control, in her poems, as it broke forth, not always under control, on more than one notable occasion in her life. In his first (and perhaps best) book, *The Birth of Tragedy*, Nietzsche overturned the traditional view of the classical Greeks, admired as they had previously been for their adherence to moderation, as expressed in their proverb 'nothing in excess'. There is nothing to admire, he argued, in people with mild and moderate urges controlling them. It was precisely their difficulty in controlling their wild, destructive and immoderate Dionysian tendencies that led the Greeks to value the surface control and calm of Apollo, and gave an eternal look to their poetry.

NOTES

[1] In a private letter to Mark Jacobs dated June 21 1973 she made a specific comment on 'Forgotten Girlhood', relevant and valuable here:

> Though as a poet I could from the earliest suspend my gravity, I was nowhere merely playing…The first poem in Collected Poems is a tale of *knowledge of the rough of experience penetrating through a very young consciousness without ruffling it into perturbation.* (Italics added; letter in Nottingham Trent University archive).

[2] This phrase derives from John Knox's diatribe in 1588 entitled *The First Blast of the Trumpet Against the Monstruous Regimen of Women*. Appropriately enough for our discussion here 'monstruous' for Knox meant 'unnatural, deviating from natural order', and 'regimen' meant rule or regulation by women.

[3] The first passage recalls the 'Before-time of being' in Laura (Riding) Jackson, *The Telling* (London: Athlone Press, 1972), 30. I have taken the phrase from passage 28, but more relevant to this poem are the later passages 45-55. In the passage below she sets out her vision of how to bring to an end 'the cycles of disunion':

> Calling on 'God' speaks the wish of men that cycles of disunion die in us, as we are men and women living out the war of men with men. But the cycles of disunion have their nexus in us as we are men and women living out the whole unmasking of being and remaking of it in ourselves as men and women. And what we have to do is not for 'Man' (which includes 'Woman' counted Nought) or 'God', and not for ourselves, but is for Being. Being, which was first ever all-one, waits to be made all-one again, through our being: it waits for our soul to recreate Soul. (Passage 45, page 44).

[4] This looks forward to 'Tale of Modernity' lines 31-32: 'Truth seemed love grown cool as a brow| And young as the moon, grown girl to self.'

[5] *Collected Poems*, 197. While the poem is addressed to men in general, it is easy to imagine this part of the poem – 'I moved the soldier-lusts in you' – being inspired by Graves in particular. The themes are taken further in the opening 'Poem Continual', 'The Last Covenant', the longest poem of the main body of *CP*.

Chapter 10

'Come, Words, Away': words without music

COME, WORDS, AWAY

Come, words, away from mouths,
Away from tongues in mouths
And reckless hearts in tongues
And mouths in cautious heads—
Come, words, away to where
The meaning is not thickened
With the voice's fretted substance,
Nor look of words is curious
As letters in books staring out
All that man thought strange   10
And laid to sleep on white
Like the archaic manuscript
Of dreams at morning blacked on wonder.

Come, words, away to miracle
More natural than written art.
You are surely somewhat devils,

COME, WORDS AWAY

But I know a way to soothe
The whirl of you when speech blasphemes
Against the silent half of language
And, labouring the blab of mouths,   20
You tempt prolixity to ruin.

It is to fly you home from where
Like stealthy angels you made off once
On errands of uncertain mercy:
To tell with me a story here
Of utmost mercy never squandered
 On niggard prayers for eloquence—
The marvelling on man by man.
I know a way, unwild we'll mercy
And spread the largest news   30
Where never a folded ear dare make
A deaf division of entirety.

That fluent half-a-story
Chatters against this silence
To which words, come away now
 In an all-merciful despite
Of early silvered treason
To the golden all of storying.

We'll begin fully at the noisy end
Where mortal halving tempered mercy   40
To the shorn utterance of man-sense;
Never more than savageries
Took they from your bounty-book.

Not out of stranger-mouths then
 Shall words unwind but from the voice

That haunted there like dumb ghost haunting
Birth prematurely, anxious of death.
Not ours those mouths long-lipped
To falsity and repetition
Whose frenzy you mistook 50
For loyal prophetic heat
To be improved but in precision.

Come, words, away—
That was an alien vanity,
A rash startling and a preening
That from truth's wakeful sleep parted
When she within her first stirred story-wise,
Thinking what time it was or would be
When voiced illumination spread:
What time, what words, what she then. 60

Come, words, away,
And tell with me a story here,
Forgetting what's been said already:
That hell of hasty mouths removes
Into a cancelled heaven of mercies
By flight of words back to this plan
Whose grace goes out in utmost rings
To bounds of utmost storyhood.

But never shall truth circle so
Till words prove language is 70
How words come from sound far away
Through stages of immensity's small
Centring the utter telling
In truth's first soundlessness.

Come, words, away:
I am a conscience of you
Not to be held unanswered past
The perfect number of betrayal.
It is a smarting passion
By which I call—   80
Wherein the calling's loathsome as
Memory of man-flesh over-fondled
With words like over-gentle hands.
Then come, words, away,
Before lies claim the precedence of sin
And mouldered mouths writhe to outspeak us.

1

'Come, Words, Away' is the first of the poems from the book *Poet: A Lying Word* (*PALW*) to appear in *Collected Poems*, placed toward the end of 'Poems of Immediate Occasion'. By contrast, in *Poet: A Lying Word* it appeared late, in the fourth of the five sections; its placement much earlier 'in the story' of *Collected Poems* is clearly for artistic reasons, to which we shall return shortly. The poet made numerous mostly minor alterations of word and phrase in that version, deleting the odd line, and separating into ten sections what had been a continuous flow in the original. There are though no substantial changes, no sections added or omitted. On the other hand, in the poet's *Selected Poems: In Five Sets* (1970), in the unsentimental editorial fashion unique to her, just over half the poem appears, the fourth, fifth, seventh, ninth and tenth sections being omitted.[1]

'Come, Words, Away' concentrates for almost the first time in *Collected Poems* on the subject of words. There are incidental, unobtrusive mentions in earlier poems, but only 'Hospitality to Words'*,* the first full poem of 'Immediate Occasion' (after the brilliant collection of fragments, 'Echoes') takes words for a subject, and, rather as with 'The Quids' in relation to the poet's thought on the cosmos, that poem can be superficially appreciated as playful, whimsical, rather than literal and integral to the poet's wider thought. 'Come, Words, Away' begins (in the poems) an uncovering of the poet's thought on words, thought which was eventually to take her on to various iterations of work on a dictionary, then a book on language, the final version of which was eventually published after her death.[2]

The poem begins briskly, almost trippingly, with a series of regular iambic trimeters. The pace is moderated by passages with less regular rhythm, but momentum is re-injected at intervals by the seven-fold repetition of the opening phrase 'come, words, away'. This prompts the observation that characteristically Laura Riding uses a refrain, often with variation and development, often irregularly, at the beginning or in the middle of a passage, rather than at the end, in contrast with poets such as Hardy and Yeats.[3] The effect is of a pulsing, renewed, exploratory, cumulative energy rather than the conclusive, often ironic statement made by end-refrains.

As ever there is memorable and sometimes beautiful, sometimes strange or grotesque phrasing, as in the following passages:

> As letters in books staring out
> All that man thought strange
> And laid to sleep on white
> Like the archaic manuscript
> Of dreams at morning blacked on wonder.
>
> * * *
>
> It is to fly you home from where
> Like stealthy angels you made off once
> On errands of uncertain mercy:
>
> * * *
>
> To which words, come away now
> In an all-merciful despite
> Of early silvered treason
> To the golden all of storying.
>
> * * *

COME, WORDS AWAY

> Not out of stranger-mouths then
> Shall words unwind but from the voice
> That haunted there like dumb ghost haunting
> Birth prematurely, anxious of death.
>
> * * *
>
> How words come from sound far away
> Through stages of immensity's small
> Centring the utter telling
> In truth's first soundlessness.
>
> * * *
>
> Wherein the calling's loathsome as
> Memory of man-flesh over-fondled
> With words like over-gentle hands.
>
> * * *
>
> Before lies claim the precedence of sin
> And mouldered mouths writhe to outspeak us.

The poem, though not formally divided into two, can be taken as two halves, each of five sections. The first half sets the scene for the more complex and intense latter part.

2

The first thing to note is that words are addressed as sentient beings capable of response to the poet's invocation – a word used here advisedly. [4] 'Invocation' is the action of calling upon a deity (or someone) for aid or protection, or the action of conjuring or summoning a devil or spirit by incantation.[5] This idea of 'invocation' is supported by the use of the terms 'somewhat devils' (16) and 'stealthy angels' (23) to describe words.

Words are called away, in succession, from mouths, from tongues, from 'reckless hearts' and from 'mouths in cautious heads'. Initially it seems (one wants to think!) that the poet is calling words away from talk, where they are used without due consideration, but it soon becomes apparent, in a wonderful passage, that she is equally calling for words to come away from books:

> Come, words, away to where
> The meaning is not thickened
> With the voice's fretting substance,
> Nor look of words is curious
> As letters in books staring out
> All that man ever thought strange
> And laid to sleep on white
> Like the archaic manuscript ['pantomime' in *PALW*]
> Of dreams at morning blacked on wonder.
> Come, words, away to miracle
> More natural than written art. (5-15)

This reminds one of 'The Troubles of a Book' which opens the 1970 selection, the last stanza especially:

> The trouble of a book is chiefly
> To be nothing but book outwardly;
> To wear binding like binding,
> Bury itself in book-death,
> But to feel all but book;
>
> To breathe live words, yet with the breath
> Of letters; to address liveliness
> In reading eyes, be answered with
> Letters and bookishness.

In a rare published remark on an individual poem the author commented: To comment on the poem 'The Troubles of a Book': lest it be mistaken for an exercise in poetic playfulness, I pause to characterize it as one that rises through stages of sense of the queer nature of a book, as a hybrid of external and internal actualities, to perception of its essentially tragic nature'.[6]

To return to the poem in hand, although words are first described as 'somewhat devils' the poet knows the way 'to soothe | The whirl of you when speech blasphemes against the silent half of language':

> It is to fly you home from where
> Like stealthy angels you made off once
> On errands of uncertain mercy: (22-24)

'Mercy' seems a strange word to be introducing in this context, but it reappears in various forms five more times in the poem. The primary meaning of the word is 'forbearance and compassion shown by one person to another who is in his power and who has no claim to receive kindness'.[7] The next use of it comes two lines later:

> To tell with me a story here
> Of utmost mercy never squandered
> On niggard prayers for eloquence—
> The marvelling on man by man. (25-28)

The idea of marvelling on man by man may seem a harmless, indeed praiseworthy activity, but that is not the intended sense here. This is confirmed by the lines in the earlier version published in the book *Poet: A Lying Word*: 'On niggard prayers for eloquence | In man's marvelling of man.'[8] This version is unambiguous in a helpful way, where the *Collected Poems* version with its dash after eloquence leaves it confusingly unclear whether 'the marvelling on man by man' relates to the story as well as the prayers for eloquence.

And in the following line 'mercy' appears as a verb:

> I know a way, unwild ['alone' – *PALW*] we'll mercy
> And spread the largest news
> Where never a folded ear dare make
> A deaf division of entirety. (29-32)

As a verb 'mercy' is virtually a neologism; it is listed as obsolete in OED.[9] Perhaps the most straightforward reading here would take the main meaning as to 'deliver compassionate forbearance', in line with the normal meaning of the noun, but with a hint of the power held in abeyance, so that 'never a folded ear *dare* make | A deaf division of entirety' (italics added).[10]

The connection is not simple, and as usual the contrast is as revealing as any likeness, but I think the use of the word 'mercy' was suggested by its use by in the work of the great visionary, William Blake:

> Time is the mercy of Eternity; without Times swiftness
> Which is the swiftest of all things: all were eternal torment [.][11]

Both Blake and Riding were concerned with origin, with what we can know of whence we came. Along with the use of 'mercy' the 'devils' and 'angels' in 'Come, Words, Away' may have been suggested by Blake's cosmology in which his 'devils' are forms of energy, his 'angels' forms of reason, necessary contraries in his system. On the other hand Riding would reject Blake's view that without Time all 'were in eternal torment.' For her, by contrast, Time has reached its end, as in the lines she wrote to open *Epilogue* (which title of course implies that time has ended):

> Now time has reached the flurrying curtain-fall
> That wakens thought from historied reverie
> And gives the word to uninfected discourse.[12]

To return to the poem, words are envisaged as once having made off from 'home' (their eternal home, I would suggest) on 'errands of uncertain mercy', but they are now being recalled.

The obsession, as throughout the poems and the work in general is with *wholeness*. Three times in seventeen lines similar points have been made:

> The whirl of you when speech blasphemes
> Against the silent half of language (18-19)
>
> * * *
>
> Where never a folded ear dare make
> A deaf division of entirety. (31-32)
>
> * * *
>
> That fluent half-a-story
> Chatters against this silence (33-34)

Nothing but the whole is good enough. These lines lead into the concluding lines of the fourth section of the poem, wrapping up, as it were, the themes of the incompleteness of the treatment of words in books and talk, and of a merciful mission to tell the 'golden all of storying':

> To which, words, come away now
> In an all-merciful despite
> Of early silvered treason
> To the golden all of storying. (35-38)

The point about 'halving' is made yet again in the fifth section, with 'noise' again contrasted implicitly with 'the silent half of language'.

> We'll begin fully at the noisy end
> Where mortal halving tempered mercy
> To the shorn utterance of man-sense;
> Never more than savageries
> Took they from your bounty-book. (39-43)

In this case the 'mortal halving tempered mercy', which I read as meaning that mercy is made less forgiving to the 'shorn utterance of man-sense' – a reading reinforced by the strongly critical term 'savageries'. The 'treason' (elsewhere described in the poem as 'blasphemy' or 'sin') is associated explicitly with men, who took never more than savageries from words' 'bounty-book'. 'Bounty', while indicative of goodness in general, is associated with gifts, with generosity, but also with bounty-hunters, men on the make.

By contrast with most of the earlier poems (by which I mean the 'Poems of Mythical Occasion' and 'Poems of Immediate Occasion') which tend on the whole to make their points concisely, 'in one go', and with remarkable economy and internal consistency of language, the first part of this poem is expansive, eloquent, demonstratively rich with variations exploring the same theme, using different terms for different nuances of similar meaning. Given the theme this eloquence is somewhat paradoxical.

There is more than a hint of Riding as Prospero in *The Tempest* (a play she loved) in the conjuring up of angels and devils.

The contrast of the noise of speech with the silent half of language parallels the poet's paradoxes in relation to visibility and sight, sun and darkness, in the little poem 'How Blind and Bright'. There men are blinded by brightness, can only 'see', while those who look inward, (who 'bide the night' – to introduce a phrase from 'Echoes 5'), achieve 'sight'.[13] Here the noise of speech may, implicitly, lead one to make 'a deaf division of entirety', unable to 'hear' the 'silent half of language'.

3

After the account of why words should come away from mouths and from books the opening words of the second half of the poem begin to reveal the source of words and truth:

> Not out of stranger-mouths then
> Shall *words* unwind but from the *voice*
> That haunted there like *dumb* ghost haunting
> Birth prematurely, *anxious* of death. (44-47; italics added)

In the original version, in *Poet: A Lying Word*, the last three lines are slightly different and as elsewhere help clarify, in a complementary way, the sense of the final version:

> Shall *truth* unwind but from the *words*
> That haunted there like ghosts haunting
> Birth prematurely, *impatient* of death. (Italics added)

We are now unambiguously on new and peculiar ground. How can 'the voice' or 'the words' be like dumb ghost, or ghosts haunting birth prematurely? How can ghosts haunt birth? The dictionary lists a range of meanings of 'ghost', amongst the most relevant of which are: the spiritual or immaterial part of a person; the active essence of God, the Holy Spirit; the soul of a dead person which manifests itself visibly or audibly to the living.[14] If the ghost or ghosts here are anxious or impatient of death, what does that mean? That they are incomplete, remain immaterial, without death, for which birth is the essential prerequisite.

Words, and truth, are becoming closely identified, and truth, not having been directly mentioned in the first half, is increasingly a focus in the latter part of the poem. In what follows we shall concentrate on what the poet is saying positively about truth and words, although she proceeds through contraries, urging words away from falseness or failing before adumbrating, in contrast, their origins and potential for truth. After the first of these passages (on false prophecy, lines 48-52) we come to:

> Come, words, away—
> That was an alien vanity,
> A rash startling and a preening
> That from truth's wakeful sleep parted
> When she within her first stirred story-wise,
> Thinking what time it was or would be
> When voiced illumination ['the eternal wildfire' –
> *PALW* version] spread:
> What time, what words, what she then. (53-60)

'Truth' is here 'personified', to use the standard literary term; and although this is an entirely different context we are oddly reminded, through the phrase 'wakeful sleep', of the fairy tale figure of the Sleeping Beauty, first evoked in our reading of 'The Tiger'. We are also reminded, again from a different context, of the figures of the Monoton and the quids, in an early poem; there the Monoton is veiled (one is tempted to say) as an 'it', whereas here, 'past the half-way mark in the poems' truth is revealed as 'she', unambiguously.[15] And in the eighth section we are back with the first person singular:

> Come, words, away,
> And tell with me a story here (61-62)

'She', 'truth' and 'me' are closely interrelated, if not identical.

Unless you are one of the few to read the poems before reading *The Telling* it will hardly be possible to read the following passage without the intervening lens of her 'personal evangel', the following passage.[16]

> By flight of words back to this plan
> Whose grace goes out in utmost rings
> To bounds of utmost storyhood.
>
> But never shall truth circle so
> Till words prove language is
> How words come from far sound away
> Through stages of immensity's small
> Centring the utter telling
> In truth's first soundlessness. (66-74)[17]

This poem, though, is her first substantial statement of the theme. In the abbreviated version in *Selected Poems* it ends, appropriately enough, at 'utmost storyhood'. The story of the ninth section, lines (69-74 above), is effectively paralleled in 'The Flowering Urn' which is the next poem but one in *Selected Poems*,[18] and to which we shall return in Chapter 13. The concluding section begins:

COME, WORDS AWAY

> Come, words, away:
> I am a conscience of you
> Not to be held unanswered past
> The perfect number of betrayal.
>
> ['The perfect number of our
> Difference from each other' – *PALW*]

'Conscience' is a word with complex meaning here. As its chief meanings OED gives us (I) inward knowledge, consciousness; inmost thought, mind; (II) consciousness of right or wrong; moral sense; conscientiousness of practice, observance; tenderness of conscience: all of which are encompassed here. The 'I' of the poet, the 'she' of truth hold words answerable for any betrayal – or blasphemy, or niggard prayers for eloquence, or deaf division of entirety, or silvered treason, or savageries, or falsity and repetition, or alien vanity, or sin.

The preceding 78 lines of the poem do not prepare us for the strangeness, even grotesquery, of its final lines:

> It is a smarting passion
> ['It is a passion such as death' – *PALW*]
> By which I call—
> Wherein the calling's loathsome as
> Memory of man-flesh over-fondled
> With words like over-gentle hands.
> Then come, words, away,
> Before lies claim the precedence of sin
> And mouldered mouths writhe to outspeak us.
> ['Before corruption claims a sinner's share
> And mouldered mouths outspeak us.' – *PALW*] (79-86)

The poem has been studded with words and phrases with religious connotations throughout; in this final section it began with 'conscience' and 'betrayal' (harking back to the 'silvered treason' of line 37, with its suggestion of Judas) and continues with 'passion' (as in Christ's passion and death) and 'sin' (as in sin against the Holy Spirit). The poet's meanings are not, of course, those of the Judaeo-Christian tradition, but she has to go back to and through that tradition, and the millennia of thinking implicit in their use, in order to 'rinse' them clean for her own meaning.[19] In this she goes beyond the dictionary 'origins' to her own account of the origins of words and language, as in this poem as a whole. It was this, in part, to which she referred in *Anarchism Is Not Enough*:

> Words have three historical levels. They may be true words, that is, of an intrinsic sense; they may be logical words, that is of an applied sense; or they may be poetical words, untrue and illogical in themselves, but of supposed suggestive power. The most the poet can now do is to take every word he uses through each of these levels, giving it the combined depth of all three, forcing it beyond itself to a death of sense where it is at least safe from the perjuries either of society or poetry.[20]

As before, the first version of the last two lines of the poem complement and helps clarify the more gnomic final version. In both versions the vision is of medieval ghastliness, conjuring up dead, rotted mouths (from which words had been called away at the outset) 'writhing' (in agony, perhaps, or with worms) to 'outspeak', to speak more forcibly than, 'us'. 'Us' is the first use of the first person plural in the poem. The plural includes not fellow human beings (one's first thought) but words, which (as in the quote above) the author is taking beyond themselves to a place where they are 'safe from the perjuries either of society or poetry'.

Why should the calling be loathsome? And why should the loathsomeness of the calling be likened to memory of man-flesh over-fondled? The calling is loathsome because she envisages words being called out of the mouldered, writhing mouths, and it is that which elicits the repellent memory of the man-flesh over-fondled in the throes of another 'sin', that of lust.

The poem, then, ends with the poet pulling up the trapdoor – the words go with her into the silence. Unless, perhaps, I (or you) the reader, dangerously choose to include myself (or yourself) in the 'us' of the poem's final word.

NOTES

[1] See the essay on 'One Self' for more on this ruthless editing of her poems not just in *Selected Poems* but also in the culling of fragments from much larger poems for other collections.

[2] Laura (Riding) Jackson and Schuyler B. Jackson, *Rational Meaning* (Charlottesville: University Press of Virginia, 1997). The genesis of this work is described by Elizabeth Friedmann in the authorised biography, *A Mannered Grace*, (New York: Persea Books, 2005), Ch 36.

[3] Perhaps 'An Ageless Brow' could be seen as an exception, where the final line's 'never, never, and now, now' repeats the phrase at the end of the third stanza.

[4] Just as the letters making up the words 'stare out' (at the reader, at the world?) in line 9. One is reminded of the term 'poem-person' used in *A Survey of Modernist Poetry*, and the treatment of 'poems' generally in the preface to *Poems: A Joking Word*. See the essay on *One Self* for further discussion.

[5] Shorter OED, 1 and 2.

[6] In Excerpts from a Recording, 1972, published as Appendix V to the 2001 edition of the poems, p496.

[7] OED, 1.

[8] Confirmed too by a passage in *Contemporaries and Snobs*, in which Riding attacks, in her inimitable fashion, the 18th century conception of '. . . the natural man, the common-sense antithesis to the erratic person. . . .'

Serving as a literary and sociological convenience, he did not act originally; he did not act at all. It was his function to be observed. "The proper study of mankind is man."' 12-13 in 1928 edition.

[9] 'Unwild' is certainly a neologism in the same line! How much notice has been paid to the often (though not always) unobtrusive use of new or obsolete words in this poet's work? Once you start looking the poems are studded with them.

[10] The idea of withheld punishment or power occurs elsewhere in the poems. See Mark Jacobs' analysis of 'An Ageless Brow', as an example, and its line 14 in particular: 'The stroke withheld from trouble'.

[11] William Blake, *Milton*, 24.72-73

[12] Reprinted in Laura Riding and Robert Graves, *Essays from 'Epilogue'* 1935-1937 (Manchester, Carcanet: 2001), 1. A key difference between her and Blake is in her belief in words as integral with origin and the eternal, earlier than the Bible which was Blake's ultimate reference point;

and Blake, for all his original and creative use of language believed primarily in vision and imagination, not words. On the other hand his point about the need to see not *with* but *through* the eyes in order to see Eternity chimes (I think) with her caution about the eyes.

And they have in common the belief in a Fore-being accessible by unforgetting (in Riding's case), or by opening the doors of perception (in Blake's case).

[13] See the essay on 'How Blind and Bright'.

[14] Relevant meanings taken from the Shorter OED.

[15] The Quids is an early poem, first published in 1924. For the author's commentary see the 2001 edition of the poems, Appendix V, p498. The relevant parallels are firstly, in the concept of an all-encompassing figure composed of contributory beings, secondly the references to grammar (*The Quids*) and words *(Come, Words, Away)*.

[16] The quote is from the preface to *The Telling*, Athlone Press, 1972, p1.

[17] The last two lines in *PALW* are: 'Centring the soundless telling/In truth's still ever-watch', which by transposition of 'soundless' sharpens the paradox.

[18] As it was too in the original publication in *PALW*, but not in *CP*, where it is placed 85 pages later.

[19] I have borrowed this word from Alan J. Clark's *Where Poetry Ends*, PN Review, 1981, No 22, p27: '... the clear air of her poems, their freedom from mistily implicative reverberation, is one of their perception-rinsing elements...'.

[20] Cape, 1927, in the opening section, *The Myth*, p12.

Chapter 11

'Tale of Modernity': a cosmogony unveiled

TALE OF MODERNITY
1

Shakespeare knew Lust by day,
With raw unsleeping eye.
And he cried, 'All but Truth I see,
Therefore Truth is, for Lust alone I see.'

By night Lust most on other men
Its swollen pictures shone.
And the sun brought shame, and they arose
Their hearts night-stained, but faces lustless.

They in the sun to themselves seemed well.
The sun in guise of Truth gave pardon.   10
Hypocrisy of seeming well
Blamed the sore visions on bed and night.

But Shakespeare knew Lust by day,

By day he saw his night, and he cried,
'O sexual sun, back into my loins,
Be night also, as you are.'

2

Shakespeare distinguished: earth the obscure,
The sun the bold, the moon the hidden—
The sun speechless, earth a muttering,
The moon a whispering, white, smothered.   20

Bishop Modernity, to his spent flock cried,
'She is illusion, let her fade.'
And she, illusion and not illusion,
A sapphire being fell to earth, time-struck.

In colour live and liquid and earth-pale,
Never so near she, never so distant.
Never had time been futured so,
All reckoning on one fast page.

Time was a place where earth had been.
The whole past met there, she with it.   30
Truth seemed love grown cool as a brow,
And young as the moon, grown girl to self.

3

Bishop Modernity plucked out his heart.
No agony could prove him Christ,
No lust could speak him honest Shakespeare.
A greedy frost filled where had been a heart.

And that disdainful age his flock,
Resolved against the dream-delight
Of soft succession another world to that,
Like women slipping quiet into monk-thoughts,   40

Went in triumph of mind from the chapel,
Proud interior of voided breast,
To Heaven out, or Hell, or any name
That carnal sanctity bestows.

Home they went to heartless memories of wives
And appetites of whoredoms stilled
In lustful shaking off lust,
Of knowledge-gall, love's maddening part.

4

Bishop Modernity in the fatal chapel watched
And end-of-time intoned as the Red Mass   50
Of man's drinking of the blood of man:
In quenched immunity he looked on her

Who from the fallen moon scattered the altar
With thin rays of challenged presence—
The sun put out there, and the lamps of time
Smoking black consternation to new desire.

Then did that devilish chase begin:
Bishop Modernity's heart plucked out
In old desire flew round against and toward her—
And he but shackled mind, to pulpit locked.   60

Which stirred up Shakespeare from listening tomb,
Who broke the lie and seized the maid, crying, `
Thou Bishop Double-Nothing, chase thy soul—
Till then she's ghost with me thy ghostly whole!'

1

'Bishop Modernity', an earlier version of this poem, was published in *Poet: A Lying Word* in 1933. It was an outwardly rebarbative, studiedly grotesque poem in that edition and despite detailed, mostly minor, verbal variations it fully retains those characteristics, together with its overall form, in the final version, albeit with a great deal of highly memorable, sometimes beautiful, phrasing, as in the following passages:

Shakespeare knew Lust by day,
With raw unsleeping eye. (1-2)

By day he saw his night, and he cried,
'O sexual sun, back into my loins,
Be night also, as you are.' (14-16)

And she, illusion and not illusion,
A sapphire being fell to earth, time-struck.
In colour live and liquid and earth-pale
Never so near she, never so distant. (23-26)

Truth seemed love grown cool as a brow,
And young as the moon, grown girl to self. (31-32)

And that disdainful age his flock,
Resolved against the dream-delight
Of soft succession another world to that,
Like woman slipping quiet into monk-thoughts, (37-40)

> Home they went to heartless memories of wives
> And appetites of whoredoms stilled
> In lustful shaking off lust,
> Of knowledge-gall, love's maddening part. (45-48)

In form it is outwardly regular, uniquely so for one of this author's *Collected Poems*, which should alert us to what is going on. The form is 4 cubed: four sections each of which contains four stanzas each of which has four lines. It is tempting to describe this regular outward form as appropriately brutalist, by analogy with the inhuman architecture of the time, and in accordance with the inhuman chapel, the 'Proud interior of voided breast' and the 'Red Mass | Of man's drinking of the blood of man' within the poem itself.

Inwardly, though, the lines, while mostly iambic, are not at all regular – with the ironical exception of the heroic couplet which rounds off the poem. Each line, in fact, finds its own irregular 'natural size' to suit the thought, despite the imposed, external, artificial regularity.[1]

In the book *Poet: A Lying Word* the poem heads up a powerful sequence of four highly original poems: 'Bishop Modernity'; 'Two Loves, One Madness' ('The Dilemmist' in *Collected Poems*); 'The Unthronged Oracle'; and 'Come, Words, Away'. In *Collected Poems* it is the penultimate poem of 'Immediate Occasion', followed by 'Midsummer Duet'. The brutalist construction, grotesque action, uneven rhythms and unpleasant but memorable language of 'Modernity' make a bizarre contrast with the rather sickly and forgettable conventional invocation of 'nature' in 'Midsummer Duet', its whimsical Georgian language and its di-dah, di-dah, di-dah rhythms.[2]

2

Whilst the details, and the complexity of the overall meaning, are much less graspable, the outline of the 'tale', the argument, is clear enough, at least in the first, third and final sections of the poem, and may be summarised as follows. Shakespeare, unlike other men – who experienced lust at night and were hypocritical about it by day – was 'honest' about lust and saw it with his eyes open. This first section is full of the words 'sun', 'day' and 'night'. The second section introduces the moon. Bishop Modernity cried out to his flock 'She is illusion', but in the form of a sapphire being 'she' fell to earth, time-struck. In the third section Bishop Modernity plucked out his heart: 'No agony could prove him Christ | No lust could speak him honest Shakespeare'; and his flock resolved against 'the dream-delight | Of soft succession another world to that' and went home to 'heartless memories of wives | And appetites of whoredoms stilled | In lustful shaking off lust'. In the final section Bishop Modernity presided over a Red Mass of man's drinking the blood of man, looking on 'her' in 'quenched immunity' (to her attractions presumably); then, while his mind remained shackled to the pulpit, his plucked-out heart flew 'round against and toward her'. This stirred up Shakespeare who 'broke the lie and seized the maid', denouncing the Bishop as Double-Nothing and urging him to chase his soul.

In the next sections we attempt to explicate the poem further, section by section.

3

> Shakespeare knew Lust by day
> With raw unsleeping eye

The subject of lust is first directly broached in the course of *Collected Poems* in 'The Tiger'. In our essays on that poem and on 'The Rugged Black of Anger' we made reference to Riding's (and Graves') profound reading of Shakespeare's Sonnet 129 in Chapter III of *A Survey of Modernist Poetry* (Th'expence of Spirit in a waste of shame/Is lust in action...).[3] Some detailed quotation from her interpretation of the sonnet is essential to an understanding of 'Tale of Modernity', particularly of the first section.

By Riding's reading of the sonnet lust is both a bliss and a woe both during and after the 'proof' (the sexual consummation). But the most radical reinterpretation, resulting from their re-instatement of the punctuation, was focused on line 12 of the 1609 edition:

> Had, hauing, and in quest, to have extreame,
> A blisse in proofe and proud and very wo,
> Before a joy proposed behind a dream,
> All this the world well knowes yet none knowes well
> To shun the heauen that leads men to this hell. (10-14)

These lines had been officiously re-punctuated in other editions, including this from the Oxford Book of English Verse:

> Had, having, and in quest to have, extreme;
> A bliss in proof, and proved, a very woe;
> Before, a joy proposed; behind a dream.
> All this the world well knows; yet none knows well
> To shun the heaven that leads men to this hell.

Riding argues:

> The important thing about this line [line 12, with the restored punctuation and liberated meaning of the 1609 edition] is that it takes all the meanings in the poem one stage further. Lust in the extreme goes beyond both bliss and woe; it goes beyond reality. It is no longer lust *Had, having and in quest*, it is lust face to face with *love*. Even when consummated, lust still stands before an unconsummated joy, a proposed joy, and proposed not as a joy possible of consummation but one only to be desired through the dream by which lust leads itself on, the dream behind which this proposed joy, this love, seems to lie. This is the final meaning of the line.[4]

She argues that the revised punctuation restricts the meaning to: 'In prospect lust is a joy; in retrospect a dream', and continues:

> Though a possible contributory meaning, as the *only* meaning it makes the theme of the poem that lust is impossible of satisfaction, whereas the theme is, as carried on by the next line, that lust *is* satisfiable but that satisfied lust is in conflict with itself. The next line, if unpunctuated except for the comma Shakespeare put at the end, is a general statement of this conflict: the man in lust is torn between lust as he well-knows it with the world and lust in his personal experience, which crazes him to hope for more than lust from lust.[5]

And further:

> The character and the moral of lust the world well knows, *but no one knows the character and the moral really well unless he disregards the moral warning and engages in lust, no one knows lust well enough to shun it because, though he knows it is both heavenly and hellish, lust can never be recognised until it has proved itself lust by turning heaven into hell.*[6] (Italics added)

Whilst we shall never know for certain that the punctuation in the 1609 edition was Shakespeare's own, or that this interpretation would be his own, this is an amazingly subtle and convincing reading of the poem as originally published.

For Riding poetic reality can only be achieved by 'disregard of the anti-poetic pressure of social reality'.[7] In a subsequent comment on the analysis Riding makes it clear that she was defending only Shakespeare's 'justifiable attempt' to achieve 'poetic reality', not the 'results of attempt'.[8] Nevertheless, with that caveat, the account of lust as ascribed here to Shakespeare does help us with our reading of her own poem.

It is worth pausing a moment to consider what 'lust' means. It would be easy to read the poem as using the term simply in the negative senses of a sensuous desire leading to sin, or strong (uncontrollable) sexual appetite; but it also has the senses of vigour, life, passionate desire for or to do, passionate enjoyment; and these senses (taken all together) are consistent with the reading of Shakespeare's sonnet, and need to be born in mind in reading this poem. 'Shakespeare' is the apparent hero of the tale. He has had the bravery to experience the bliss and the woe of 'Lust' and the honesty to report it:

> And he cried, 'All but Truth I see'
> Therefore Truth is, for Lust alone I see.' (2-4)

He has not, though, so far been able to go beyond the experience of Lust. In the fourth quatrain of the first section, following an account of the failure of other men to face the truth about lust (and themselves) the poet repeats, with variation and development:

> But Shakespeare knew Lust by day,
> By day he saw his night, and he cried,
> 'O sexual sun, back into my loins,
> Be night also, as you are.' (13-16)

'Loins' is of course a biblical expression meaning both the part of the body that should be covered by clothing and the seat of physical strength and reproductive power. To 'gird up one's loins' is to prepare for strenuous exertion. By returning the sexual sun to his loins 'Shakespeare' would return lust to its 'proper' place – as the physical expression of the biological drive to reproduce. At this stage in the poem lust has not gone 'beyond reality' as it has in the sonnet, where it is 'face to face with love'. There is no mention of love thus far, and no mention of woman. The first part of the poem is all about men's (and Shakespeare's) experiences *with themselves*.

4

> Bishop Modernity plucked out his heart.
> No agony could prove him Christ,
> No lust could speak him honest Shakespeare.

> A greedy frost filled where had been a heart. (33-36)

What are we to make of the figure of Bishop Modernity? A bishop, of course, is a spiritual overseer or governor in the Christian church; here the 'Bishop' figure stands for assumption of spiritual authority.

As to 'Modernity', at its etymological root is the Latin 'modo' or 'just now'; with the implication of a religious leader in tune with the spirit of his time, Riding's anathematised Zeitgeist.[22] It does not here refer specifically to poetic modernism: the key idea is in the implicit opposition between modern (up-to-date, recent) and ancient (antiquated, long past). The Bishop, in asserting his modernity, in effect denies 'the old, original dust'[23] – as he denied the reality of the female figure of the moon – and 'plucked out his heart', which, as we shall explain in our essay on 'Earth', the poet associates with 'earth'. He is detached both from the roots of his religion ('No agony could prove him Christ') and from the poetic reality of Shakespeare. 'A greedy frost' (an ugly mixed metaphor surely, this), a cold rapacity, fills the hole left by his heart.[24]

The remainder of the third section describes the consequent behaviour, resolutely resistant to 'lust' and thoughts of woman, of the Bishop's flock:

> Resolved against the dream-delight ['dream-terribleness' in *PALW*]
> Of soft succession another world to that,
> Like woman slipping into monk-thoughts,
> Went in triumph of mind from the chapel,
> Proud interior of voided breast, (38-42)

This exclusive masculinity reminds one of the puritans, their demolition of the human figures in the churches and their suppression of the cult of that sapphire blue figure, the Virgin Mary, mother of god. Blue is also, of course, the literal colour of Earth as seen from space.

The final lines of this section read:

> Home they went to heartless memories of wives
> And appetites of whoredoms stilled
> In lustful shaking off lust,

> Of knowledge-gall, love's maddening part. (45-48)

'Knowledge-gall' is a memorable phrase. A 'gall' was originally a painful swelling, then a sore produced by rubbing or chafing, then a person or thing which irritates, vexes or harasses. Lust should be the irritant, love's maddening part, which spurs one on (as in the interpretation of Shakespeare's sonnet) to knowledge. But for the 'spent flock' their 'lustful shaking off lust' conjures up masturbation, as do the second and third stanzas of the first section of the poem.

5

> Bishop Modernity in the fatal chapel watched
> And end-of-time intoned as the Red Mass
> Of man's drinking of the blood of man:
> In quenched immunity he looked on her (49-52)

In the church a red mass is 'usually one of the Holy Ghost'[25] at which the priest wears red vestments. For all its grotesque, pantomimic quality this final section of the poem concerns matters of spirit and soul. The Bishop intoned end-of-time as (in the capacity of) the Red Mass of man's drinking of the blood of man. Of course, in the Christian Eucharist bread and wine are consumed as Christ's body and blood, but what may be implied here is something more actually bloody, recalling the horrors of totalitarianism.

Again 'in quenched immunity' (spiritual thirst apparently quenched or extinguished by the drinking of the blood of man, leading to immunity to the temptations posed by the female figure) he looks on 'her' –

> Who from the fallen moon scattered the altar
> With thin rays of challenged presence— (53-54)

Her very presence is challenged – in dispute, denied, but she makes it felt at the altar at which the Eucharist is celebrated.

The next stanza is relatively straightforward action, strange though it is.

Bishop Modernity's heart 'in old desire' (by contrast with the 'new desire' of line 56) flew round against and toward 'her' while his mind remains shackled. This leads to the final stanza:

> Which stirred up Shakespeare from listening tomb.[26]
> Who broke the lie and seized the maid, crying,
> 'Thou Bishop Double-Nothing, chase thy soul—
> Till then she's ghost with me thy ghostly whole!' (61-64)

The female figure has now become 'the maid' of the final lines of the second section when:

> Truth seemed love grown cool as a brow
> And young as the moon, grown girl to self. (31-32)

Shakespeare broke the lie – that 'she is illusion' (22). The Bishop is Double-Nothing because he's neither Christ nor poet, he is in denial of woman, and he has torn out his heart. Until the Bishop chases his soul:

> Till then she's ghost with me thy ghostly whole. (64)

What do the terms 'ghost' and 'ghostly' mean here? As we have seen (for example in 'The Signature') Riding uses the terms throughout the *Collected Poems*. She uses them paradoxically and characteristically. At its simplest a ghost is an appearance without substance, and in that sense a ghost can be 'alive' in the usual sense, but not whole. Typically she uses the term with the implication of someone whose approach to the *spiritual* excludes the *material* elements.[28] Introduced here is the additional association with the Holy Ghost of the Christian trinity, for whom the red mass is normally celebrated.

These complex final lines sum up the themes of the poem as a whole. Unless Bishop Modernity succeeds in the pursuit of his soul, recognising the 'maid', the ghost 'she' who is illusion but not illusion, then she will remain, the Bishop's 'ghostly' (i.e. spiritual) whole with Shakespeare, and his poetic reality.

7

Only three poems from the collection *Poet: A Lying Word* were placed in 'Poems of Immediate Occasion' in *Collected Poems*. All three appear toward the end of that section and they are, in order of appearance, 'As to a Frontispiece', 'Come, Words, Away' and 'Tale of Modernity'. 'Poems of Final Occasion' comprises the remainder of the book *Poet: A Lying Word*[29], the only additional poem being the final one, 'Disclaimer of the Person'.

The importance of 'Tale of Modernity', as we have seen, is that it breaks new ground, preparing the way for a different order of poetry 'past the half-way mark' in *Collected Poems*. Just as 'The Rugged Black of Anger' marked the end of 'Poems of Mythical Occasion', and epitomised the more analytical, austere type of poetry which was to follow, so 'Tale of Modernity' unveiled the elements of a new cosmology that was explored further in many of the poems that followed. It also introduced elements of the grotesque and indelicate, which pave the way for greater bluntness, unpleasantness and even ugliness in some of the ensuing poems. (On the other hand some of those poems, the shorter ones in particular, appear more at ease than hitherto with an accomplished poetic beauty of imagery and elegance of expression).

NOTES

[1] For a further discussion of regularity and irregularity of form see the essay on 'The Tiger', which refers to Chapter II, *The Problem of Form and Subject-Matter*, in *A Survey of Modernist Poetry*, reprinted by Carcanet, 2002, pp17-28.

[2] Why was this uncharacteristic and occasional poem, which could unkindly be described as a *folie a deux*, included in *Collected Poems?* Possibly it was to provide a contrast in style while humanising and personalising the account of love and lust, as in Riding's teasing lines to Graves:

Shall you against the lull of censoring mind
Not let the bones of nature run
On fleshlorn errands, journey-proud—
If ghosts go rattling after kisses,
Shall your firmed mouth not quiver with
Desires it once spoke beauty by? (*CP*, 147)

Or possibly it was to expose Graves' rather abject self-abasement?

> And what of jest and play—
> If caution against waggishness
> (Lest I look backward) makes my mood too canting?
> Shall you not mock my pious ways
> Finding in gloom no certain grace or troth,
> And raise from moony regions of your smile Light spirits, nimbler on the toe
> Which nothing are—I no one? (*CP*, 148)

[3] Mark Jacobs has demonstrated beyond any reasonable doubt that of the two authors of *A Survey* Riding was both originator and driving force behind this analysis of Shakespeare, despite the fact that Graves reprinted some of the account in *The Common Asphodel* and despite subsequent malicious refusal of others, William Empson chief among them, to recognise her as the main author. Hence in my account I refer to Riding as the sole author. Mark Jacobs, 'Contemporary Misogyny: Laura Riding, William Empson and the critics — a survey of mishistory', *English*, Summer 2015, 64 (245).

[4] *A Survey of Modernist Poetry*, op cit, Chapter III, 35.

[5] Ibid

[6] Ibid, 36

[7] Ibid.

[8] In 1935, in an essay 'On Poems and Poets' which marks a further development of her approach to criticism; reprinted in Laura Riding and Robert Graves, *Essays from 'Epilogue' 1935-1937* (Manchester: Carcanet, 2001), 49.

[9] The final 'Poem of Final Occasion', the only poem in that section not published previously in the collection *Poet: A Joking Word*. 'Disclaimer of the Person' had been printed individually, in two separate parts as *The First Leaf* (in 1933) and *The Second Leaf* (in 1935). Its position in *Collected Poems*, and the separate publication, indicate the importance given to the poem. The quotation is from p255.

[10] In Appendix V, 2001 edition of *CP*, 496.

[11] See my essay on that poem.

[12] The meaning of 'earth the obscure' relates to the fact that night causes man to doubt his reality, his world, the earth. Suddenly the earth becomes 'obscure', until daylight again, that is.

[13] In the third line of 'Throe of Apocalypse':
And in that shrill antithesis of calm
The goaded brain is struck with ague,
By a full moon of waste sublimely sweats.

[14] From the final section, 'All the Way Back', *CP*, 7-8.

[15] It is hinted at by Graves' lines in 'Midsummer Duet', quoted at note 2 above.

> Shall you not mock my pious ways Finding in gloom no certain grace or troth,
> And raise from moony regions of your smile Light spirits, nimbler on the toe
> Which nothing are—I no one?

[16] *CP*, 219 and 311.

[17] Is there an echo here of the slang term 'bishop' for erect penis, which derives from the latter's resemblance to the chess piece? This would make Bishop Modernity a prick, which would certainly fit the context. Is there not, too, an echo in Shakespeare's 'raw unsleeping eye' of Chaucer's sly opening lines in The Canterbury Tales, of the birds 'that slepen al the nyght with open ye'? There are in the neighbouring poem, 'Come Words Away', some pretty indelicate, or indecorous lines: 'Wherein the calling's loathsome as / Memory of man-flesh once overfondled/With words like gentle hands' – which the poet could have avoided if she'd wanted to, and of which 'Nor love loathe / Nor loathing fondle' are a precursor, in 'All Nothing, Nothing'. (See *CP*, 139 and 101).

[18] This is evident from the earlier version, where line 29 reads: In colour live, pale as earth's paleness. Both versions mix up the attributes of earth and moon.

[19] I am grateful to Mark Jacobs for many of the ideas in this section. He points out the links between these two lines in particular and the poem 'An Ageless Brow' (*CP*, 72).

[20] I am conscious that I am at this point bypassing lines 23-26, which open up wider discussion on the poet's conceptions of time and space, which are covered in some detail in the account of the poem 'Earth'.

[21] To go further with this quotation would take us beyond the poem under discussion.

[22] See the core essay 'Poetry & the Literary Universe' in Laura Riding, *Contemporaries and Snobs* (London: Cape, 1928), 9-121.

[23] See essay on 'Incarnations'.

[24] The idea reappears in the next poem in *Poet: A Lying Word*, 'Two Loves, One Madness' ('The Dilemmist' in

CP). 'Nor does his shivering heart one icy line remember'. (*CP*, 220)

[25] OED

[26] Taken literally this would place the action in Westminster Abbey.

[27] See the essay on 'The Signature' for further discussion.

[28] As in 'the old original dust' of 'Incarnations'; the full material of 'in my material' of 'Prisms'.

[29] With the exception of the extracts from *Laura and Francisca* and one poem which was omitted, 'Memory of the World'. The latter poem also explores ideas in relation to sun, moon and earth, and is interesting for that reason, but is not one of her better poems.

Chapter 12

'Earth': the name of the place of human life

EARTH

Have no wide fears for Earth:
Its universal name is 'Nowhere'.
If it is Earth to you, that is your secret.
The outer records leave off there,
And you may write it as it seems,
And as it seems, it is,
A seeming stillness
Amidst seeming speed.

Heavens unseen, or only seen,
Dark or bright space, unearthly space,   10
Is a time before Earth was
From which you inward move
Toward perfect now.

Almost the place it is not yet,
Potential here of everywhere—

EARTH

Have no wide fears for it:
Its destiny is simple,
To be further what it will be.

Earth is your heart
Which has become your mind   20
But still beats ignorance
Of all it knows—
As miles deny the compact present
Whose self-mistrusting past they are.
Have no wide fears for Earth:
Destruction only on wide fears shall fall.

1

In Riding's penultimate collection, *Poet: A Lying Word*, there were studded a number of perfect short poems, islands of serenity achieved amidst the strenuous struggles and experimentation of the longer poems. 'Earth', 'With the Face' and 'The Flowering Urn' are some of the most beautiful and fully-realized poems we have.

'Earth' is a 'Poem of Final Occasion' in the *Collected Poems*. As such it is the first poem of our selection from 'past the half-way mark'.[1] The earliest published version in 1930, in *Twenty Poems Less,* was significantly altered and developed in the 1933 version in *Poet: A Lying Word* with further minor amendments in the *Collected Poems* version. This latter version was also chosen by Laura (Riding) Jackson, unaltered, for her 1970 *Selected Poems*.

At 26 lines it is one of the shorter poems in the second half of *Collected Poems*. Within this relative brevity there is considerable repetition, despite the impression of conciseness, and there is also parallelism, both features that help further the poem's momentum and develop the meaning. The first line is repeated in the penultimate line and echoed in the seventeenth; there is a further repetition of the phrase 'wide fears' in the concluding line; the phrase 'as it seems' is repeated in lines 6 and 7.

Alongside the repetition is the parallelism noted in the essay on 'The Tiger' as a feature of Riding's poetic technique. Here, the opening stanza as a whole, with its references to Earth and its universal name 'Nowhere', is roughly paralleled by the second, with its contrasting references to heavens and space, unearthly space. Within that overall parallelism there is a particular parallel/contrast between:

> If it is Earth to you, that is your secret.
> The *outer* records leave off there. (3-4, italics added)

And:

> From which you *inward* move
> Toward perfect now. (12-13, italics added)

There are images of space and movement which help give the poem its sensation of serenity, again proceeding by contrasts and parallels. The vast outer space and time implicit in the 'Heavens unseen, or only seen... a time before Earth was' of lines 9-11 are in contrast both with the inward movement toward the 'perfect now' of lines 12-13 and with the lines from the final stanza, which knot together the outer and inner worlds in a gnomic utterance:

> As miles deny the compact present
> Whose self-mistrusting past they are. (23-24)

The knot is then untied at a stroke in the final lines, which return us first to the assurance of the opening line only to drop the bombshell of the unexpected final line:

> Have no wide fears for Earth:
> *Destruction only on wide fears shall fall.* (25-26, italics added)

There are beautiful and memorable phrases in the poem, in the following passage in particular:

And as it seems, it is,
A seeming stillness
Amidst seeming speed.

Heavens unseen, or only seen,
Dark or bright space, unearthly space
Is a time before Earth was
From which you inward move
Toward perfect now. (6-13)

2

Good opening questions for many of the poems of Laura Riding are 'What?' and 'Why?' What, on earth indeed, does the poet mean by 'Earth'? Without a context, without wider reference to her other poems, and 'the large coherence of thought behind them'[2], and reference in this case also to her prose works, this would surely be baffling, although there is a typically direct statement at lines 19-20 which should help, if only we can bear with it:

Earth is your heart
Which has become your mind

The reader's first impression is that the poet is using (and indeed mixing) metaphor or symbol here. However, as we have seen, the author flatly denied the use of symbols (and she elsewhere deprecated the special value given by many to metaphor in poetry[3]):

Nowhere should I be taken as speaking by what are called 'symbols'. If, for instance, I say 'the sun which multiplied' or 'the moon which singled', as I do in one poem, I am endeavouring to indicate actualities of physical circumstance in which our inner crucialities of human circumstance are set. My moon may look like the old tired poetical symbol, and I like an old tired poetic romanticist, but I truly meant that the moon's being where it is

intervenes in our outer circumstances as a negator of the sun's
fostering excessiveness in our regard, both lush and destructive –
– as a tempering counter-agency, relatively little but near.
However foolishly mystical this may seem, nothing so far learned
by astronauts disproves this.

The continuity of Laura Riding's thought is evident in much of her later work as Laura (Riding) Jackson. One must always be cautious in extrapolating backwards, but it is legitimate to see whether the later, post-poetic work sheds light upon the earlier.[5] *Rational Meaning*, the work to which she and her husband devoted their lives together, and which was only published in 1997 six years after her death, contains a chapter, 'Words and Things', several pages of which are devoted to 'Earth', a chapter to which we had recourse in our essay on 'Incarnations' with reference to the poet's use of 'dust'.

Although the argument of 'Words and Things' is driven towards linguistic conclusions, the whole of the intricate thought of the chapter is of interest in relation to a consideration of her poems in general and this poem in particular. The following statements are a sample only:

> The name "Earth" or "earth" ought not to appear in any dictionary
> as one of the "meanings" of the word "earth" but only as a name,
> the name of the place of human life. […]
>
> And the matter of time, and that of space, inject themselves into
> far-flung efforts to calculate or to imagine possibilities "out there"
> from "here." Time and space are disposed in various unimaginable
> combinations, in these efforts, to which the Einsteinian time-space
> dimensional contraption provides no relief, linguistically or
> otherwise.[6]

In her poetry a use of the word 'earth' comparable with that in the poem 'Earth' itself appears in *Laura and Francisca*, which first appeared, in book form, in 1931, in the same period as *Twenty Poems Less* (excerpts from it were also published in *Poet: A Lying Word*):

> This [Mallorca] is not heaven, but the smallest earth. [...]
> There are many habitable islands.
> To be habitable is an island:
> The rest is space, childhood of the mind [...]
>
> Exact Mallorca, least everywhere,
> Most earth-like miniature
> Of a too heavenly planet [...]
> I lie from Deya inward by long leagues
> Of earthliness from the sun and sea
> Turning inward to nowhere-on-earth.[7]

3

To come back to our second question: why? Why is the poet telling us to have no (wide) fears for Earth? And as a supplementary question, why should destruction fall on wide fears? Seeking the answer one recalls the reference to astronauts in her 1972 recording. Implicitly the poem is a criticism, not of science *per se*, but of the impact of misapplied scientific thinking, astronomy in this case, upon our values and our concepts of ourselves and the place we live.

This brings to mind Riding's pungent critique of (the impact of modern) psychology in her preface to 'Homiletic' Studies in *Epilogue II*. It is seldom referred to, and needs to be read whole as an epitome of her thought on this area; what follows are extracts:

> Psychology has disintegrated the natural person, disentangled the constitutional strands, and attempted to recompose them again not into constitutions but into patterns of behaviour. In the old homily tradition which preceded psychology, the determination of qualities, the resolution of character, was a process dependent on personal choice. The natural person was an inviolable unit: all modification or strengthening must take place from within, be an act of character. [...]

> Psychology dispenses entirely with the notion of character. […] Psychology has thrown away the person, our guarantee that what is being done and said is peculiarly, personally, of now, and plunged event and truth back into its primitive state of chaotic detail. […]
>
> Our persons have grown ghostly under the influence of psychological analysis, which composes a common, public person out of the old privately vested qualities. […] Event and truth must be public realities; but they cannot be this unless apprehended by a personally identifiable population, each of us grounded in private integrity of consciousness.[8]

Laura Riding did not simply disparage science. In her 'Nonce Preface' to *The Telling*, for example, she shows respect to the power of scientific criticism and approves the question 'Have I checked the results of my operations for nonsense?' that science's criticism 'makes one rudely ask oneself'.[9] Scientific rigour was not unwelcome to her, then, and she was familiar with scientific thought. She was, however, most perturbed by the disorder created by what she believed to be the misapplication of scientific ideas.

One of the better reviews of *Collected Poems* at the time of their first publication was that of the poet and great translator of Homer, Robert Fitzgerald, who wrote:

> The authority, the dignity, of truth telling, lost by poetry to science may gradually be regained. If it is, these poems should one day be a kind of *Principia*.[10]

To return to the poem, her criticism is that unnecessary and inappropriate fears for Earth have been generated by the adoption of an external scientific time-space perspective in which Earth, along with its human inhabitants, is an accidental and temporary by-product of the universe. There is an alternative, inward (and she would say true) perspective; this is one in which Earth and the humans who live there are central, the unifying culmination of the universe's processes of becoming. This is set forth early in the main body of *The Telling*, with such innocence that the thought's profundity, and its implications, might easily be missed:

> For science, the explanation of the first life-forms, or earliest matter-patterns, is a main end of knowledge. But the explanation of these cannot be the explanation of ourselves. *My thought is that the explanation of ourselves can be the explanation of such mysteries* — that in the missing story of ourselves can be found all other missing stories.[11] (Italics added)

4

The first version of 'Earth' was simpler but less elegant than the later versions, like a preliminary sketch, but its unambiguous simplicity helps clarify the author's intentions when read alongside the finished version. Given the rarity of the edition, limited to 200 copies and never reprinted, it will be helpful to reproduce the full 1930 version of 'Earth' here:

> Have no fears for earth.
> The universal name of it is Nothing.
> If it is Earth to us, that is our secret.
> The outer records leave off here,
> And we may write it as it seems to us,
> And as it seems, it is,
> Being so still and reasonable
> Amidst great speed and strangeness.
>
> For that which is unseen, or only seen,
> That which is space, unearthly space,   10
> Is a time before Earth was,
> And we move only inwards,
> Towards ourselves and it.
> From which it is a place of places,

> An onlywhere of everywhere.
> And have no fears for it,
> Its destiny is simple,
> To be further what it is.
> How long this means in present miles we know,
> Though not in coming hours. 20
>
> But we are not tired yet,
> Nor need be while we count as always
> In the lazy scale of ever.
> So have no fears.[12]

In the first line 'wide' does not qualify fears, and the poem lacks the final line of the finished version, with its statement that 'Destruction only on wide fears will fall'; to that extent the criticism is less trenchant (or humorous). The use of the first person plural rather than the second person somehow gives a more homely feel to lines 3, 5, 12 and 13. It is 'we', how 'it seems to us', which is important:

> If it is Earth to us, that is our secret.
> The outer records leave off here,
> And we may write it as it seems to us,
> And as it seems, it is,
> Being so still and reasonable
> Amidst great speed and strangeness. (3-8)

The inclusion of 'reasonable' as an adjective for Earth (and by extension for us), and of 'strangeness' as an attribute of the 'unearthly space', emphasises and clarifies the nature of the difference.

All the great universe, that which is unseen or only seen, is a space and time before Earth was:

> And we move only inwards,
> Towards ourselves and it. (12-13, 1930 version)

> From which you inward move
> Toward perfect now. (12-13, 1938 version)

The two versions complement each other. While the first version is simpler and makes it clearer that we move inwards towards earth as well as ourselves, the second takes the idea of what the inward move means further, into a concentration of time and space into the 'now'.

The following stanzas in the two versions are more similar:

> From which it is a place of places,
> An onlywhere of everywhere.
> And have no fears for it, Its destiny is simple,
> To be further what it is. (14-18, 1930 version)

> Almost the place it is not yet,
> Potential here of everywhere—
> Have no wide fears for it:
> Its destiny is simple,
> To be further what it will be. (14-18, 1938 version)

The first version has the attractive coinage 'onlywhere' (compare 'least everywhere' of Mallorca, in one of the passages cited above from *Laura and Francisca*) which successfully conveys the uniqueness and singularity of Earth, but this is sacrificed in the second version for a more qualified and less comfortable image of a place that is not quite there yet, but that will be. The final stanzas are very different in the two versions:

> How long this means in present miles we know,
> Though not in coming hours.
> But we are not tired yet,
> Nor need be while we count as always
> In the lazy scale of ever.
> So have no fears. (19-24, 1930 version)

> Earth is your heart
> Which has become your mind
> But still beats ignorance
> Of all it knows—
> As miles deny the compact present
> Whose self-mistrusting past they are.
> Have no wide fears for Earth:
> Destruction only on wide fears shall fall. (19-26, 1938 version)

The first version lacks the defining statements about Earth, and the final invocation of destruction on wide fears. It appears blander, less conclusive than the final version. The line 'But we are not tired yet' indicates that we may not be ready for 'death', as in the final lines of 'Intelligent Prayer':

> If you are tired—good. Tiredness is to pray to death,
> That it shall think for you when speechlessness
> Tells how you lie so full of understanding each,
> Sorry of life in his own grave of mind each.

Lines 19-24 are the core of the final version of the poem, which focuses on ignorance, but this is 'ignorance | Of all it knows', which implies that unforgetting will be the key to knowledge, not science.[13] (This idea is reminiscent of the line in 'Incarnations': 'Death does not give a moment to remember in' and also of the climax to 'The Tiger', where it is implied that only by closing her eyes will the lady wake up.)

Earth (as heart) still beats ignorance (as mind) of all it knows:

> As miles deny the compact present
> Whose self-mistrusting past they are. (23-24)[14]

The 'compact present' is close to, but has not yet quite achieved, the 'perfect now' of line 13. The 'miles' – that is the external distances of the measured universe – are the self-mistrusting past of the compact present, which compact present they 'deny'. That is why 'you' should –

> Have no wide fears for Earth:
> Destruction only on wide fears shall fall. (25-26)

The use of 'wide' has a dual application here. In a more ordinary application to the noun 'fears' it has the obvious but secondary meaning of 'far-reaching'. However, the primary meaning of 'spacious' and 'extensive' are particularly relevant to fears generated by a 'universal' perspective of earth. By qualifying the noun in the later versions of the poem it allows the notion that we should indeed have some sort of fear for Earth. Could this be, in line with the less confident tone of final stanza in the later versions, that we *may* fear that it (and we) will not fulfil its (and our) destiny, unless we can overcome our ignorance?

5

This account of Heaven and Earth by the poet subverts the account of astronomy, without denying the validity of science within its own field. In part the poet's argument rests on the fact that science cannot tell us about origins even in its own terms, namely, it cannot tell what there was before the Big Bang. When, in the mid-20th century, the theory of black holes was developed the term 'singularity' was appropriated by scientists as the name for: 'a region in space-time at which matter is infinitely dense'.[15] The concept seems peculiarly apt, if by inversion and by analogy only, to this poem. The word 'singularity' has a range of other historic and current meanings many of which also seem (if more mundanely) apposite to Laura Riding's poems and to her person more generally, including: singleness of purpose; the quality or fact of being one in number; a special or particular kind of something; dissent or separation from something; and the fact or condition of being alone or apart from others, solitariness.[16] By analogy, in the poem, the 'region in space-time at which matter is infinitely dense' would be your mind, the poet's mind, the compact present and the perfect now.[17]

Some months after first drafting this essay I came across the following passage, by Yuval Noah Harari:

> Physicists define the Big Bang as a singularity. *It is a point at which all the known laws of nature did not exist. Time too did not exist.* [Italics added]

Thus far the poet would follow; but Harari goes on to say:

> We may fast be approaching a new singularity, when all the concepts that give meaning to our world – me, you, men, women, love and hate – will become irrelevant. Anything happening beyond that point is meaningless to us.[18]

The poet's conclusions were completely the reverse.

NOTES

[1] See 'Excerpts From A Recording (1972) Explaining The Poems', published as Appendix V to the centenary edition of Collected Poems, *The Poems of Laura Riding* (New York: Persea Books, 2001) 496, where the author makes comments on the change in her poems. This is discussed in the introduction to this book.

[2] From the rear dust wrapper of the original edition of Laura Riding, *Collected Poems* (London: Cassells, 1938). [3] See 'The Matter of Metaphor', published as a supplementary essay in Laura (Riding) Jackson and Schuyler B. Jackson, *Rational Meaning: A New Foundation for the Meaning of Words* (Charlottesville, Virginia: University Press of Virginia: 1997), 506-509, of which the following is an excerpt:

'The use of metaphor effects no expansion of the meaning-potentialities of a language. [...] It is, as a common feature of linguistic practice, an incidental expediency, a homely administering of first-aid by mother-wit to jams or halts in expression suddenly confronting speakers, with no respectable linguistic solution immediately in sight.' (507).

[4] From Appendix V, 1980 and 2001 editions of her collected poems, 490 in 2001 edition. The poem referred to is 'Disclaimer of the Person'.

[5] I have felt freer in use of Laura (Riding) Jackson's post-poetic criticism and commentary in respect of the poems 'past half-way', in her words; this roughly equates to the 'Poems of Final

Occasion' and 'Poems Continual', all first published after 1929. There is something in the nature of a category shift in the latter part of her poetic career, briefly but suggestively summed up in the 1972 recording referred to in notes 1 and 4 above.

[6] *Rational Meaning*, 1997, 399, 400. The following passages are also of interest, if less directly relevant here:

> And "human," identifying creatures knowing themselves as the characteristic beings of the place in which they found themselves, has become varyingly a term theological, biological, historical, yet ever one verging upon the status of a *word*. But as a word it acquires a meaning so eloquent with happy self-knowledge as to make the creatures shy back, uncomfortably, as from ridiculous claiming themselves creatures of Heaven [...]

> And what of the other words, and terms, or names, that rise in minds, from mouths, in considerations of universal possibilities from the vantage of a sense of earth-location, superficially sophisticated in its intellectual expression, linguistically slipshod, inwardly all a stodgy, sluggish bewilderment? Universe? Heaven? Hell? The Sky, skies? The Moon, moons? The Ocean, oceans? The Horizon, horizons? And what of the religious implications of "earthly" as in "earthly life," "earthly nature," with contrastive "heavenly" at hand? (*RM*, 400).

And we are reminded also of the following passage, quoted in the essay on 'Incarnations':

> For Earth, which is reverenceable as the human place of being, is also, as the site of the physical engendering of human beings, a materiality out of which they have had to extract themselves: the humble fact of this is a sobering element of the dignity of being human. The dust of Earthly createdness clings to, still falls from the beautiful reality of human identity. (*RM*, 419)

[7] These excerpts can be found in *Collected Poems*, 398, 399, 400, 413. The last of these quotations is followed immediately by:

> A rumoured place? That takes us to the moon? Let it be moon. The moon was never more Than a name without a place to match it. . . .

[8] Reprinted in Laura Riding and Robert Graves, *Essays From Epilogue* (Manchester: Carcanet, 2001), 78-79.

[9] Laura (Riding) Jackson, *The Telling* (London, Athlone Press: 1972), 2-3.

[10] 'Laura Riding' in *Kenyon Review*, 1 (Summer 1939), 341-345.

[11] *The Telling*, 9, passage 2.

[12] Laura Riding, *Twenty Poems Less*, (Paris, Hours Press: 1930), 3.

[13] Again, in *The Telling*, memory is identified as the key:

> To know the spirit within the whole we must learn what we are in the whole, and be according to that, so that we know it in ourselves. And as this knowledge experience seems to me [...] memory is the key [...]

> In every human being there is secreted a memory of a before-oneself; and if one opens the memory, and the mind is enlarged with it, one knows a time which might be now, by one's feelings of being somehow of it. (From passages 21 and 22, pages 24-25)

Passages 21-28 deal at length with the role of memory, culminating in passage 28, quoted elsewhere, which begins:

Yes, I think we remember our creation! — have the memory of it in us, to know. (Passage 28, page 30)

[14] The second version of *Earth*, in the 1933 collection *Poet: A Lying Word*, otherwise very close to the final version has a variation in line 23:

As present miles deny the compact man

[15] Shorter OED 2002.

[16] OED, 1971.

[17] Mark Jacobs points out the following relevant passage of Laura Riding's thought, from her major essay 'The Idea of God' in *Epilogue I* (p25 in the 2001 selection):

The scientific universe is the assurance that there is a next moment because there is this moment and because the next moment has its start in this, is guaranteed in this, is really the same as this. And this free, perfect moment is not of space: it is only one moment, always the same next moment in the same position, though it has infinite occurrence. Variety of position means only numerical extent, as if to say: 'Let us reduce earth to the smallest conceivable space, so small that it cannot be called space.

Then, though there are many of us, and only one spot, nevertheless we are all standing there; and it cannot even be called a spot, because, since all of us are standing on it, the notion of space is eliminated.' Nor is this free, perfect moment one of time: because, while there is a succession of moments, all the moments are equally this moment. They succeed each other in the sense that one is the logical predecessor of the other, but no new moment is entered into. It is already the new moment—already as new, as different, as 'next' as it can be in being the perpetuated same moment.

[18] Yuval Noah Harari, *Sapiens: A Brief History of Humankind* (London: Vintage, 2011), 461.

Chapter 13

'The Flowering Urn': the virgin sleep of Mother All

And every prodigal greatness
Must creep back into strange home,
Must fill the hollow matrix of
The never-begotten perfect son
Who never can be born.

And every quavering littleness
Must shrink more tinily than it knows
Into the giant hush whose sound
Reverberates within itself
As tenderest numbers cannot improve.   10

And from this jealous secrecy
Will rise itself, will flower up,
The likeness kept against false seed:
When death-whole is the seed
And no new harvest to fraction sowing.

Will rise the same peace that held
Before fertility's lie awoke
The virgin sleep of Mother All:
The same but for the way in flowering
It speaks of fruits that could not be.   20

1

This serene, perfect poem bears little resemblance, other than in the opening stanza, to its rather raw-seeming forerunner, under the title 'Zero', which was published as the final poem of *Twenty Poems Less* in 1930.[1] Its next incarnation, in *Poet: A Lying Word* in 1933 is almost identical to the version in *Collected Poems*, the only variations being that in the latter 'shrink' replaced 'pale' in line 7 and 'harvest' replaced 'season' in line 15. The poem was published in the author's *Selected Poems* in 1970 with just one amendment to the 1938 *Collected Poems* version (not carried forward to the later editions of *CP*), 'Will rise the secret' replacing and clarifying 'Will rise itself' in line 12.

The poem is in four five-line stanzas; whilst the rhythm is not completely regular its basis, as Roy Fuller pointed out of Laura Riding's verse in general '. . . is the four-beat line, which has claims to be the most natural (i.e. speakable) measure in English poetry, and her good ear enables her to make convincing transitions to shorter or more irregularly accented lines.'[2] Supple movement and momentum are created by a combination of this flexible rhythm with the pulsing repetitions and parallels of imagery and phrase. For example 'Must', 'Must' and 'Must' drive the first two stanzas, as 'Will', 'will' and 'Will' drive the third and fourth. The poem's opening two lines are closely paralleled and contrasted by the first two lines of the second stanza; the parallels become more distant as the second stanza progresses, but there is an echo or parallel of 'the hollow matrix' in 'the giant hush'.

The third stanza begins in a way that suggests there will be another close parallel, with the second repetition of 'And', but then '*this* jealous secrecy' (italics added) refers us back to the previous stanzas to see what is meant, and we then contrast the rising up of the flower with the creeping back of the prodigal greatness and the shrinking of the quavering littleness in the first half of the poem.

There are further repetitions with variation – 'Will rise itself, will flower up' and 'Will rise the same peace'; 'the same peace' and 'the same but for the way in flowering' – that help gather and resolve the tensions and thoughts in the poem.

The most striking repetition is of the word 'And' which begins each of the first three stanzas, with a further echo in the last line of the third stanza. To start a poem with 'And' is unusual, though not unique. It breaks the stylistic rule drummed into schoolchildren of never beginning a sentence with 'And' or 'But'. It returns us to the strong simplicity of biblical storytelling, at least that of the King James translation. There, especially in the translation of the limpid Greek of the New Testament, every other verse seems to begin with 'And'.[3] Blake's 'Jerusalem', of course, begins portentously with 'And', and lines 3, 5, and 7 of that poem repeat the motif. For once the Oxford English Dictionary gives no adequate account of this usage. Used occasionally it has a powerful effect, as though a deep undercurrent of continuous thought is breaking surface into a poem.

2

The poem's title, 'The Flowering Urn', encapsulates the theme of life out of death – an urn, of course, being a vase used to store the ashes of a cremated person, as opposed to the normal use of a vase for flowers. Ashes remind us of the 'dust' of the poem 'Incarnations' and of the very first lines of *Collected Poems*:

> The stove was grey, the coal was gone
> In and out of the same room
> One went, one came.
> One turned into nothing.
> One turned into whatever
> Turns into children.[4]

We said that the title encapsulated the theme of 'life out of death'. However, this is misleading and inadequate. The words 'flower' and 'flowering' have connotations divergent from those of the word 'life'. A flower is, most concretely, the seed-bearing part of a plant, a meaning referred to in lines 12- 15, and also in the opening line of 'Doom in Bloom' (which has a similarly oxymoronic title): 'Now flower the oldest seeds.' Figuratively a flower may be, in an old-fashioned way, virginity (indirectly perhaps alluded to in 'The virgin sleep of Mother All'); it is commonly used to denote the most vigorous period of a person's life. More to the point, to flower is, again figuratively, to be in or to attain one's fullest *perfection*, not merely to 'live'.

The tensions in the poem are between ideas of flowering and of fertility, of perfection and fecundity. Put simply the poet, contrary to traditional ideas of womanhood and of motherhood, finds fulfilment in the former and not in the latter, which are seen as delusory. Against 'flowering' is set 'fertility's lie', which may be associated with the sun in 'Signs of Knowledge', and in 'Disclaimer of the Person', as in the lines:

> I am a woman.
> I am not the sun which multiplied,
> I am the moon which singled
> I am not the moon but a singling.
> I am I.
> I am my name.
> My name is not my name,
> It is the name of what I say.

The idea expressed in the phrase 'fertility's lie' can also be found in the concluding lines of 'On a New Generation':

> And in such silence may enough centuries fade
> For all the loud births to be eloquently unmade.

There is an example of a similar thought in lines 5-10 of 'Care in Calling':

> Child is the first man still
> Man is the last man not yet.
> And the first man is seed,
> And the last man is seed silenced.
> The last man is womanish:
> Woman which before man
> Was silent word alone—
> That breeding silence she.

3

There is a reminder of the prodigal son of the parable in the first stanza, the reckless spendthrift (compare the 'reckless hearts in tongues' of 'Come, Words, Away', and the much later phrase 'the aggressively free word-spenders'[5]) who is yet received with joy by his father on his return home. In this case the prodigal greatness must creep back not to a father but to a mother-figure, a strange home, a womb, to fill:

> The hollow matrix of
> The never-begotten perfect son
> Who never can be born. (3-5)

There never can be a perfect son, or a perfect man; this gives an elegiac air to the poem (for a man, perhaps, if not for the poet). 'Matrix' is a more technical word than 'womb'; most basically it means a place or medium in which something is bred, a point of origin and growth, by extension it means a mould in which something is cast or shaped. It is a word denoting the feminine principle, which appears further on in the poem in the form of 'Mother All.'[6]

> And each over-beautiful lady of the year
> Must die must yield to reason [...]

In the later version the second stanza parallels the prodigal *greatness* with the quavering *littleness*. The 'quavering littleness' is more inclusive in its reference than the female 'over-beautiful lady of the year'. It may include the 'prodigal greatness', already reduced in the first stanza, now shrinking further; it may include both men and women, as in 'each over-beautiful lady of the year'.

The language of this stanza has complex associations. 'Quavering littleness' radiates suggestions of human awe and fear,[7] of music and of the power of minute particulars: 'quavering' (trembling and vibrating; but also the tiny note, the quaver), the hush whose 'sound reverberates' and 'numbers'. 'Numbers' itself has complex connotations; it may refer to the classification of word forms, to (the principles of) harmony, or to the conformity of verse or music to a regular rhythm. The tenderest[8], most subdued and sensitive song, cannot improve on the reverberant sound of the original giant hush. This thought brings us back to the ninth section of 'Come Words Away':

> But never shall truth circle so
> Till words prove language is
> How words come from far sound away
> Through stages of immensity's small
> Centring the utter telling
> In truth's first soundlessness.

'Numbers' also involves ideas of 'telling', as in a bank-teller as well as story-teller; and all numbers in *The Telling* lead to Zero (the One), in the final passage of that book.[9] The first version of the poem, given in the first endnote here, was entitled 'Zero', being the last, in a count-down, of the *Twenty Poems Less*.

> And from this jealous secrecy
> Will rise itself, will flower up,
> The likeness kept against false seed:[10]

Then death-whole is the seed
And no new harvest to fraction sowing. (11-15)

The shrinkage back to a seed-core of authenticity is consistent with the image of an 'inch of wholeness' from 'Celebration of Failure'. The final stanza takes us forward to the past:

> Through pain the land of pain,
> Through tender exiguity,
> Through cruel self-suspicion:
> Thus came I to this inch of wholeness.
>
> It was a promise. After pain I said,
> An inch will be what never a boasted mile.
> And haughty judgement,
> That frowned upon a faultless plan,
> Now smiles upon this crippled execution,
> And my dashed beauty praises me.

The hollow matrix and the giant hush taken together create an image of an inward secret feminine universe. The word 'jealous' contains the notions of possessiveness and watchfulness, but also, of God, demanding absolute faithfulness and exclusive worship; although we are not here in the realm of the Heavenly Father of the Bible, rather that of Mother All.[11]

> [And from this jealous secrecy]
> Will rise the same peace that held
> Before fertility's lie awoke
> The virgin sleep of Mother All:
> The same but for the way in flowering
> It speaks of fruits that could not be. (16-20)

'Fertility's lie' awaking the 'virgin sleep of Mother All' reminds us (as in

'The Tiger' but in a different context) of the fairy tale figure of Sleeping Beauty. The virgin sleep of Mother All also provides us with an image that contrasts with the picture of Winter's dream of productivity conjured up by Coleridge in 'Work Without Hope':

> And Winter slumbering in the open air,
> Wears on his smiling face a dream of Spring!

There is though here a (for Riding, untragic) sense of the acceptance of impossibility, of the conditions of existence, as in the following passage from *Anarchism Is Not Enough*:

> The only productive design is designed waste. Designed creation results in nothing but the destruction of the designer: it is impossible to add to what is; all is and is made. Energy that attempts to make in the sense of making a numerical increase in the sum of made things is spitefully returned to itself unused. It is a would-be-happy-ness ending in unanticipated and disordered unhappiness. Energy that is aware of the impossibility of positive construction devotes itself to an ordered using-up and waste of itself: to an anticipated unhappiness which, because it has design, foreknowledge, is the nearest approach to happiness. Undesigned unhappiness and designed happiness both mean anarchism. *Anarchism is not enough.*[12]

My reading of 'the fruits that could not be' is that they represent what is here described as 'designed creation'; there will only be the (unfertile) flower; there need never be a harvest (nor a fruitful season).

4

The complexity and compactness of the second stanza here gives pause for reflection on the nature of this poet's use of words and images. The poet herself, of course, in the climax to her preface 'To the Reader', insists that her poems must be read 'literally, literally, literally, without gloss, without gloss, without gloss. So read, so exist.' In a careful article marking publication of the second edition of *Collected Poems* Alan Clark, commenting upon the author's insistence that she should nowhere be taken as speaking by symbols, said that 'the clear air of the poems, their freedom from mistily implicative reverberations, is one of their perception-rinsing elements.' And Robert Nye commented, with acute perceptiveness, that he found 'in due course that here were not so much spells as acts of verbal *disenchantment*, inspired unravellings of the world's riddle.'

Some of the poems clearly do unravel mystery, are 'disenchantments'. In that category, clearly, are poems such as 'Signs of Knowledge' and the first part of 'Disclaimer of the Person', and other poems have seemed, in the course of our reading, to detonate our assumptions and our illusions. Equally, it has not been hard to find umpteen examples of clarity of word-use, based on profound knowledge, to justify Clark's statement about the 'clear air' of the poems. However, in some poems, or parts of poems, the words and ideas are ravelled up, by contrast into a complex in which different meanings of words, and ideas and images are compacted into a unitary density that is, at least for long, baffling, and could lead to accusations of mixing of metaphors. Here are two examples, from 'Earth' and from 'Tale of Modernity':

> *Earth is your heart*
> *Which has become your mind*
> *But still beats ignorance of all it knows—*
> As miles deny the compact present
> Whose self-mistrusting past they are [...] (Italics added)

.   .   .

> And she [the moon], illusion and not illusion,
> *A sapphire being fell to earth, time-struck.*
> *In colour live and liquid and earth-pale,*
> Never so near she,
> never so distant.

> Never had time been futured so,
> All reckoning on one fast page.
> Time was a place where earth had been.
> The whole past met there, she with it.
> *Truth seemed love grown cool as a brow,*
> *And young as the moon, grown girl to self.* (Italics added)

The sections on poetry in *Anarchism Is Not Enough* are the nearest we have to a primer as to how to understand her own poetry. She speaks there, in a paragraph I have already quoted elsewhere, of how words are used in (by implication, her) poetry, being taken through 'three historical levels':

> They may be true words, that is of an intrinsic sense; they may be logical words, of an applied sense; or they may be poetical words, of a misapplied sense, untrue and illogical in themselves, but of supposed suggestive power. The most a poet can now do is to take every word he uses through each of these levels, giving it the combined depth of all three, forcing it beyond itself to a death of sense where it is at least safe from the perjuries either of society or poetry.[13]

This takes us only so far. It helps explain the complexity of use of individual words, but what we have in the examples given above is a dynamic in which one word or concept seems to become another and to acquire characteristics of a third. In the second stanza of 'The Flowering Urn' 'littleness' quavers, shrinks (or pales). 'Earth' is blithely described as being your heart which has become your mind which 'still beats ignorance of all it knows.' In the two italicised passages from 'Tale of Modernity', first the unnamed moon acquires the characteristics ('sapphire', 'earth-pale') of the earth in falling to earth, then in two short lines 'Truth' seems like love, like the moon, which is described as young, then 'grown girl to self.'

These passages are not aberrations, and they are deliberate. They are the product of a woman writing in the full confidence of her vision:

We can get truth — how things are as a whole — only from woman: man operates through the sense of difference, woman through the sense of unity.[14]

NOTES

[1] As the book is not readily available, even from libraries, I include the poem here in this endnote for ease of reference:

ZERO
And every prodigal greatness
Must creep back into the womb
And fill the empty matrix of
The never-begotten perfect son
Who never need be born.

And each over-beautiful lady of the year
Must die must yield to reason
That has promised such a one
As will not work love or
Any other softness or enchantment.

And all fear and custom
And all frankness and confusion
Must become a smile of shame
On the sad face of history
Lying where it lay.

And be it known that I, proud name,
Have found my knees and am in prayer,
The prayer of the dispersed multitude
Which never yet was gathered -
For by its broken breath they lived.

[2] Roy Fuller, 'The White Goddess', *The Review*, 1970, No. 23, 9.

[3] See for example Luke 2, v33-52, a passage selected almost at random, in which all but one of the 15 verses begins either with 'And', or in one case 'But'.

[4] *Forgotten Girlhood*, lines 1-6.

[5] Laura (Riding) Jackson and Schuyler B. Jackson, *Rational Meaning* (Charlottesville and London: University Press of Virginia, 1997), 565, use this phrase of the author Norman Mailer.

[6] The mother figure appears in *Back to the Mother Breast*, and more relevantly to this context in *That Ancient Line*. She also appears in various guises in *Forgotten Girlhood*: Old Trouble, Mother Damnable, Mother Mary and her Magdalenes, Mother and Moon and Old Trouble.

⁷ Perhaps because of the way this poem proposes a 'Mother All' rather than a 'Heavenly Father' the 'quavering littleness' reminds me, by contrast, of the meek of Christianity, who shall inherit the earth.

⁸ We are reminded, here, of the language of Riding's firm rejection of analogies between poetry and music: 'This mutual tenderness leads to false critical analogies between poetry and music; to the deliberate effort to use the creative method of one art in the other. (*Anarchism Is Not Enough*, Cape 1928, p32) Riding tends to use 'tenderness', as in this quotation, satirically or somewhat ironically as in *Chloe Or* . . . 'Yet they [the girls] have been used so tenderly [by the men]' (*CP*, p17).

⁹ Laura (Riding) Jackson, *The Telling* (London: Athlone, 1972), e.g. 53 (passage 60) and the book's final statement at 56 (passage 62):

> ([…] And none will be missing from the count of those: it will tally perfectly with ONE.)

¹⁰ 'The likeness kept against false seed' reminds one of the Platonic theory of forms. The key difference, as so often, is that for Riding the original 'dust' or 'likeness' is material, not just an idea but a thing.

¹¹ *Rational Meaning*, 1997, 401 (and the related note, 469) has an instructive commentary on our use of 'Mother Earth' and how it does *not* parallel our use of 'Heavenly Father'.

¹² *Anarchism Is Not Enough,* Cape 1928, pp18-19.

¹³ Ibid, 12.

¹⁴ Laura (Riding) Jackson, *The Word "Woman"* (New York: Persea, 1993), 40-41; from the title essay originally written around 1934.

Chapter 14

'Poet: A Lying Word': a riposte to Arthur Rimbaud

POET: A LYING WORD

[1] You have now come with me, I have now come with you, to the season that should be winter, and is not: we have not come back.

[2] We have not come back: we have not come round: we have not moved. I have taken you, you have taken me, to the next and next span, and the last—and it is the last. Stand against me then and stare well through me then. It is a wall not to be scaled and left behind like the old seasons, like the poets who were the seasons.

[3] Stand against me then and stare well through me then. I am no poet as you have span by span leapt the high words to the next depth and season, the next season always, the last always, and the next. I am a true wall: you may but stare me through.

[4] It is a false wall, a poet: it is a lying word. It is a wall that closes and does not.

[5] This is no wall that closes and does not. It is a wall to see into, it is no other season's height. Beyond it lies no depth and height of travel, no partial courses. Stand against me then and stare well through me then. Like wall of poet here I rise, but am no poet as walls have risen between next and next and made false end to leap. A last true wall am I: you may but stare me through.

[6] And the tale is no more of the going: no more a poet's tale of going false-like to a seeing. The tale is of a seeing true-like to a knowing: there's but to stare the wall through now, well through.

[7] It is not a wall, it is not a poet. It is not a lying wall, it is not a lying word. It is a written edge of time. Step not across, for then into my mouth, my eyes you fall. Come close, stare me well through, speak as you see. But oh, infatuated drove of lives, step not across now. Into my mouth, my eyes shall you thus fall, and be yourselves no more.

[8] Into my mouth, my eyes, I say, I say. I am no poet like transitory wall to lead you on into such slow terrain of time as measured out your single span to broken turns of season once and once again. I lead you not. You have now come with me, I have now come with you, to your last turn and season: thus could I come with you, thus only.

[9] I say, I say, I am, it is, such wall, such poet, such not lying, such not leading into. Await the sight, and look well through, know by such standing still that next comes none of you.

[10] Comes what? Comes this even I, even this not-I, this not

lying season when death holds the year at steady count—this every-year.

[11] Would you not see, not know, not mark the count? What would you then? Why have you come here then? To leap a wall that is no wall, and a true wall? To step across into my eyes and mouth not yours? To cry me down like wall or poet as often your way led past down- falling height that seemed?

[12] I say, I say, I am, it is: such wall, such end of graded travel. And if you will not hark, come tumbling then upon me, into my eyes, my mouth, and be the backward utterance of yourselves expiring angrily through instant seasons that played you time-false.

[13] My eyes, my mouth, my hovering hands, my intransmutable head: wherein my eyes, my mouth, my hands, my head, my body-self, are not such mortal simulacrum as everlong you built against very-death, to keep you everlong in boasted death-course, neverlong? I say, I say, I am not builded of you so.

[14] This body-self, this wall, this poet-like address, is that last barrier long shied of in your elliptic changes: out of your leaping, shying, season-quibbling, have I made it, is it made. And if now poet-like it rings with one-more-time as if, this is the mounted stupor of your everlong outbiding worn prompt and lyric, poet-like—the forbidden one-more-time worn time-like.

[15] Does it seem I ring, I sing, I rhyme, I poet-wit? Shame on me then! Grin me your foulest humour then of poet-piety, your eyes rolled up in white hypocrisy—should I be one sprite more of your versed fame—or turned from me into your historied brain, where the lines read more actual. Shame on me then!

[16] And haste unto us both, my shame is yours. How long I seem to beckon like a wall beyond which stretches longer length of fleshsome traverse: it is your lie of flesh and my flesh-seeming stand of words. Haste then unto us both. I say, I say. This wall reads 'Stop!' This poet verses 'Poet: a lying word!'

[17] Shall the wall then not crumble, as to walls is given? Have I not said: 'Stare me well through'? It is indeed a wall, crumble it shall. It is a wall of walls, stare it well through: the reading gentles near, the name of death passes with the season that it was not.

[18] Death is a very wall. The going over walls, against walls, is a dying and a learning. Known death is truth sighted at the halt. The name of death passes. The mouth that moves with death forgets the word.

[19] And the first page is the last of death. And haste unto us both, lest the wall seem to crumble not, to lead mock-onward. And the first page reads: 'Haste unto us both!' And the first page reads: 'Slowly, it is the first page only.'

[20] Slowly, it is the page before the first page only, there is no haste. The page before the first page tells of death, haste, slowness: how truth falls true now at the turn of page, at time of telling. Truth one by one falls true. And the first page reads, the page which is the page before the first page only: 'This once-upon-a-time when seasons failed, and time stared through the wall nor made to leap across, is the hour, the season, seasons, year and years, no wall and wall, where when and when the classic lie dissolves and nakedly time salted is with truth's sweet flood nor yet to mix with, but be salted tidal-sweet—O sacramental ultimate by which shall time be old-renewed nor yet another season move.' I say, I say.

1

The book *Poet: A Lying Word*, published in 1933, was Laura Riding's only collection named after one of the poems.[1] That is one indication of the special place, the pride of place that the poem occupies in her work. It stands out, too, as the only prose poem in the main body of *Collected Poems*, which was published in 1938, being set out in paragraphs rather than in verses.[2] The text of the original version was subject to quite a few, mostly minor, amendments to words, phrases and punctuation but remained as twenty paragraphs in *Collected Poems*. This latter version was subsequently included whole and without further amendment in the author's *Selected Poems*. That is further confirmation of the importance of the poem to the author, or rather to the overall story she has to tell in the poems, as it is the only long poem to appear there thus, unabridged.[3]

The title of both book and poem *might* be read as further provocation to the literary world, following the title of *Poems: A Joking Word,* with its extraordinary introduction.[4] The title *might* also be read as a precursor of the 'renunciation' of poetry which eventually followed, but we must remember that five years later a most passionate and unequivocal defence of poetry was offered in the 1938 preface to *Collected Poems*.

Unlike *Poems: A Joking Word*, for which the preface provided a detailed explanation of the title's meaning (and in which it is made clear, odd though it may seem, that 'joking' is not a word of disparagement of poems), there is no such introduction to the book *Poet: A Lying Word*, for all that it is the most elaborately organised of her collections. The book is set out in five parts, each with a mysterious rubric referring to the seasons, and hinting at their imminent demise. The poem in view is in the fifth and final part of the book, entitled 'Failure of Season', and paragraphs 1-3, 8, 10, and 12 of the poem itself all refer to the seasons.

The final part of *Poet: A Lying Word* consists of four long poems in the following order: 'Signs of Knowledge', 'Poet: A Lying Word', 'Benedictory Close' and 'Apocryphal Numbers'. In *Collected Poems* the same poems are also placed together, in nearly the same order, preceding the ultimate poem of final occasion, 'Disclaimer of Person'.[5] Taken together the four poems are the culmination of *Poet: A Lying Word* the book, with 'Signs of Knowledge' leading up to 'Poet: A Lying Word' and 'Benedictory Close' and 'Apocryphal Numbers' (renamed 'Three Sermons to the Dead' in *Collected Poems*) having a post-climactic and posthumous role in the sequence. Whilst each of the four poems is distinctive in form and mood there is throughout a language of ending and of re-beginning, of simultaneous, solemnly ecstatic, renunciation and affirmation: the language of a religious sensibility, in short. This is consistent with her first full post-poetic commentary:

> The last poems I wrote are contained in my *Collected Poems*, published in 1938. I can be seen, in that book, to be striving to find at once the poetic extreme *and*, the mark of human fullness of utterance – and to be heading towards finalities of proof of poetry, and of the poet-rôle itself. There is also to be seen there a movement of developing sensibility, above the personal or professional, reflecting consciousness-at-large of the approach of human life in the whole to a term, and of there being, to come, *something after*. The relation of the sense of a something-after to the striving is, precisely, that of religious sensibility giving itself into the keeping of poetic sensibility, which has a partial identity with it, but is also, otherwise engaged. Poetry invited vision of a lasting, living fact awaiting our arrival at a state of grace in which we know it, *speak* it; it is also the patron of a historic love of the patterning of words with a physically ordered nicety, pleasing to human pride. I forced the issue, in my poems, of the spiritual serviceability of what has been regarded in all past human ages, and automatically continues so to be in this, as the universal type of the spiritual best in language.[6]

For this essay, because of the poem's (and the essay's) length, the poem has been printed both whole at the beginning and then again in sections preceding relevant commentary and analysis. In those sections variants from the original

1933 version are noted in the text, in square brackets. For ease of reference the paragraphs, unnumbered in the poem as published, have been numbered here, also in square brackets.

2

Why are the poem and the book entitled 'Poet: A Lying Word'? There are at least three potential, not unrelated, explanations. The first relates to special characteristics of poetic form; the second relates to the etymology of the word 'poet'; and the third relates to the special rôle assumed by the poet.

At its most obvious the title could be taken as referring to the fact that the poet has chosen to set out the poem itself as a non-metrical composition without verse form, contradicting the normal expectation of a poem. On the other hand setting out a poem in prose form was not a radical move in itself, and a prose poem may retain many of the characteristics of 'normal' poetry. Baudelaire wrote many prose poems, and subsequently Rimbaud (of whom more later) wrote his poetic masterpiece and finale, *Une Saison en enfer,* predominantly in prose. As noted in the essay on 'The Tiger', Chapter 2 of *A Survey of Modernist Poetry*, entitled 'The Problem of Form and Subject-Matter in Modernist Poetry', draws attention to prose passages from the authorised version of the Bible where the original text was in poetic form, with the comment: 'The effect of regularity is here again achieved by the recurrence of ideas in varying alternations to show the movement of the poem.'[7]

Riding and Graves identify parallelism of phrases, imagery and lines as a means of development and enrichment of those ideas, particularly relevant in maintaining internal unity in longer poems, which would otherwise collapse under the strain of maintaining outward regularity (of metre, in particular). Few of Riding's poems are metrically regular; in fact, in most of her poems, especially the longer ones, she uses the techniques of parallelism and recurrence, often with variation, of phrases and lines to good effect, in creating or maintaining momentum and internal coherence, and in the development of ideas.[8] In this poem the opening phrase 'You have now come with me, I have now come with you' is repeated in paragraph 8; the last phrase of paragraph 1 is repeated as the opening phrase of paragraph 2; 'Stand against me then and stare well through me then' from the middle of paragraph 2 is repeated at the beginning of paragraph 3 and twice in paragraph 5. These are just three of many examples.

This poem could conceivably have been set out in verse form. The initial phrases are anapaestic and set the tempo for the poem, which is slow and deliberate, almost hypnotic in the main, but broken up by passages of great vividness and intensity. However, the choice of a prose form does feel more appropriate, somehow. There is some figurative 'poetic' language, as in the use of 'seasons' and 'wall', but no rhyme, no systematic assonance; there is a directness and immediacy of address, as though we were in the same room – which of course we are, with the 'poem-person' at any rate.[9]

One is tempted to say (with reference back to the quotation towards the end of the first section of this essay) that there is a strongly ritualistic flavour, in the systematic use of repetition with variation and development, but ritualistic more in its resemblance to a religious than a poetic form. In using the term 'ritual' here I do not mean that the poet is carrying out a rite in the sense of following a conventional or habitual form of behaviour, still less a compulsive behaviour, but that she is marking a solemn occasion in a rhythm and a form resembling those of religious ritual. ('Benedictory' makes an interesting comparison; there it could be said that the verse form is more traditionally 'poetic' but the title and language are more overtly 'religious'.)

The second explanation for the title concerns the etymological derivation of the word 'poet', which is from the Greek for making, composing *something*. For Riding the poet (in creating a poem) makes *nothing*, or a vacuum; hence 'poet: a lying word'. This was expressed with characteristic vigour in *Anarchism Is Not Enough*:

> What is a poem? A poem is nothing. By persistence the poem can be made something; but then it is something, not a poem. [. . .] It cannot be looked at, heard, touched or read because it is a vacuum. [. . .] If it were possible to reproduce it in an audience the result would be destruction of the audience.[10]

This thinking is reflected in much of her earlier criticism and in the content of many of the poems, for example in the title of *Twenty Poems Less*, the final poem of which is 'Zero', as if at the end of a countdown to nothing. It was, perhaps, implicit in her earliest, most romantic poetic credo:

> But if they [modern poets] are to succeed, their constitution must contain some of the elements that went to make up Francis Thompson – the magic at the start (*non murato, ma veramente nato*), the power of wonder that begets wonder, and miracle, and prophecy.[11]

As noted in the introductory chapter the quotation in Italian means, roughly translated, 'not builded [or 'walled'], but really born'. It will be referred to later on in this essay. 'The magic at the start' reminds us of 'Forgotten Girlhood', and in particular of 'Incarnations', those two poems acting as a sort of nativity at the beginning of *Collected Poems*. Romantically expressed as it may be in this passage, the idea that the poet is born and not made persists through the unfolding of the poet's career[12], and can be evidenced in the post-poetic work.[13]

Consistent with these ideas, that a poem is nothing, or a vacuum, and that a poet is born and not made, is a passage from the author's introduction to the 1938 edition of the poems, entitled 'To the Reader':

> A poem is an uncovering of truth so fundamental and general a kind that no other name besides poetry is adequate except truth.[14]

The word 'uncovering', a quieter word than 'revelation', but close in meaning, is used on several subsequent occasions in the introduction.

The third explanation for the title, and the most pertinent, concerns the poet-rôle. The arrangement of the poem into paragraphs makes an interesting comparison with the style of *The Telling*, which Laura (Riding) Jackson described as 'breaking the spell of poetry'.[15] Of that she wrote:

> Readers may have wondered over the style in which *The Telling* is written: how to characterize it? Some may tend to think it 'poetic'. As it is veritably so, it has slipped from my hold. But 'poetic' is a greedy classification — it will take whatever is put into it. I myself think the linguistic character of *The Telling* more accurately describable in terms of *diction* than of those of style. Diction I consider to be the actual substance of style; and style, to be a vague, figurative identification of — a literary name for – diction. I view myself as having spoken to the page, in *The Telling*, not engaged in a kind of writing.[16]

The use of the word 'diction' in preference to 'style' is highly significant and beautifully apt. 'Diction' includes in its meaning not just the choice of words in speech or writing but also the manner of enunciation in speaking, which she regards herself as doing here. Mark Jacobs recalls a later conversation in which she suggested to him that 'Poet: A Lying Word' offered clues as to the meaning of *The Telling*.[17] Although the paragraphs of the poem as published are not numbered, as are the 'passages' of *The Telling*, and they are mostly shorter, one can appreciate that its form is a step in the direction of that of the later work, moving yet further away from the traditional accoutrements of verse. There are also similarities in terms of the content. The poem progresses from a self-description as 'a written edge of time' (paragraph 7) to the repeated 'I say, I say' (paragraphs 8, 9, 12, 13, 16, 20), very much a 'speaking to the page' by the final paragraph. There are other parallels between the two works. There is the conversational approach, the companionship of travellers together, suggested in the poem by the opening lines – 'You have now come with me, I have now come with you' – and in *The Telling* such passages as: 'You will perhaps be wondering, who have come with me thus far, if I expect you to anticipate a change in the world and in yourselves of a universal magnitude?'[18]

In spite of her 'renunciation' of the poet-role Laura (Riding) Jackson returns to the subject again and again. Later in *The Telling*, in the 'Preface for a Second Reading' she wrote at some length on the subject, from which the following are extracts:

> Late in my own poetic professionalism I renounced the satisfaction of poetic success in words. *The Telling* is descended from that renunciation. [. . .] Poems can seem to the silent laity to fill the void of their non-speaking, to be their speaking on the Subject. [...] When I abandoned the poet-position, I took up place in the lay position. Authority, then, required transposition from the poetic to the lay region: it had to be looked for wherever personhood, from which comes the ability to say 'I', is.[19]

The first sentence makes it clear that the process of renunciation had begun during and not after her poetic practice. That helps make sense of what otherwise reads rather strangely in the preface to her *Selected Poems*:

> And just what is the sequel to my poems? [...] With my poems and the commentary I point to the predicament in which poetry locks tongue, ear, the organs of feeling and intelligence, and even the sum of being, the soul; *my poems are good illustrations of poetry, and as such may be considered to be also part of the sequel*.[20] [Italics added]

For all the parallels the style (or diction) of 'Poet: A Lying Word' is clearly different from that of *The Telling*. The characteristic (in her poetry) use of repetition, of parallelism, of riddling, paradoxical and apparently contradictory statements remains. She would not, in her post-poetic work, in the lay position, speak thus, and nor would she deploy such poetic figures of speech as 'the seasons', or 'a wall', without apology or further explanation. There is, to my mind, loss as well as gain in the transition to the 'post-poetic' prose, even the wonderfully lucid and intricate prose of *The Telling*. In this poem, for example, amidst the cumulative and progressive power of statement, there are periodically startling and vivid irruptions as in the following:

> It is a written edge of time. Step not across, for then into my mouth, my eyes, you fall. [...] and be yourselves no more [Paragraph 7]
>
> My eyes, my mouth, my hovering hands, my intransmutable head [...] [Paragraph 13]
>
> Does it seem I ring, I sing, I rhyme, I poet-wit? Shame on me then! Grin me your foulest grin of poet-piety, your eyes rolled up in white hypocrisy [...] [Paragraph 15]
>
> [...] where when and when the classic lie dissolves and nakedly time salted is with truth's sweet flood nor yet to mix with, but be salted tidal-sweet—O sacramental ultimate by which shall time be old-renewed nor yet another season move. [Paragraph 20]

These passages have an immediacy unmatched in the later prose; passages like them are studded throughout the later poems. They shake us up.

3

> [1] You have now come with me, I have now come with you, to the season that should be winter, and is not: we have not come back.
>
> [2] We have not come back: we have not come round: we have not moved. I have taken you, you have taken me, to the next and next span, and the last—and it is the last. Stand against me then and stare well through me then. It is a wall not to be scaled and left behind like the old seasons, like the poets who were the seasons.

The opening statements imply a journey, a pilgrimage, or more precisely, a *quest*. The reader[21] is depicted as having accompanied the poet thus far. Taken literally, whence have they travelled? In one sense this refers to the whole experience of her writing and our reading of the poems. It may also, and helpfully, be taken as referring more literally and specifically to the place where the previous poem left us. As noted above, in both *Poet: A Lying Word* and in *Collected Poems*, the preceding poem is 'Signs of Knowledge'. That poem deploys the figure of the *grail*, a word derived from the medieval legend, in which the Holy Grail denotes the vessel used by Joseph of Arimathea to receive blood from Christ's wounds at the Cross. Figuratively the grail is the elusive object of a long and difficult quest. The poem describes how 'the world' could never fill the grail; it may be filled – characteristic paradox here – only by being emptied of the world:

> By words the world has end,
> By words which brought
> From first articulation, wordless stir,
> To the last throbbing phrases. [...]
>
> By one sign shall you first know All,
> See more than world of much contains:
> The sign of emptiness,
> An empty grail, an empty world
> Of world drained to be world-full. [...]
>
> By two signs shall you know you see. [...]
>
> The first sign of the two signs
> Shall be unlove of the sun.
> The second sign of the two signs
> Shall be unlife of the earth.
> And the first with the second sign locked
> Shall be undeath of the moon. [...]
> When the first and the second sign are one sign
> Shall you see the grail, know the moon-sense,
> Shall there be whole-world pouring brimful
> Into an empty grail, an empty world,
> An empty whole, a whole emptiness.[22]

To return to the opening lines of 'Poet: A Lying Word': the language suggestive of a quest in the preceding poem ('Signs Of Knowledge') [23] brings to mind the great, optimistic, medieval epic, *The Divine Comedy*. There, after the rigours of Hell and Purgatory, are depicted the persons of Beatrice and Dante, the idealised woman the guide, the other, the poet viewing and 'speaking as he sees' the revelation of Paradise.

Here, by contrast, Laura Riding is the poet who asks the reader, after the successful filling of the grail of the previous poem, to interpret for themselves, to 'stare me well through, speak as you see' (paragraphs 5, 7). This invokes an evangelical tradition of individual responsibility that in poetry is represented by William Blake. Christopher Rowland, a Professor of Theology at Oxford University, noted that Blake's famous poem 'And did those feet in ancient time' is followed in the preface by a quotation from Numbers 11, xxix: 'Would to God that all the Lord's people were prophets, and that the Lord would put his spirit upon them', and argues that this includes everyone in the task of speaking out about what they saw:

> Prophecy for Blake, however, was not a prediction of the end of the world, but telling the truth as best a person can about what he or she sees, fortified by insight and an "honest persuasion" that with personal struggle, things could be improved. A human being observes, is indignant and speaks out: it's a basic political maxim which is necessary for any age. [24]

The first paragraph of our poem begins by announcing the end of the association of 'you' and 'me' with the round of the seasons. 'We' are no longer moving with the outer 'natural' world, unlike the poets who were (moved by, identified with) the seasons, the apparently fixed round of the seasons. The 'unlove of the sun' and the 'unlife of the earth' of the preceding poem, 'The Signs of Knowledge', have taken poet and reader to this point. The detachment from, the lack of precedence given to, the natural world was explicit in Laura Riding's first poetic credo, 'A Prophecy or a Plea', in which she praises Frances Thompson's stance in his lines:

> Lo, here stand I and Nature, gaze to gaze,
> And I the greater![25]

The second paragraph reinforces the finality of that move into a fifth unchanging 'season', reminding us of an earlier poem:

> I have come with Amalthea in my veins
> Into a fifth season.
> Time is more than slow.
> For winter is over, yet I see no summer.
> Now it is always snow.[26]

What does the poet mean by her reference to 'the poets that were the seasons'? Our first thought would be that she refers to poets who, unlike Francis Thompson, depend upon nature for their subject matter, or identify with or celebrate it in their work – poets like Wordsworth and Keats, James Thomson and Clare with his Shepherd's Calendar. They treat the round of the seasons as a fundamental 'given', their return to be relied upon, as in *Ode to the West Wind* by Riding's early favourite, Shelley, in the concluding lines of which the poet identifies himself with the force that drives the seasons' changes:

> Be through my lips to unawakened earth
> The trumpet of a prophecy! O, Wind,
> If Winter comes, can Spring be far behind?

More relevant still is the link with that most precocious prodigy of modern poetry, Rimbaud, one altogether less dependent on the seasons, whose final, desperate, work *Une Saison en enfer*, was also (mainly) in prose-poem form. In *A Survey of Modernist Poetry* Rimbaud is described approvingly as a 'natural poet' endowed with a 'natural poetic mind'. He is numbered in Laura Riding's *Contemporaries and Snobs* with the romantic absolutists (quite a good thing) but one who 'made intellectual monstrosity the first condition of poetic finality – an *"immense et raisonné dérèglement de tous les sens"* (an evil thing). [27]

She also, much later, took the trouble to make a firm distinction between Rimbaud's quitting of poetry and her own, in her preface to her *Selected Poems*:

> In the poetic adventure, I had a structure of hope for shelter, whatever happened; and my inspiration came from everywhere. He was inspired by desperation; he flung it out, it narrowed fast back upon him, and would have destroyed him eventually had he not run away from it. For me the essence of the adventure was in the words; he used them as the stuff from which to distil an elixir giving power to make happiness out of unhappiness.[28]

Her interest in Rimbaud had extended to helping Norman Cameron with his celebrated translations.[29] Initially the connection with Rimbaud's *Une Saison en enfer* seems thin – just the word 'season'. However, the final poem of that book, 'Adieu' ('Farewell' in Cameron's translation) contains several striking connections – and contrasts – with 'Poet: A Lying Word':

> Autumn already. But why long for an everlasting sunshine, if we are engaged in the discovery of a divine light – far from the people who die according to the seasons? […]
>
> And I dread winter because it is the season of comfort. […]
>
> I have created all festivals, all triumphs and all dramas. I have tried to invent new flowers, new stars, new kinds of flesh, new languages. I thought I had acquired supernatural powers.
>
> Ah well, I must bury my imagination and my memories. A fine fame as artist and narrator all swept away!
>
> I – I who called myself magus or angel, exempt from all morality, am now given back to the soil, with a duty to pursue and a wrinkled reality to embrace – peasant!

Am I mistaken? Would charity be for me the sister of death?

Well, now, shall I ask forgiveness for having fed on lies? And let me be off. But not one friendly hand? And where shall I find succour?

[...] One must be absolutely up to date ['moderne', in the original].

No hymns – hold the yard one has gained. [...] Spiritual combat is as brutal as battle between men. But the vision of justice is the pleasure of God alone. [...]

Did I speak of a friendly hand? One great advantage is that I can laugh at the old lying loves, and put to shame those lying couples – I have seen the women's hell down below. And I shall be permitted *to possess truth in a soul and a body*. [30]

Some of the differences between the poets are alluded to in the passage from the preface to *Selected Poems* quoted above (and there is more in the brief passages cited from *Contemporaries and Snobs*). However, these passages from Rimbaud's final poem remind us of qualities and aspirations that the two poets had in common. Both were youthful prodigies; both combined phenomenal courage with exceptional talent; both could be outrageous and rejected social norms in favour of poetic reality; both had aspirations to immortality; and both renounced poetry at the peak of their poetic achievements. Rimbaud's 'I thought I had acquired supernatural powers' is echoed (albeit that the meanings are different) by Riding's quotation from Francis Thompson in 'A Prophecy or a Plea'. His sentence 'I had tried to invent new flowers, new stars, new kinds of flesh, new languages' resembles, but is superseded by, her description of the new poet, the new sort of romantic poet:

He is the maker of beauty, since all form originates in him, and of meaning, since he names the content. Life is create with him. [...]

> Confronted by a terrifying, absorbing, fascinating universe, it does not cry out: 'How big, how terrifying, how fascinating!' and permit itself to be overcome by it, but answers it, since this universe, a thing apart, can be answered in no other way, atom for atom in a recreated universe of its own, a universe defiantly intelligible.[31]

Rimbaud's references to the seasons, to having 'fed on lies', the questioning of the self-adopted role of magus or angel, the lack of a friendly hand, the idea of possession of truth in a soul and a body – all have echoes in 'Poet: A Lying Word', albeit that the conclusions reached, and the directions taken by each poet are so different. In part Riding's poem can be read as a riposte to Rimbaud's, and the prose-poem form gives a signal that this is the case. Unlike Rimbaud she never gave up on the idea of companionship in her (our) enterprise, as the poem and *The Telling* demonstrate, but the thrice repeated (and concluding) phrase from another poem from *Poet: A Lying Word*, 'The Unthronged Oracle', 'Is this to be alone?' makes it clear how lonely that enterprise could be.

Connections and contrasts with Rimbaud's 'Adieu' extend to the poem which precedes 'Poet: A Lying Word', 'Signs of Knowledge', which begins with a passage in which, in characteristic fashion, Riding simultaneously evokes and negates an apocalyptic vision of world's end:

Not by water, fire or flesh
Does the world have that end
Which have it must in being, having been,
A world so privileged to begin
And long increase of self to spin,
And long outspinning, spinning out
To end of thread to have—

Not by water, fire or flesh,
Not by drinking back of self,

> Not by flaming up of self,
> Not by lavish plague to lie down
> Sainted, rotted, rendered.
> By words the world has end
> By words which brought
> From first articulation, wordless stir,
> To the last throbbing phrases.

The graphic phrase 'Sainted, rotted, rendered' replaced the equally startling if less pithy 'Sainted, innocented, cruelly gloried' in the 1933 version. That version seems to respond to 'A fine fame ['gloire', in the Rimbaud's original] as artist and narrator all swept away!' The whole passage could be a response to, and negation of, the grim second paragraph of Rimbaud's poem, which itself resembles a medieval Last Judgement. Part of it reads:

> Ah, the rotted rags, the rain-soaked bread, the drunkenness, the thousand loves that have crucified me! She will never have done, then, this ghoul [poverty], who is queen over millions of souls and bodies that are dead *and will be judged*. I see myself again with skin gnawed by mud and pestilence, with hair and armpits full of worms, and with still bigger worms in my heart, stretched out amongst strangers without age or feeling... I might have died there... Frightful image! I detest poverty.[32]

To which Riding's answer in 1933 was: by words the world has end, not by mud and pestilence; the empty grail is filled with words; and she, not Rimbaud's female personification of poverty, will be the judge.

4

The second paragraph also introduces a new idea of herself (person, poet and/or poem) as a wall (or not a wall), an idea to which the poem returns again and again in the remaining paragraphs:

[2] […] It is a wall not to be scaled and left behind like the old seasons, like the poets who were the seasons.

[3] Stand against me then and stare well through me then. I am no poet as you have span by span leapt the high words to the next depth and season ['always' *after* 'season' *not in 1933 version*], the next season always, the last always, and the next ['always' *after* 'next' *in 1933 version, omitted 1938*]. I am a true wall: you may but stare me through.

[4] It is a false wall, a poet: it is a lying word. It is a wall that closes ['halts' *1933*] and does not.

[5] This is no wall that closes ['halts' *1933*] and does not ['halt' *in 1933 version, omitted 1938*]. It is a wall to see into, it is no other season's height. Beyond it lies no depth and height of ['human' *in 1933, omitted 1938*] travel, no partial courses. Stand against me then and stare well through me then. Like wall of poet here I rise, but ['I' *in 1933, omitted 1938*] am no poet as walls have risen between next and next and made false end to leap. A last true wall am I: you may but stare me through.

[6] And the tale is no more of the going: no more a poet's tale of going false-like to a seeing. The tale is of a seeing true-like to a knowing: there's but to stare the wall through now, well through.

In normal figurative use a wall is a barrier, impediment or obstacle to communication, interaction, etc. To 'bang your head against a (brick) wall' is to have one's efforts repeatedly rebuffed, whereas to 'see through a (brick) wall' requires unusual intelligence or perceptiveness – which may well be the case here! It brings us back to the quotation from Vasari: 'murato' can mean 'walled' as well as 'builded' as we have translated it earlier.

'Scaling' a wall implies a ladder (as opposed to simply 'climbing'), with just a suggestion of Jacob's ladder from earth to heaven, but of course it is negated: 'not to be scaled'. The word 'height' is used repeatedly in negated phrases: 'no poet as you have span by span leapt the high words to the next depth and season', 'no depth and height of travel', and 'no other season's height'.

In section 2 of this essay, contrasting the style of the poem with that of *The Telling*, we pointed out the characteristic use (particularly marked in her later, longer poems) of repetition, of parallelism, of riddling, paradoxical and apparently contradictory statements. The progression in the successive statements of these paragraphs is a good example:

i   'I am a true wall' (last sentence of 3);
ii 'It is a false wall, a poet: it is a lying word. It is a wall that closes and does not.' (paragraph 4);
iii 'This is no wall that closes and does not.' (first sentence of 5); and then back again to i)
iv 'A last true wall am I' (last sentence of 5).

What are we to make of this sequence?[33] Initially the struggling here reminds one of the conflict or distinction between poems and the poet's life, as expressed in the preface to *Poems: A Joking Word*:

> My poems then are instead of my life. I don't mean that in my poems I escape from my life. My life by itself would be nothing but escaping, or anybody's. I mean that in my poems I escape from escaping. And my life reads all wrong to me and my poems read all right.[34]

The attempt in the later poems is for the poet to escape from escaping finally and *continually*, for there to be nothing but poems: 'Poems of Final Occasion' and 'Poems Continual'. However, what is happening in 'Poet: A Lying Word' is a further shift, going beyond 'escaping from escaping' in poems, and preparing to abandon the poet-position, as described in *The Telling*, in the 'Preface for a Second Reading' quoted in section 2 of this essay:

> Late in my own poetic professionalism I renounced the satisfaction of poetic success in words. *The Telling* is descended from that renunciation. [...] Poems can seem to the silent laity to fill the void of their non-speaking on the Subject. [...] When I abandoned the poet-position, I took up place in the lay position. Authority, then, required transposition from the poetic to the lay region: it had to be looked for wherever personhood, from which comes the ability to say 'I', is.[35]

This enables us to make sense of the apparent contradictions in statements i) to iv) above. The 'I' of statements i) and iv) above, and the 'this' of iii) could be taken as referring to the *personhood* of Laura Riding. Statement ii) on the other hand would refer to the *poet-rôle*.

4

> [7] It is not a wall, it is not a poet. It is not a lying wall, it is not a lying word. It is a written edge of time. [':' *1933*] Step not across, for then into my mouth, my eyes you fall. Come close, stare me well through, speak as you see. But oh, infatuated drove of lives, step not across now. Into my mouth, my eyes shall you thus fall, and be yourselves no more.
>
> [8] Into my mouth, my eyes, I say, I say. I am no poet like transitory wall to lead you on into such slow terrain of time as measured out your single span to broken turns of season once and once [*no second* 'once' *in 1933*] again. I lead you not. You have now come with me, I have now come with you, to your last turn and season [', which stand you still against me' *in 1933, not 1938*]: thus could I come with you, thus only.

With paragraph 7 we reach the first culmination in the poem, the first unequivocal statement, with the revelation that 'It is not a wall, it is not a poet. It is not a lying wall, it is not a lying word. *It is a written edge of time*' (italics added). It is living, concentrated poetic reality; it is a nothing, a vacuum, a singularity.

We are then immediately told 'Step not across', but rather to 'Come close, stare me well through, speak as you see'. The next statement could be considered absurd given the lack of interest in or understanding of her poetry shown by most readers, including her closest companions, at the time: 'But oh, infatuated drove of lives, step not across now. Into my mouth, my eyes shall you thus fall, and be yourselves no more'. Where was this 'infatuated drove of lives', presumably lovers of poetry, coming from?

We are reminded of her earlier statement in *Anarchism Is Not Enough,* quoted above in section 2, about the nature of a poem:

> It cannot be looked at, heard, touched or read because it is a vacuum. […] If it were possible to reproduce it in an audience the result would be destruction of the audience.[36]

It may seem far-fetched but for this reader the phrase 'infatuated drove' conjures up a Christian story and a Homeric one. The bible story is that of the Gadarene swine, in which the local people, having invoked Christ's spiritual powers to cure two insane men, came to regret it after the destruction of a large herd of swine resulting from the transfer of the evil spirits in the madmen into the pigs. The Homeric tale is that of Circe, the witch, who transforms Odysseus' men into swine by drugging their wine with a magic potion.

What is the power that shall transform the infatuated drove so that we shall be ourselves no more? There is a suggestion that we are in the presence of (as she put it in the earlier poem, 'Rejoice Liars') 'the witch of truth', but a witch concerned lest her formidable power leads to destruction.[37] The readers here are then addressed directly for our own good, and to warn us of the precipice rather than to precipitate us over it. Thus far and no further; remain yourselves: 'I lead you not'. It is this renunciation, the renunciation of the magical powers implicit in the poet-role to which she referred later in her preface to her *Selected Poems*, in what would otherwise seem a strange

221

thing to say: 'I have written that which I believe *breaks the spell* of poetry' (italics added).[38]

In this context I am reminded of Robert Nye's penetrating comment on the impact of Laura Riding's poems upon him:

> For whatever reason, or for reasons beyond reason, as the words and their rhythms worked upon and then within me, I found in due course that here were not so much spells as acts of verbal *disenchantment*, inspired unravellings of the world's riddle [....] Here is work that reads the person reading it.[39]

These reflections help to explain an apparent paradox in the friendships and partnerships of Laura Riding. She drew people into her orbit, and expected reciprocal personal loyalty and adherence to principles; where these were perceived to have been breached, dissociation and sometimes denunciation ensued. But however closely she drew people to her, it was never to clone or imitate her own literary qualities (unlike the imitations of 'The Waste Land' that Eliot actually endorsed). There are no pale imitations of Laura Riding's work by her chosen associates such as Graves, Reeves and Cameron; in fact it is striking how distinct in both style and content their works are; if one did not know it, one would not assume a connection. Those like Auden and Ashbery, who chose to imitate or claimed to be influenced by her, without consulting her, are another matter.

A conversation recorded by Mark Jacobs, in his memoir, is also relevant here. Mrs Jackson was commenting on the well-known poem by Robert Frost:

> 'And that's exactly where he and poems are wrong,' she said. 'Fences do make good neighbours. They keep us apart to live neighbourly and not mix each other up in our lives too much so that we don't know where we stand. They keep us civilized.'

She was and is – with all her radicalism, her assertion of individual poetic reality against social reality – a profoundly conservative poet of *order*, of civilization *going beyond* anarchy.[40]

5

[9] I say, I say, I am, it is, such wall, such poet, such not lying, such not leading into. Await [*replaces* 'Wait on'] the sight, and [*no* 'and' *in 1933*] look well through, know by such standing still that next comes none of you.

[10] Comes what? Comes this even I, even this not-I, this not lying season when death holds the year at steady count—this every-year.

[11] Would you not see, not know, not mark the count? What would you then? Why have you come here then? To leap a wall that is no wall, and a true wall? To step across into my eyes and mouth not yours? To cry me down like wall or poet as often your way led past down- falling height ['heights'] that seemed?

[12] I say, I say, I am, it is: [*replaces* ','] such wall, such end of graded travel. And if you will not hark, come tumbling then upon me, into my eyes, my mouth, and be the backward utterance of yourselves expiring angrily through instant seasons that played you time-false.

Paragraph 9 recaps (in the circling or spiralling fashion noted below in note 34) the previous three paragraphs and concludes with a new statement: '[…] know by such standing still that next comes none of you.' By standing still, as instructed, staring 'me' well through, and speaking as you see: *next* comes *none of you* but 'even this I, even this not-I', only the person and/or the poet, the not-lying season. Then follows a new note: 'when death holds the year at steady count—this every-year.' We are back in the place where time and space have become concentrated in the moment-to-moment person of the poet, in the written edge of time, as in earlier poems 'Smile, death, O simultaneous mouth' ('One Self') or 'the compact present' ('Earth'). We are back to passages from *Anarchism Is Not Enough*, the first from 'The Myth':

> Poetry (praise be to babyhood) is essentially not of the Myth. It is all the truth it knows, that is, it knows nothing. It is the art of not living [...] In the art of not living one is not ephemerally permanent but permanently ephemeral.[41]

And the second passage is from the central essay 'Jocasta':

> The poem dances the dance of reality, but with such perfect artificiality that the dance, from very perfection, cancels itself and leaves, as far as reality is concerned, Nothing. But as far as the poem is concerned, Nothing is a dancer walking the ruins; character, by the ascetic nature of its energy, surviving gesture.[42]

The words for distance in the poem are notable for their human scale: 'span' – the distance between the tip of the thumb to extended tip of little finger; 'graded travel' – from the Latin for step; and 'scale' itself, implying hand over hand, foot by foot climbing.

The motives of reader (and poet) are under scrutiny in this poem, from paragraph 2 onwards. There 'me' becomes 'it' in: 'It is a wall not to be scaled and left behind like the old seasons, like the poets who were the seasons.' We read, it is implied, in order to scale 'a wall', to conquer the height, and then to move beyond both 'it' and the poet. Riding will have none of it! We, the readers, should only come close and stare well through, speaking as we see.

In paragraph 11 she issues the challenge: 'What would you then? Why have you come here then? To leap a wall that is no wall, and a true wall? To step across into my eyes and mouth not yours? To cry me down like wall or poet as often your way led past down-falling height that seemed?' Stylistically this pugnacious squaring up to the reader is reminiscent of Baudelaire's line from *Au Lecteur*, adapted by Eliot at the end of Part I of *The Waste Land*: 'Hypocrite lecteur, – mon semblable, – mon frère.'

6

[13] My eyes, my mouth, my hovering hands, my intransmutable head: wherein my eyes, my mouth, my hands, my head, my body-self, are not such mortal simulacrum as everlong you builded against very-death, to keep you everlong in boasted death-course, neverlong? I say, I say, I am not builded of you so.

[14] This body-self, this wall, this poet-like ['poet-wise' 1933] address, is that last barrier long shied of in your elliptic changes: out of your leaping, shying, season-quibbling, have I made it, is it made. And if now poet-like ['poet-wise'] it rings with one-more-time as if, this is the mounted stupor of your everlong outbiding worn prompt and lyric, ['worn' *removed in 1938*] poet-like—the forbidden one-more-time worn time-like.

Here we have another irruption into our reading mind: a vivid self-portrait of the poet – at work with her hands hovering over the typewriter perhaps. Is it perverse to be reminded of the beautiful self-portrait of Dylan Thomas at work in his writing-shed?

> And the rhymer in the long tongued room,
> Who tolls his birthday bell,
> Toils towards the ambush of his wounds [. . .]
> He in his slant, racking house
> And the hewn coils of his trade[43]

Her 'hovering hands' she describes elsewhere, in fragment 11 of 'Echoes', as 'mending it', whenever something breaks:

> Then with my hands washed clean
> And fingers piano-playing
> And arms bare to go elbow-in [...]

And this connection helps us, perhaps, to make sense of 'Echo 1':

> Since learning all in such a tremble last night—
> Nor with my eyes adroit in the dark,
> But with my fingers hard with fright,
> Astretch to touch a phantom, closing on myself—
> I have been smiling.

It may seem odd, but in pursuing this imagery, of hands making discoveries, of mending by doing, I seem to find an echo of the thought in a passage from Jacob Bronowski's *The Ascent of Man*, although Mrs Jackson might have disparaged the title:

> We have to understand that the world can only be grasped by action, not by contemplation. The hand is more important than the eye. […]
>
> I have described the hand when it uses a tool as an instrument of discovery.[44]

The next key phrase in this passage is 'my intransmutable head'. 'Intransmutable' is an uncommon word meaning unchangeable, but with specific reference: it was used in chemistry or alchemy and applied, for example, to metals such as gold or quicksilver, or to principles governing the universe. In *Collected Poems* we first come upon a form of the word in that key early poem, 'Incarnations', in the extraordinary image of a 'statue's too transmuted stone' suggesting, after a detailed analysis of the context, transmutation into immortality of the poet in the poem.

The third key phrase, 'not such simulacrum', reinforces the impression that we are in the presence of – permanently ephemeral – immortality. The original meaning of 'simulacrum' is of a material image or representation of a person or god, then a thing with the appearance but not the substance or proper qualities of something. Hence the passage means that Laura Riding is the 'real thing', the appearance does not belie the substance.

So she is 'not such mortal simulacrum as everlong you builded against very-death, to keep you everlong in boasted death-course, neverlong?' She is unlike the reader, she strongly implies, although the (unexpected) question-mark at the end of the sentence allows readers the chance to answer 'No, I'm like you!' – if they only dare.

The idea of *building* the mortal simulacrum clearly refers to the idea of 'wall' that has been reiterated throughout the poem up to this point. It enables us to connect back to the quotation from 'A Prophecy or a Plea' given in section 2 of this essay, and to the idea that if modern poets are to succeed their constitution must contain the magic at the start (*non murato, ma veramente nato*). As noted there the quotation in Italian, roughly translated, means 'not builded [or walled], but really born'. I take this to mean that there is no chance of *constructing* a self that will survive death, immortality can only be achieved by unforgetting our creation, as in 'Incarnations', and as subsequently in *The Telling*:

> Yes, I think we remember our creation! — have the memory of it in us, to know. Through the memory of it we apprehend that there was a Before-time of being from which being passes into what would be us.[46]

Paragraph 14 conjures up images of the reader(s) continually circling, leaping, shying away from the poet or the person Laura Riding in whom time has come to a halt and space has compacted. This is conveyed in the word 'elliptic', beautifully deployed, as noted in the introduction, in a manner reminiscent of Milton. The word *derives from* the Greek for falling short, deficient (as in the grammatical term 'ellipsis' to indicate something missing), but is mainly *used* in English to describe the oval orbit of the planets around a centre of gravity – like readers orbiting herself. [47] The word carries both senses here; readers for ever orbiting the poet and falling short, or missing the full point.

7

[14][…] And if now poet-like it rings with one-more-time as if, this is the mounted stupor of your everlong outbiding worn prompt and lyric, poet-like – the forbidden one-more-time worn time-like.

[15] Does it seem I ring, I sing, I rhyme, I poet-wit? Shame on me then! Grin me your foulest humour then of poet-piety, your eyes rolled up in white hypocrisy—should I be [phrase *replaces* 'for I may be' *in 1933*] one sprite more of your versed fame ['legend' *in 1933*]—or turned from ['against' *in 1933*] me into your historied brain, where the lines read more actual ['shrewdly' *in 1933*]. Shame on me then!

[16] And haste unto us both, [replaces ':'] my shame is yours. How long I seem to beckon ['invitation' *deleted from 1933*] like a wall beyond which stretches longer ['further' *in* 1933] length of fleshsome traverse: it is your lie of flesh ['lie of flesh' *replaces 1933* 'fleshsome shame'] and my flesh-seeming stand of words. Haste then [*replaces* 'therefore' in *1933*] unto us both. I say, I say. This wall reads 'Stop!' This poet verses 'Poet: a lying word!'

The first phrase of the last sentence of paragraph 14 now perhaps justifies, in its imagery of a body ringing like a bell, our reference to the Dylan Thomas poem at the beginning of the previous section: 'And if now poet-like it [this body-self, this wall] rings with one-more-time as if'. For the author ringing, singing, rhyming are all suspect; all are returns to the 'poet-like' and not to truth. This makes a further link between the poem and *The Telling*. 'Truth rings no bells' she writes in passage 11 of that work, and then explains, in a substantial note:

> That which 'rings a bell', as the saying goes, excites, according to the implication of the saying, admiring wonder, brings one fast to wrapt [*sic*, presumably 'rapt' is meant] attention. But, while the tendency is to treat the proverbial bell-ringing thing or being as

something exceptional, one knows nothing except that one has been forced to give ear — or eyes or mind – to an insistence. An advent of truth will not provoke wonder, admiration, forcefully seize attention. Truth's nature is to fill a place that belongs to it when the place becomes cleared of a usurping occupant. It slips into place, then, with a quiet of natural fitness, perfectly not-astounding in the rightness of its being there.[48]

This is not a 'post-poetic' idea only. We have seen in section 3 of this essay, in the passage from 'Signs of Knowledge', the way in which a 'place is cleared' by the poem of a 'usurping occupant' in order for truth to slip into place:

When the first and the second sign are one sign
Shall you see the grail, know the moon-sense,
Shall there be whole-world pouring brimful
Into an empty grail, an empty world,
An empty whole, a whole emptiness.[49]

To return to paragraph 14, there is another telling phrase: 'mounted stupor'. 'Mounted' reminds us of a 'wall not to be scaled and left behind' (paragraph 2); 'no poet as you have span by span leapt the high words to the next depth and season' (paragraph 3); 'no depth and height of further travel' (paragraph 5). 'Stupor', as well as its common meaning of stunned bewilderment, implies failure of sensibility or consciousness. Here 'mounted stupor' conjures up the elevated language of lyric poetry, its failed attempts on truth, as in Yeats' memorable image of the poet 'dressed to impress' on stilts, as Malachi Stilt-Jack, in his poem 'High Talk'.[50]

In paragraphs 15 and 16 the assault upon herself as poet, and on her readers (and fellow poets) reaches its zenith. The first two sentences, after our reading of the preceding parts of the poem, seem simple enough: shame on me if I seem to deploy the traditional methods of poetry. There follows another irruption into the reading mind:

> Grin me your foulest humour then of poet-piety, your eyes rolled
> up in white hypocrisy — should I be one sprite more of your
> versed fame — or turned from me into your historied brain, where
> the lines read more actual.

How are we to understand the violence of this language, this unequivocal and colourful rejection of the traditional accoutrements of poetry? Again we are reminded of Rimbaud's 'Adieu', 'Farewell' in Cameron's translation:

> Ah well! I must bury my imagination and my memories. A fine
> fame as artist and narrator all swept away!

In Riding's case she also rejects the idea of becoming either 'one sprite more' of the reader's 'versed fame' (where that phrase plays on the various meanings of 'versed' – expert, knowledgeable, practised versifier – to place her in a poetic hall of fame, as in the Oxford Book of English Verse) or 'turned from herself' into the reader's 'historied brain, where the lines read more actual' – in other words, to lose her poetic reality and to become part of time, of social reality and to be converted into literary history to be 'more actual', more 'contemporary', part of the *Zeitgeist* so eloquently rejected in her first book of criticism, *Contemporaries and Snobs*.[51]

> In the next paragraph the poet introduces another simile:

> How long I seem to beckon like a wall beyond which stretches
> longer length of fleshsome traverse: it is your lie of flesh and my
> flesh-seeming stand of words.[52]

The biblical connotations are most relevant here: 'the days of his flesh' referring to Christ's incarnation, the period of his earthly life; all human and animal life is transitory: For 'All flesh is as grass, and all the glory of man as the flower of grass. The grass withereth, and the flower thereof falleth away: but the word of the Lord endureth for ever.'[53]

We are reminded again of the faith of the poet – far 'outbiding' her poetic career – in words. And we are reminded again of her belief in her own permanence, as stated in paragraph 8: 'I am no poet like transitory wall' albeit that she is 'permanently ephemeral' in the 'art of not living'. [54]

8

[17] Shall the wall then not crumble, as to walls is given? Have I not said: 'Stare me well through'? It is indeed a wall, crumble it shall. It is a wall of walls, ['it is a page of very-death, the first.' *Deleted from 1933 version*] stare it well through: ['it is the next and next,' *deleted from 1933 version*] the reading gentles near, the name of death passes with the season that it was not.

[18] Death is a very wall. ['.' *replaces* ':' *in 1933* version] The going over walls, against walls, is a dying and a learning. Known death is truth sighted at the halt. The name of death passes. The mouth that moves with death forgets the word ['forgets the word' *replaces* 'stands still the spoken side of truth: it reads and says'].

[19] And the first page is the last ['last' *replaces* 'unlettering'] of death. And haste unto us both, lest the wall seem to crumble not, to lead mock-onward. And the first page reads: 'Haste unto us both!' And the first page reads: 'Slowly, it is the first page only.'

* * *

We are now, yet again, in the realm of 'death', familiar from so many of this poet's poems, and yet so difficult to incorporate into our understanding. The 'death' she speaks of is not the death of the mortuary slab, but it results from the emptying of the consciousness in order to fill it. Nor is it the 'second death', the loss of spiritual life by which lost souls are punished in traditional religious belief. In fact it is the reverse of that spiritual death. The 'death' of which the poet writes initiates what might be called, loosely, spiritual learning, what she calls in 'Signs of Knowledge' the filling of the (emptied) grail, and refers to elsewhere as 'unforgetting'. It resembles, on a grander scale, the *'petite mort'* of the sexual climax in that it results from an intensification of experience. As she wrote in her preface to *Selected Poems*:

> With my poems I point to the predicament in which poetry locks tongue, ear, the organs of feeling and intelligence, and even the sum of being, the soul [...][55]

9

[19] [...] And the first page reads: 'Haste unto us both!' And the first page reads: 'Slowly, it is the first page only.'
[20] Slowly, it is the page before the first page only, there is no haste. The page before the first page tells of death, haste, slowness: how truth falls ['prophecies fall' *1933*] true now at the turn of page, at time of telling. Truth one by one falls true. And the first page reads, the page which is the page before the first page only: 'This once-upon-a-time when seasons failed, [*no* ',' in *1933*] and time stared through the wall nor made to leap across, is the hour, the [*no* 'the' *in 1933*] season, seasons, year and years, no wall and wall, where when and when the classic lie dissolves and nakedly time salted is with truth's sweet flood nor yet to mix with, but be salted ['ensalted'] tidal-sweet [*omitting* 'true taste, new taste of true' *from 1933*] —O sacramental ultimate ['ultimate' *replaces* 'true-and-false and sweet-and-salt'] by which shall time be old-renewed nor yet another season move.' I say, I say.

The poem ends with a beginning, with 'the page before the first page only'. We can recognise the development of a similar idea, expressed somewhat differently, in *The Telling*:

Yes, I think we remember our creation! — have the memory of it in us, to know. Through the memory of it we apprehend that there was a Before-time of being from which being passed into what would be us. And the Soul was gone, that had been the entire Form of Life, become transmuted into formless Spirit. But, spirit working where matter spread in Soul's place, and farther, into emptiness, dispersed being was contained in a saving possibility of *souls* — souls to fill Soul's absence with a new One-being, risen up out of plurality:... each soul shining the Form of Life on the other. [...] Souls there were not until there were bodies in which, each, diversity's extremes were brought into a union... another and another and another, to that rounding-in and exhaustion of diversity which is human. Thus from physicality emerge persons — ourselves.[56]

The page before the first page reads 'This once-upon-a-time', the traditional beginning of a fairy tale, where the classical rules are suspended. Therewith we have the final startling irruption:

[...] where when and when the classic lie dissolves and nakedly time salted is with truth's sweet flood nor yet to mix with, but be salted tidal-sweet [...]

The imagery here, at the end of this most complex long poem, reminds us of the apparently much simpler, more lyrical, but equally intense poem, 'The Wind Suffers':

The wind suffers of blowing,
The sea suffers of water,
And fire suffers of burning,
And I of a living name.
* * *
How for the wilful blood to run

> More salt-red and sweet-white?
> How for me in my actualness
> To more shriek and more smile?
>
> By no other miracles,
> By the same knowing poison,
> By an improved anguish,
> By my further dying.[57]

Only by going back to before the beginning of life can one experience incarnation. 'Death' and 'dying', for this poet, are, as ever, signals of the greatest intensity of feeling, of consciousness – of being born by returning to before the beginning.

NOTES

[1] The book *Poet: A Lying Word* (London: Arthur Barker, 1933) has never been reprinted, but a few copies are available second-hand. With amendments, usually fairly minor, all but one of the poems were reprinted in *Collected Poems* (London: Cassell, 1938), all but three of those in the section entitled 'Poems of Final Occasion'.

[2] That the poet was entirely comfortable with the production of 'unversed' poetry is clear from the form of the poem written when she was only twenty, a 'pride of the workshop', published in book form as *Voltaire: A Biographical Fantasy* (London: Hogarth, 1927). Prose-poem pieces were also interspersed with verse in the highly experimental *Though Gently* (Majorca: Seizin, 1930), although none of the pieces in prose made it into *Collected Poems*.

[3] Of the other seven long poems selected for her *Selected Poems* two are represented by one complete part of three ('Memories of Mortalities' and 'Three Sermons to the Dead'). There are several segments cut from each of the remaining five.

[4] *Poems: A Joking Word* (London: Cape, 1930). Again, only a few second-hand copies are available. See my essay on 'One Self', available on Nottingham Trent University's Laura (Riding) Jackson website for an account of the book's preface.

[5] 'Benedictory' is placed after 'Three Sermons to the Dead' (the retitled 'Apocryphal Numbers') in *Collected Poems*.

[6] From the preface by Laura (Riding) Jackson *Selected Poems: In Five Sets* (London: Faber, 1970) 13-14.

[7] Laura Riding and Robert Graves, *A Survey of Modernist Poetry* (London: Heinemann, 1927). Quotation is from the Carcanet edition of 2002, 23.

[8] Good examples are 'The Tiger'; 'Come, Words, Away'; and 'The Signs of Knowledge'.

[9] The expression 'poem-person' is borrowed from a passage in *A Survey*, p73. In Laura Riding, *Contemporaries and Snobs* (London: Cape, 1928) 62, we are told: 'The only difference between a poem and a person is that in a poem *being* is the final state, in a person the preliminary state.'

[10] These quotations are from 'What Is A Poem?' in Laura Riding, *Anarchism Is Not Enough* (London: Cape, 1928) 16-17.

[11] 'A Prophecy or a Plea' was first published in *The Reviewer*, no, 5 (1925) 1-7. It is now most readily available as Appendix C in *First Awakenings*, (Carcanet: 1992) 274-280; this passage is from 278.

[12] See, for example *Contemporaries and Snobs*, 124: 'As the poet, if a true poet, is one by nature and not by effort'.

[13] See especially 'The Person I Am', the second essay in the first volume of the collection *The Person I Am* (Nottingham: Trent Editions, 2011) 48-76.

[14] *Collected Poems* (1938) xviii; Centennial edition, *The Poems of Laura Riding*, (New York: Persea, 2001) 484.

[15] *Selected Poems*, 1970, 15.

[16] Laura (Riding) Jackson, *The Telling*, (London: University of London, Athlone Press, 1972) 67-68.

[17] This is verified in a letter from James Mathias to Jacobs in the Nottingham Trent University Archive. Matthias reminded Jacobs of the conversation, at which he had been present, and asked whether Jacobs should undertake a piece of work on the poem to link it to *The Telling*.

[18] *The Telling*, passage 59, 52.

[19] Ibid, 66-67.

[20] *Selected Poems*, 1970, 15-16.

[21] It feels as though one is being addressed individually at the start of the poem, although in paragraph 7 we are most definitely plural – a 'drove of lives'.

[22] 'Signs of Knowledge', *Collected Poems* 229-233. The poem deploys a cosmology of sun, earth and moon first unveiled, in *CP*, in 'Tale of Modernity', and subsequently used in 'Disclaimer of Person'. The language of the poem is strange and unbeautiful; I am not aware of any poem in English that is so thickly studded with neologisms coined by the author (as in the passage quoted: 'unlove', 'unlife', 'undeath'). There are literally scores of examples. In the 1933 version this is even starker; the 1938 version mitigates the practice somewhat by hyphenating many of the compounds.

[23] Not just the language of the grail, but the apocalyptic language at the beginning of the poem:

> Not by water, fire or flesh
> Does the world have that end . . .
> Not by flaming up of self,
> Not by lavish plague to lie down
> Sainted, rotted, rendered...

[24] Christopher Rowland, 'William Blake: a visionary for our time' (openDemocracy.net, 2007). Compare this and to some extent contrast it with Riding's essay 'In Defence of Anger' reproduced in Laura Riding and Robert Graves, *Essays from Epilogue* (Manchester: Carcanet 2001) 88-99, and with her poem, 'The Rugged Black of Anger'.

[25] In *First Awakenings*, 277 (see note 11). The quotation by Riding comes from Thompson's 'Of Nature: Laud and Plaint' and can be found in *Poems of Francis Thompson*, (Boston: Boston College, 2001) 341.

[26] From 'Goat and Amalthea', *CP*, 36.

[27] *A Survey*, 14 in Carcanet 2002 edition; *Contemporaries* 1928, 39, also 43.

[28] 'Preface' to her *Selected Poems*, 15.

[29] Originally published as *A Season in Hell* (London: John Lehmann, 1949) but reissued in *Arthur Rimbaud: A Season in Hell & Other Poems*, translated by Noman Cameron (London: Anvil, 1994), the edition I refer to here. I owe the perception of the connection between *Une Saison en enfer* and 'Poet: A Lying Word', and the information about Riding's involvement with Cameron's translation, to Mark Jacobs. Riding and Cameron began collaborating on a translation sometime in the mid-1930s.

[30] *Rimbaud* (Cameron translation), 1994, 192-195; the italics are in the original.

[31] A Prophecy' in *First Awakenings*, 279.

[32] *Rimbaud* 1994, 193.

[33] In her valuable essay, 'Laura (Riding) Jackson: Against the Commodification of the Poem' (http://coldfrontmag.com/laura-riding-jackson-against-the-commodity-of-the-poem-part-1/), Andrea Rexilius analyses the first part of the poem 'Disclaimer of the Person', in which there is a similar progression from statement to contradiction, from claiming to disclaiming:

> Time and space are collapsed and her saying becomes circular, or spiral, so that each new statement is slightly different than the previous one. At the peak of this spiral we find the lines, "What is one thing?/ It is all things myself/ And each as myself/ And none myself". Now the disclaimer sets in. "Myself is the one thing only [claiming] / I am not I [claiming and disclaiming at once] / I am the one thing only / Which each thing is [disclaiming the person or being]. (AR's square brackets)

[34] *Poems: A Joking Word*, 10.

[35] *The Telling*, 66-67.

[36] *Anarchism Is Not Enough*, 1928, 17.

[37] In 'Rejoice Liars' 'the witch', having initially 'perished' and 'had a mortal laming' ultimately 'Takes on substance, shedding phantomness.' *Collected Poems*, 130.

[38] *Selected Poems*, 15, referring to *The Telling*, of course.

[39] 'Preface' *A Selection of the Poems of Laura Riding* (Manchester: Carcanet, 1994) 5.

[40] This can be seen, for example, in her introduction to 'Homiletic Studies' in *Essays from Epilogue*, 2002, 78- 79), and in her 1980 introduction to *CP*, reprinted in the 2001 edition, where at xxxiv-xxxviii she compares her moral purpose with that of Matthew Arnold, the author of *Culture and Anarchy*. And of course, for her anarchism would never be enough.

[41] *Anarchism Is Not Enough*, 11.

[42] Ibid, 120.

[43] 'Poem on his Birthday'. The evocative word here is 'tongued', which conjures up a complex three-fold image: Thomas sticking out his tongue as he makes the effort to write, 'tasting his words' on his tongue as he works on the poem, and then standing and pacing in the room envisaging himself like the 'tongue' in a bell.

[44] Jacob Bronowski, *The Ascent of Man* (London: Book Club Associates, 1973), 115-116. Bronowski stayed and worked with Laura Riding from 1932, when he was only 24, to 1934. As Elizabeth Friedmann points out in her biography, *A Mannered Grace*, 2005, p230 and the note 58 on p508), Bronowski appears to have put his collaborative work with Riding to good use in his first two books, *The Poet's Defence* (1939) and *William Blake: A Man Without a Mask* (1943). I find possible echoes of Riding's thought in some of Bronowski's thinking in *The Ascent of Man*: the interest in Blake, the development of the brain through the use of the hand, and a unitary approach to emotion and intellect.

[46] *The Telling*, passage 28, page 30.

[47] This recalls a passage from Mark Jacobs' memoir where Jim Mathias, the president of the Guggenheim Foundation laments that he will not be able to keep up with Laura (Riding) Jackson, saying: "The most I'll be is a burnt-out satellite circling the moon."

[48] Ibid, 16 and the note on 149. For a similar idea compare the poem, 'Ding-Donging', which begins: 'With old hours all belfry heads/Are filled, as with thoughts'.

Collected Poems, 96.

[49] *CP*, p231. The way in which 'a place is cleared' can be seen in other poems, such as 'Incarnations', 'The Tiger', 'One Self'.

[50] Yeats had a correspondence with Riding in respect of his edition of *The Oxford Book of English Verse*, on which he himself comments revealingly in his letters to Dorothy Wellesley. 'You are right about Laura Riding. I had rejected her work in a moment of stupidity but when you praised her I reread her in *The Faber Book of Modern Verse* and was delighted in her intricate intensity'. (*Letters On Poetry From W. B. Yeats To Dorothy Wellesley*, 1940, 58) His request for some of her poems to be included in the anthology was rejected, after which he commented facetiously:

> 'I wrote today to Laura Riding, with whom I carry on a slight correspondence, that her school was too thoughtful, reasonable & truthful, that poets were good liars who never forgot that the Muses were women who liked the embrace of gay warty lads. I wonder if she knows that warts are considered by the Irish peasantry a sign of sexual power?' (Ibid, 69)

Quoting this correspondence Mark Jacobs and Alan J Clark comment:

> In other quarters her work was disliked as taking upon itself too much in what it said of the fundamental issues of poetic practice, and in its demanding from poets greater concern with the moral principles implicit in poetry, rather than the poetic-technique principles fostered by literary criticism.
>
> 'The Question Of Bias: Some Treatments of Laura (Riding) Jackson',; *Hiroshima Studies in English Language and Literature*, Vol. 21, Nos. 1 and 2, 1971; http://www.ntu.ac.uk/laura_riding/scholars/58471gp.html

[51] See the first essay in *Contemporaries and Snobs*, 'Poetry and the Literary Universe', 9-96.

[52] As an aside, note the succession of neologisms so typical of her later poetry: 'everlong', 'outbiding', 'historied' and now 'fleshsome'. 'Flesh' appears in similar contexts (in various forms) in 'Incarnations', 'One Self' ('O fleshfold dress': another neologism), 'The Virgin', and by implication and by contrast with 'bone' in 'Back to the Mother Breast'.

[53] 1 Peter 1, xxiv-xxv, quoting from Isaiah, 40, xi-viii.

[54] *Anarchism Is Not Enough*, 11.
[55] *Selected Poems*, 1970, 16.
[56] *The Telling*, passage 28, page 30.
[57] *Collected Poems,* 95.

Chapter 15

'After So Much Loss': how to live with what we know

AFTER SO MUCH LOSS

After so much loss—
Seeming of gain,
Seeming of loss—
Subsides the swell of indignation
To the usual rhythm of the year.

The coward primroses are up,
We contract their diffuse mildness.
Women with yet a few springs to live
Clutch them in suppliant bouquets
On the way to relatives, 10
Who, no, do not begrudge
This postponement of funerals.
And, oh, how never tired, and tired,
The world of primroses, how spring
The bended spirit fascinates

With promise of revival,
Leaving more honest summer to proclaim
That this is all—a brighter disappointment
Time has to give to an implacable—
Persuasion of things lost, wrongly.   20

Is it to wonder, then,
That we defy the unsuspecting moment,
Release our legs from the year's music,
And, to the reckless strum of hate,
Dance—grinding from primroses the tears
They never of themselves would have shed?
None dances whom no hate stirs,
Who has not lost and loathed the loss,
Who does not feel deprived.
Slyest rebellion of the feet,   30
The chaste and tremulous disport
Of children, limbs in passionless wave—
None dances whom no hate stirs,
Or shall not stir.

As sure as primrose spring betides,
After so much loss,
The hate will out, the dance be on,
And many of their rage fall down.
It is as easy as spring to yield to the year,
And easy as dance to break with the year.   40
But to go with the year in partition
Between seeming loss, seeming gain,
That is the difficult decorum.
Nor are the primroses unwelcome.

1

'After So Much Loss' is one of the 'Poems Continual' and seems likely to have been written in 1937, making it one of the last poems she wrote. The poem may have been a response, as Elizabeth Friedmann suggests, to a letter from Montague Simmons:

> He had compared the interaction of the male and female sides of an individual to a "dance of complementaries" and called for "all the world" to dance […][1]

In that context Riding's identification of the cause of 'dance' as 'hate', hate of loss, rather than love or a catharsis, may seem the action of a spoil-sport.

'After So Much Loss' was included by the author in the final section of her *Selected Poems: In Five Sets*, and that indicates its importance to the author and to the story the poems had to tell. There is a sober beauty of phrasing, unmixed with any of the studied grotesquery or extravagant neologising that we came to expect in the latter stages of 'Poems of Final Occasion'. Examples of such phrasing are:

> The coward primroses are up,
> We contract their diffuse mildness. (6-7)

> None dances whom no hate stirs,
> Who has not lost and loathed the loss,
> Who does not feel deprived.
> Slyest rebellion of the feet,
> The chaste and tremulous disport
> Of children, limbs in passionless wave […] (27-32)

And the cool and clinching final lines:

> But to go with the year in partition

> Between seeming loss, seeming gain,
> That is the difficult decorum.
> Nor are the primroses unwelcome. (41-44)

2

As 'Poems of Final Occasion' progresses there is a general increase in the length and intensity of the poems, which carries through into the beginning of 'Poems Continual', examples being 'The Last Covenant' and 'Memories of Mortalities'. After that point there is a sense of plateauing; there are fine poems, but – after the riddling and unravelling contradictions and paradoxes, the confrontations with God and the reader, the cumulative intensity, and the detonation of our illusions that characterise these major works – to come upon a poem like 'After So Much Loss' is to encounter a post-apocalyptic mood altogether plainer and more quotidian. There are several such poems in 'Poems Continual', examples being 'On a New Generation', 'Eventual Love', 'The Why of the Wind', and 'The Forgiven Past'.

There are also poems that have a more 'occasional' feel, such as 'Wishing More Dear' and, for all its remarkable beauty, 'Be Grave, Woman'.[2] Other poems, such as 'Auspice of Jewels', Divestment of Beauty', 'Doom in Bloom' and 'Nothing So Far' have a cool elegance, and demonstrate great conventional poetic accomplishment in rhythm, figurative language and even (in 'Christmas') a regular rhyme scheme. It is as though this last period of poetic activity was to some extent a lap of honour; at the same time it was a period in which she could explore the implications of her hard-won achievement: 'If what I've found out is true, then how do I, do we, live with that? How carry on from that foundation?'

'Poems Continual' was the poet's selection from poems written during her last five years as a practising poet, after her finalization of *Poet: A Lying Word*, which was published in 1933. It was a period in which, retrospectively, one can see the outlines of a post-poetic course developing; a period when Laura Riding's formidable energies were being directed into the collaborative production of *Epilogue* and when her mind was turning to the dictionary project. The mood of these later poems may be inferred from a paragraph in Mrs Jackson's 1972 recording in which she looks back upon her period of poetic production:

> A certain relaxing of the complex preoccupiedness I have described is perceptible in the very last phase. There that equanimity in the Given of which I have spoken is matched by a calm in the To Be. But there is still the difficult calm in the Not Yet—calm at this end of the poetic journey is divided against itself. But after that comes equanimity in the Next. For Next is also of the Given....[3]

3

After so much loss—
Seeming of gain,
Seeming of loss—
Subsides the swell of indignation
To the usual rhythm of the year.

Humans have always felt the passage of time acutely. Poets are often to be found lamenting their powerlessness in the face of the loss, 'as time passes' of beauty, of love, of life itself. They comfort themselves with ideas of seizing the day, slowing time down or speeding it up.[4] Alternatively they anticipate the gains promised by the end of suffering, the coming of spring or the procreation of a new generation.[5] T.S. Eliot's 'April is the cruellest month' is a new twist in that the renewal promised by the spring is lamented, the 'gain' brings pain.

Riding's ideas are different and original. 'Time' does not feature conspicuously as a subject in her early poems. However, in the long poem 'In Nineteen Twenty-Seven', which she described, in a letter to Robert Nye as 'the only poem I ever wrote in active unhappiness', her ideas about time are set out at length. Friedmann crisply summarizes the ideas in the poem thus:

> […] 'In Nineteen Twenty-Seven' is ultimately Riding's attempt to record the immediate present, to acknowledge the practical necessity of measuring time while affirming the timelessness of poetic reality.[6]

The crux of the poem comes early, in the following lines, oft quoted, which express a complex idea with a lucid and aphoristic simplicity:

> Then, where was I, of this time and my own
> A double ripeness and perplexity?
> Fresh year of time, desire,
> Late year of my age, renunciation—
> Ill-mated pair, debating if the window
> Is worth leaping out of, and by whom.[7]

The poem concludes with some sort of compromise:

> While the season fades and lasts
> I would be old-fashioned with it.
> I would be persuaded it is so,
> Go mad to see it run, as it were horses,
> Then be unmaddened, find it done,
> Summon you close, a memory long gone.
>
> So I am human, of much that is no more
> Or never was, and in a moment
> (I must hurry) it will be nineteen twenty-eight,
> An old eternity pleading refutal.

By contrast in 'Poet: A Lying Word' Riding, in declaring that the seasons have come to a halt, can be seen as taking an extreme position, in favour of poetic 'reality' (or perhaps 'actuality'), of 'renunciation', and against the siren forces of the seasons.

4

> And, oh, how never tired, and tired,
> The world of primroses, how spring
> The bended spirit fascinates
> With promise of revival,
> Leaving more honest summer to proclaim
> That this is all—a brighter disappointment—
> Time has to give to an implacable
> Persuasion of things lost, wrongly.

The world of primroses, of nature, is 'never tired' in the sense that primroses never suffer forethought or looking back – they will come up regardless, energetically. But for us the world of primroses is 'tired', we can foresuffer all the attendant emotions and associations if we allow our spirit to be 'fascinated' by the spring. The selection of primroses, as opposed to other harbingers of spring, such as daffodils or lilac, suggests the words of Ophelia:

> […] Do not as some ungracious pastors do,
> Show me the steep and thorny way to heaven,
> Whiles like a puffed and reckless libertine
> Himself the primrose path of dalliance treads,
> And recks not his own rede.[8]

Weariness of the repetitive effects of the spring and sexual desire can make the poet rail, or dissociate, or conversely he can identify (as in 'the poets who were the seasons', in 'Poet: A Lying Word') with the power and promise of the changing year. Riding in this poem neither identifies with nor rebels against the forces of time as represented in the seasons; instead she recommends that one calmly 'go with the year in partition' accepting it but not inflating its importance or letting it interfere with the spirit's independence and primacy:

It is as easy as spring to yield to the year,
And easy as dance to break with the year.
But to go with the year in partition
Between seeming loss, seeming gain,
That is the difficult decorum.
Nor are the primroses unwelcome.

NOTES

[1] Friedmann, 2005, 301.

[2] It could be argued, in contradiction, that in a sense all her poems are 'occasional' and personal, too, but some are clearly more specific to the occasion than others, less integral to the overall poetic progress.

[3] 'Excerpts From A Recording (1972), Explaining The Poems' published as Appendix V in the centennial edition of *Collected Poems*, *The Poems of Laura Riding* (New York: Persea, 2001), 495-98; this quotation from 497.

[4] Readers will have their own examples, of course. Immediately I had in mind here Herrick's 'Gather Ye Rosebuds', Marvell's 'To His Coy Mistress' and Donne's 'The Sunne Rising'.

[5] And here I had in mind Hopkins' lines (from his poem beginning 'No worst, there is none) 'all| Life death does end and each day dies with sleep', Larkin's 'The Trees' and Shakespeare's opening sonnet sequence.

[6] Elizabeth Friedmann, *A Mannered Grace* (New York: Persea, 2005), Chapter 10; this quotation and the reference to the letter to Nye from 105.

[7] This is the version in *Collected Poems*, 1938. The oscillation between the phrase 'of whom' and 'of which' in various editions of the poem is discussed in the essay on 'Chloe Or.'.

[8] *Hamlet*, 1.3.47-51.

Chapter 16

'Nothing So Far': beyond poetry

NOTHING SO FAR

Nothing so far but moonlight
Where the mind is;
Nothing in that place, this hold
To hold;
Only their faceless shadows to announce
Perhaps they come—
Nor even do they know
Whereto they cast them.

Yet here, all that remains
When each has been the universe: 10
No universe, but each, or nothing.
Here is the future swell curved round
To all that was.

What were we, then,
Before the being of ourselves began?
Nothing so far but strangeness

Where the moments of the mind return.
Nearly the place was lost
In that we went to stranger places.

Nothing so far but nearly   20
The long familiar pang
Of never having gone;
And words below a whisper which
If tended as the graves of live men should be
May bring their names and faces home.

It makes a loving promise to itself,
Womanly, that there
More presences are promised
Than by the difficult light appear.
Nothing appears but moonlight's morning—   30
By which to count were as to strew
The look of day with last night's rid of moths.

1

This poem, written, according to her authorized biography on 6 September 1937, comes very nearly at the end of the poetry, a valediction surely, although there is one further poem in *Collected Poems*, 'Christmas 1937'.[1] Significantly 'Nothing So Far' was chosen by Laura (Riding) Jackson to be the final poem in the carefully arranged *Selected Poems: In Five Sets*. It is one of a group of late poems that are rhythmically poised and elegant: less experimental, more smoothly eloquent and regular; poems to which she applied her established techniques of repetition with variation and contrast, intricate unspooling syntax and an integrated complexity of word and idea. Other poems in this category include 'Auspice of Jewels', 'Be Grave, Woman', 'Divestment of Beauty', 'Christmas', and 'Doom in Bloom' (all from 'Poems Continual').

As with so many of her poems, a pulsing and unifying energy is the use of irregular repetition with variation, based chiefly here on the opening phrase: 'Nothing so far'. The complete phrase occurs three times; in addition 'nothing' appears in three other phrases over the thirty-two lines. The poem revisits language and ideas in respect to 'moonlight', 'the universe' and 'strangeness' developed in earlier poems, and a by now familiar 'life-in-death' paradox expressed anew in 'graves of live men' and applied to 'words'. There is simple but effective phrasing throughout, as in the following:

> Only their faceless shadows to announce
> Perhaps they come—
> Nor even do they know
> Whereto they cast them. (5-8)

> Nothing so far but nearly
> The long familiar pang
> Of never having gone;
> And words below a whisper which

> If tended as the graves of live men should be
> May bring their names and faces home. (20-25)

> It makes a loving promise to itself,
> Womanly, that there
> More presences are promised
> Than by the difficult light appear. (26-29)

It finishes with startling imagery, in a puzzling poetic flourish:

> Nothing appears but moonlight's morning—
> By which to count were as to strew
> The look of day with last night's rid of moths.

2

> Nothing so far but moonlight
> Where the mind is;
> Nothing in that place, this hold
> To hold;

'Moonlight' here appears faint and distant from the strong, positive, complex associations developed in the poet's use of 'moon' in *Collected Poems*, as outlined in our introduction (and also in the essay on 'Tale of Modernity'). In 'Tale of Modernity', the moon is described by the 'villain' Bishop Modernity as illusion, but by the poet as 'she, illusion and not illusion'. She is closely identified with Truth and with girlhood, or womanhood:

> Truth seemed love grown cool as a brow
> And young as the moon, grown girl to self.[2]

In 'Signs of Knowledge' the 'locking' of the first two signs, namely the 'unlove of the sun' and the 'unlife of the earth' makes for the one sign, the 'undeath of the moon':

> When the first and the second sign are one sign
> Shall you see the grail, know the moon-sense,
> Shall there be whole-world pouring brimful
> Into an empty grail, an empty world,
> An empty whole, a whole emptiness.

And, later in the same poem's concluding *'Rubric for the Eye'*, the moon is explicitly associated with the word:

> *Let the thought see, let moon undazzle sun.*
> *Sun of world, moon of word,* […]

To return to the poem in hand, where in the lines above quoted from 'Signs of Knowledge' there is optimism in the wake of the 'undeath of the moon' and the identification of the moon with word, here, in contradiction, 'moonlight' appears, initially at least, inadequate, giving 'nothing' for the mind, that 'hold', to hold.

The word 'hold' brings attention to itself. As well as the 'hold' of a ship, and the security of a 'stronghold', there is also 'hold' as 'freehold', something given as right of possession, reminding us of 'Seizin', the name so deliberately chosen for the Riding and Graves' printing press.[3]

3

> Only their faceless shadows to announce
> Perhaps they come—
> Nor even do they know
> Whereto they cast them.

Whose are the faceless shadows, ignorant of the way they tend, on their way to a 'strange home'?[4] They may be, of course, on the one hand, human beings, perhaps the 'new' men and women for whom she waits, as in the poem 'On a New Generation':

> Yet the new girl more shines with herself,
> And the latest boy has a light in his head.
> Not unlikely they will speak to each other
> In a peculiar way and forget nature,
> Then to fall quiet like a house no more haunted.
> And in such silence may enough centuries fade
> For all the loud births to be eloquently unmade.[5]

The use of 'peculiar' in this poem reminds us of the 'peculiar earth' of 'As Well As Any Other'; the phrase 'forget nature' reminds us of 'A Prophecy or a Plea'.[6] Nowhere, yet, had Riding found equal or lasting companionship on her poetic quest. Her hope for the future remained though, characteristically expressed in the swallowing up of life and history in the elegant final couplet!

On the other hand, importantly, as well as hoped-for men and women of the future, the 'faceless shadows' refer also to *words*:

> . . . words below a whisper which
> If tended as the graves of live men should be
> May bring their names and faces home.

As we have seen, in our essay on 'Come, Words, Away', words have for Laura Riding a living being similar to the way in which poems, in her earlier criticism, are poem-persons. 'Name' had always an extraordinary significance for the poet, as we have shown in the essay on 'The Signature', there in particular reference to her own name. *Here* she is using the word 'names' in reference both to men and to words. In her later joint work, with her husband, *Rational Meaning*, as noted in our account of the poem 'Earth', 'names' are painstakingly distinguished from mere 'terms'. In the chapter 'Words and Things', a 'home' is created, a place in the mind's 'hold' is made, for 'Earth' or 'earth':

> The name "Earth" or "earth" ought not to appear in any dictionary
> as one of the "meanings" of the word "earth" but only as a name,
> the name of the place of human life.[7]

And, we remember, from the poem 'Earth', the following:

> Earth is your heart
> Which has become your mind [...]

It is easy to forget the breath-taking boldness of this poet's unitary vision!

4

> Yet here, all that remains
> When each has been the universe:
> No universe, but each, or nothing.

By the end of her poetic career Laura Riding had realised the ambition described in 'A Prophecy or a Plea', although even in setting out she recognised that the voyage might reveal a futility. That essay ends:

> If it will be argued that […] the way of analysis is the way of destruction, I can only answer that if one is faithful enough, constant enough, the analysis will induce the synthesis, the poet will come home: and he will have tramped the whole road, he will have seen. By taking the universe apart he will have reintegrated it with his own vitality; and it is this reintegrated universe that will in turn possess him and give him rest. If this voyage reveals a futility, it is a futility worth facing.[8]

This description of the poet reintegrating the universe resembles Keats' description of the world as the vale of soul-making. Much later, in 'Addendum' to *The Telling*, Laura (Riding) Jackson, in crediting Keats and Coleridge with 'phenomenal sincerity in dedication to spiritual vision' described how:

> 'Real' poetic vision may be described as vision of spiritual meanings, in poets, operating outside poems, having only scanty representation in them. Explicit representation of it is more likely to be found outside poems, in the utterances of poets — and where found will be more substantial than what their poems yield of it. When it is found, in the non-poetic writing of a poet, the difficulty of giving the expression a supporting context, a form in which it will have an authority of seriousness beyond that of marginal,

> experimental reflection, is conspicuous. [...]
>
> Thus wrote Keats, in a statement off the poetic record, so to speak. "The World is the Vale of Soul-Making." (Soul is to be distinguished from intelligence.) "There may be intelligences, sparks of divinity, in millions, but they are not Souls till they acquire identities, till each one is personally itself." How is this to be? "How but by the medium of a world like this?"[9]

These lines in the poem are not pessimistic, though they may seem so to those who have not tramped the whole road with the poet. For Riding the ultimate goal is, as outlined in the passage quoted above from 'A Prophecy or a Plea' for each to integrate the universe with his own vitality.

How are we to read the word 'nothing' in the line 'No universe, but each, or nothing'? I think we have here an ambiguity. Just as, if we have followed the poet in her forging of new meaning in relation to 'moon', we may be disorientated in encountering what seems, initially at least, a more ordinary sense of 'moonlight' so here we *could* read 'nothing' in an entirely positive sense, in line with the following crucial passage in *Anarchism Is Not Enough*:

> What is a poem? A poem is nothing. [...] It is not an effect (common or uncommon) of experience; it is the result of an ability to create a vacuum in experience – it is a vacuum and therefore nothing. [...] As nothing – well, as nothing it is everything in an existence where everything, being effect of effect and without cause, is nothing.[10]

In the poem, though, this meaning is faintly, if at all present. We appear to be returned to the more ordinary meaning of 'nothing' where 'each' has either achieved the reintegration of the universe with his own vitality, as described in 'A Prophecy or a Plea' or one is 'nothing' – one has failed to become something, one is a lost fragment of unfulfilled potential. For all the elegance and apparent 'poetic' confidence the strain in maintaining both consistency and complexity in the use of words in poetry is showing, and it may be one reason why the author would move on.

The 'future swell curved round | To all that was' could both describe the unfertile pregnancy of 'Mother All' from 'The Flowering Urn' and refer forwards to the 'loving promise' a few lines further on in this poem. It also harks forward, one might say, to passages from *The Telling*, examples being:

> But there *are* no souls, we do not *have* souls, except as we remember the Soul's before- being, in our bodily after-being.
>
> To save ourselves we must save our souls: to save ourselves we must *find* our souls....
>
> Where there is body that is the universe drawn into a littleness living beyond its great cycles of change, each such littleness has a destiny of enlargement: Soul in-little and Mind in- little await such body, as the means of presence [...]
>
> Let us look across the little identities of self, and across the great identities of kind into which we have been mercifully thrown together by fate (mortally tasting in them the common bread of One-Being, the sustenance of souls); and look with one another behind the ages and the aeons, to an all-preceding All existent only to itself, reality total, whatever it might become; and then look with one another beyond ourselves-now, less than sufficient to ourselves, to ourselves sufficient to the total reality, giving it our life to live.[11]

5

What were we, then,
Before the being of ourselves began?
Nothing so far but strangeness
Where the moments of the mind return.
Nearly the place was lost
In that we went to stranger places.

> Nothing so far but nearly
> The long familiar pang
> Of never having gone;
> And words below a whisper which
> If tended as the graves of live men should be
> May bring their names and faces home.

This question, at the core of the poem, applies to each of the first three words: 'what?', 'were?' and 'we?' The question (and answer to it) is found at the heart of the subject of *The Telling*, and its open avowal:

> In every human being there is secreted a memory of a before-oneself; and if one opens the memory, and the mind is enlarged with it, one knows a time which might be now, by one's feelings of being somehow of it.
>
> .
>
> Yes, I think we remember our creation! — have the memory of it in us, to know. Through the memory of it we apprehend that there was a Before-time of being from which being passed into what would be us. [...] Souls there were not until there were bodies in which, each, diversity's extremes were brought into a union;... another and another and another, to that rounding-in and exhaustion of diversity which is human. Thus from physicality emerge persons — ourselves.[12]

'Strange' is a word that appears in various forms in the poems, notably in 'Cycles of Strangeness' to which we shall return, and in 'The Why of the Wind', which ends:

> We must learn better
> What we are and are not.
> We are not the wind.

> We are not every vagrant mood that tempts
> Our mind to giddy homelessness.
> We must distinguish better
> Between ourselves and strangers.
> There is much that we are not.
> There is much that is not.
> There is much that we have not to be.
> We surrender to the enormous wind
> Against our learned littleness,
> But keep returning wailing '
> Why did I do this?'[13]

Strangeness is opposed to familiarity in 'Nothing So Far' with the lines 'The long familiar pang| Of never having gone' that express a deep nostalgia for the 'Before-time of being'. Using similar language, of strangeness and familiarity, of the momentary as opposed to the constant, she later expanded on these ideas in passages from *The Telling*:

> But what do we know of the spirit? We do not know the spirit yet except in strangeness. And that is why it is a fumbling spirit: denied familiarity, it is with us more than we allow, in our fumbling bodiliness (in which we reach towards it with some shrinking always, a fear of the flesh for itself).

> We look for surprise and variety in our daily encounter with the nature of our being as if it were weather-like: our curiosity towards our human-being imitates the curiosity of body we have towards the weather. But the nature of our being is not to be known as we know the weather, which is by the sense of the momentary. Weather is all change, while our being, in its human nature, is all constancy. Humanness, though belonging to many, does not vary. We are inconstant in it, and so can be curious towards it as if it were itself inconstant, weather-like. But it is to

be known only by the sense of the constant.[14]

As noted in section 3 above, there is deliberate ambiguity about the line 'May bring their names and faces home.' It refers both to words and to men. The hope is that by 'tending' words 'as the graves of live men should be' the names (of the words and the men) and the faces (of the men, and perhaps the words too) may come home.

6

> It makes a loving promise to itself,
> Womanly, that there
> More presences are promised
> Than by the difficult light appear.
> Nothing appears but moonlight's morning—
> By which to count were as to strew
> The look of day with last night's rid of moths.

'It' refers back to 'that place, this hold' 'where the mind is' at the start of the poem, but that is also where the 'moonlight' is, of the 'moon that singles,' the 'moon of word,' and of course the moon associated with woman. 'Womanly' reminds us that, to the last, we are in the poems of a woman, woman of unitary vision.[15] Therefore 'It' may also be taken as referring to 'the future swell curved round | To all that was.' She is confident that there is more to come, but perhaps, with our hindsight, not through poetry.

The poem closes with imagery that seems to refer to the poet at home, after a night at work. A passage in 'Cycles of Strangeness' may help to make sense of it. In that poem she compared the death of a man with the death of a tree, or a rock, or flies, pointing out that, of these, only when a man dies 'It is death indeed'. Turning to moths, she wrote of our false ascription to them of human emotion:

> Or of moths, how if turned outdoors
> Next morning with goodbye,

> A gratitude beyond their will
> Humanizes the unasked release,
> And an emotion reels away.
> Such insincere hysterias
> Or terrorless philosophies
> Show nature's suave proficiency in man.

Elsewhere in the poems she refers to staying up sleepless, no doubt working, with a lamp in the darkness:

> I have been assaulted by the moths
> Thick in my eyes and throat many a night
> When the thought of Amalthea was
> Tall flame in the grimy wick.

> […] If ever truth had been like night sat up with
> As one house in a city may till dawn
> With sleepless lamp eke out the night before.[16]

One does not 'count' by moths, but by words or by people. Considering 'counting', at first one thinks of numbers, then of reckoning, which is something more than numbers; and then, of course, of giving a (full) account, of weighing the whole. And then, reading backwards, as it were, there is 'telling', 'teller', someone who counts, which seems to lean forwards to *The Telling* itself. The words, the names and faces, like the moths, are 'there', but she cannot bring them forward into the morning light of prosaic day without their appearing somewhat less than they are, somehow lacking in final accent.

The promise remained. She might have felt isolated and alone in the course of her thinking, with even her friends of the time not quite following her, and the literary critics rejecting her for the most part, but she had uncovered something out of the ordinary, worth the pursuit, witnessed by the step-by-step development of the poems themselves, in which lay hope.

Indeed, the testament of her work is its hope. She had to leave this until the second period of her life, after 1940. In the very last poem of the book, 'Christmas, 1937', occur the lines:

> These things are not yet tellable
> In the tone of long-ago I would wish:
> Christmas again confounds my mouth.
>
> I speak as if in recent knowledge.
> Perhaps that is right: the tale is young,
> Though the matter old. Christmas still!

And within a year or so she gave up writing poems, and later renounced poetry altogether. While she had been able to 'tell' much within poetry, clearly, she felt that something was wrong: that there was something to tell which poetry could not.[17]

NOTES

[1] Elizabeth Friedmann, *A Mannered Grace* (New York: Persea, 2005), 304, says of 'Nothing So Far': '[...] a poem that raised the questions she was to spend the remainder of her life endeavouring to answer [...]'.

[2] See the essay on *Tale of Modernity* for a detailed account.

[3] This note on 'hold' is adapted from MJ's unpublished notes on the poem.

[4] 'And every prodigal greatness| Must creep back into strange home' – from 'The Flowering Urn'.

[5] *Collected Poems*, 316.

[6] See the essay on 'One Self', for an account of Riding's use of 'peculiar' and the essay on 'Poet: A Lying Word' for her view of 'nature'.

[7] Laura (Riding) Jackson and Schuyler B. Jackson, *Rational Meaning* (London: University Press of Virginia, 1997), 399-402; quotation from 399.

[8] Ibid, p280.

[9] *The Telling*, (London: Athlone Press, 1972), 180.

[10] Laura Riding, *Anarchism Is Not Enough* (London: Cape, 1928), 'What is a Poem?'. 16-19; quotations from 16, 17 and 18.

[11] *The Telling*, 1972, 31, 35, 36, 54 (from passages 29, 33, 34, 61).

[12] *The Telling*, 1972, 25 and 30 (from passages 22 and 28; passages 22-29 need to be read for the full expression of the ideas).

[13] *Collected Poems*, 330; see also, all from 'Poems Continual': 'We are the Resurrection', 313; 'A Letter to any Friend', 323, and 'The Forgiven Past', 345 (which immediately precedes 'Nothing So Far' in the author's *Selected Poems*.)

[14] *The Telling*, 1972, 22 and 62-63 (from passage 18 and 'Preface for a Second Reading).

[15] And what that means. For fear of distorting the proportions of the essay by elaboration, or distorting the author's ideas by abbreviation no more will be said here other than to refer to relevant passages by Laura (Riding) Jackson in *The Telling*, 1972, 44-49 (passages 45-53), and to *The Word "Woman"* (New York: Persea, 1993).

[16] 'Goat and Amalthea', and 'The Last Covenant'.

[17] The last two paragraphs have been adapted from MJ's unpublished notes on the poem.

Chapter 17

Conclusions: A futility worth facing?

This study has dealt at full length with only fifteen poems, fewer than a tenth of the 178 poems in the main body of *Collected Poems*. In the course of the analysis it has shed direct light on at least part of the meaning of perhaps thirty more, though still leaving around three-quarters of the poems largely unexplored. It will be evident, too, that as with most other readings of her poems, rather more has been said of the 'Poems of Mythical Occasion' than of the later poems, even though the poems which are most markedly peculiar to Laura Riding in content, style and technique, and the most brilliant, derive mainly from the book that marked the climax of her poetic career, *Poet: A Lying Word*, most of the poems from which appear in 'Final Occasion'. There remains, therefore, a great deal more to be told. On the other hand, we are perhaps justified in saying that a number of things have now been achieved that had not been achieved before, and that a fairly sound foundation has been laid for further work.

Appropriately enough, much of the methodology developed in the course of the readings derives from the author's own critical and explanatory writings. These are as diverse in style and tone as the poems themselves, perhaps even more so. They range from the passionate but magisterial 'A Prophecy or a Plea' through the savagely amusing and radical *Anarchism Is*

Not Enough and *Contemporaries and Snobs* to the more scholarly, practical and approachable *A Survey of Modernist Poetry*. Then there are the contrasting introductions, the feverish, inspired preface to *Poems: A Joking Word* and the sober and painstaking 'To the Reader' from *Collected Poems*, the latter acknowledging at the outset the difficulty that the poems pose, but setting out the proper approach to them. Reviewing the chapters on the poems, one is conscious of considerable repetition in reference to key passages on poetry and on poets. In part this can be defended on the grounds that each of the chapters is intended as a stand-alone essay, as well as part of a book; hence the need to establish in each case the key relevant points for a reading of the poem in view. However, the repetition may also be justified by the need to emphasise the persistently radical nature of the poet's approach, not to let it slip by 'as read'.

Complementing that has been regular recourse to the Oxford English Dictionary, both in its full and in the shorter versions. 'For me the essence of the adventure was in the words' as Mrs Jackson wrote in her first full account of her decision to quit poetry. The depth of this commitment is evident in every poem examined, and of course it carried through into the dictionary project that occupied her and her husband for the remainder of their lives.

Increasingly, as the readings followed the progress of *Collected Poems*, it became clear how frequently the post-poetic writings, particularly *The Telling* (for all that she described it as 'breaking the spell of poetry'), complement rather than contradict her poetry. Unfortunately the poet was seen by many as having shot her own fox, destroyed the object of her own quest in poetry, when she 'renounced' it, but this is, as I hope the book has demonstrated, simply not the case. Although one or two of her thoughts relating to renunciation of poetry may qualify the meaning of some of her poems – as in the case of comments on 'The Mask' in her 1970 introduction to her *Selected Poems* – by and large she stood by her poems as written, and as published in 1938 in *Collected Poems*.

In the introduction we referred for the first time since its publication to the poignant blurb on the dustcover of the original 1938 edition of *Collected Poems*, reprinted in full at Appendix A. It is worth reviewing how far we have come in recognising and evaluating the points so deftly and swiftly summed up in her own blurb:

> We can now understand why her poems have defied conventional classification. We must read them in relation to one another to appreciate the large coherence of thought behind them. Then, instead of assuming a mysterious personality at work in intellectual isolation, we recognise that here is a complete range of poetic experience controlled with sensitive wisdom.

The first point here was covered at length in the introduction, referring to her works of criticism, as outlined above. The point about reading the poems in relation to one another 'to appreciate the large coherence of thought behind them' has governed much of our approach to this book. The next sentence is less easy to grasp. It reflects, in part at least, the fact that at the time of writing she was constantly at work in intellectual company, almost in an intellectual co-operative, in Mallorca: supporting other writers with their projects; co-producing several books, and editing, and collaborating on essays for, the periodical *Epilogue*, culminating in its Volume IV, *The World and Ourselves*, in which she initiated and co-ordinated a wide correspondence on the nature of the world, and what was to be done at a time when war clouds were gathering. It also reflects, for all the strength and integrity of her personality, a deeper conviction of the need to go beyond it, something that may be inferred from the preface to *Poems: A Joking Word* (where she says that her poems make more sense than her life), from the poem 'Disclaimer of the Person', and then later on from *The Telling*, where she says:

> In describing the memory [of a 'before-oneself'], I refer to what I find in me that belongs to me not in my simple present personhood but in my intricate personless identity with all that has preceded me to the farthest, timeless reach of me.[1]

Ironically, and sadly, despite the intellectual companionship, her connectedness with the wider literary and intellectual world of her time, the recognition through publication of so much of her work, and the (wary) respect she was mainly afforded, it could be said that in one sense few poets have been so isolated, so distinct from what went before, and so unappreciated by contemporaries.

The blurb continued:

> We cannot, in fact, describe Laura Riding's poems as of such or such a type or tendency: rather, they set a new standard of poetic originality. They are undiluted: no politics or psychology, no religion or philosophical sentiment, no scholastic irrelevancies, no mystical or musical wantonness.

In part this is an implied attack on much of the poetry of the time, the 'relevant' politics and psychologising of Auden, the scholasticism and religion and philosophical sentiment in Eliot, the mystical and musical wantonness of Yeats. It summarizes the lengthy attack on poetry of the Zeitgeist in *Contemporaries and Snobs*.[2] There are essays in the same vein in *Epilogue*[3] and continued, in a way, in *The Telling*'s account of the inadequacies of religion, philosophy and psychology in the telling of the story of ourselves. In the preface 'To the Reader' inside *Collected Poems* she disowns Auden's attribution to her of the title 'the only living philosophical poet' and attacks Eliot for creating for himself a 'tailor's-dummy of religion'.[4] The reference to 'musical wantonness' recalls the sustained and brilliant attack in *Anarchism Is Not Enough* upon false analogies between music and poetry that was quoted at length in the 'Introduction'; it also recalls, if indirectly, the criticism of regularity of metre and rhyme in *A Survey of Modernist Poetry* that was used in the accounts of 'The Tiger' and other poems.

The blurb continued with a defence of her poems' qualities as poems:

> This does not mean that they lack any of the graces that it is proper to expect in poetry: they have memorable beauty of phrase, serene humour, and a rich intricacy of movement that redeems the notion of 'pure poetry' from the curse put upon it by the aestheticians.

In our readings we have recognised and sketched out, in relation to each poem treated, the qualities identified in this passage, although 'beauty of phrase' has had to be qualified by the studied ugliness and grotesquery in some of the later poems, such as 'Signs of Knowledge' and 'Tale of Modernity'. In 'Chloe Or...' the 'serene humour' is at once evident, and sustained throughout the poem, but often the humour only becomes clear once we have emerged from the struggle to make sense of the poem. Sometimes it is the 'twist in the tail', the final lines of 'Earth' ('Destruction only on wide fears shall fall') and 'After So Much Loss' ('Nor are the primroses unwelcome'). In 'The Rugged Black of Anger' it appears at the centre of the poem: 'Why crashing glass does not announce | The monstrous petal-advance of flowers.' This serenity, as in the last example given, is often, indeed characteristically, achieved against a background of magnificently articulated turbulence and anger as in 'After Smiling' and 'The Dilemmist'.

Perhaps more needs to be said about the 'rich intricacy of movement', something recognised by both Roy Fuller and W. B. Yeats, although we have discussed her changes of rhythm, her frequent and effective use of repetition, parallelism, and contrast as means both of creating the impression of regularity, of imparting momentum, and of unfolding of meaning in relation to most of the poems, notably 'The Tiger', 'Earth', and 'Come, Words, Away'.

It is interesting that she felt the need both to promote her poetry as 'pure' and to dissociate her brand of purity from that of the 'aestheticians'. Here her target was primarily the nineteenth century French poets, beginning with Gautier and Baudelaire, but culminating in Rimbaud, her equal both in poetic talent and radicalism, but without the moral compass. For Baudelaire: 'Poetry has no other end but itself. If a poet has followed a moral end he has diminished his poetic force and the result is most likely to be bad.'[5] This line became mainstream poetic currency. The comparison and contrast of Riding with Rimbaud is described at some length in the essay on 'Poet: A Lying Word'. Laura (Riding) Jackson specified the key difference between her and Rimbaud, in the context of the quitting of poetry:

In the poetic adventure, I had a structure for hope, whatever happened; and my inspiration came from everywhere. [...] *For me the essence of the adventure was in the words*; he used them as stuff from which to distil an elixir giving power to make happiness out of unhappiness. (Italics added)

Within her poems there is an acknowledged tension between beauty and truth, as in 'The Signature', a tension unstrung in the 'renunciation' of poetry, with truth the victorious party. The 'good' does not figure much (the word is hardly used) in the poems themselves,[6] but it does emerge, equated with truth, in the 'Preface to the Reader':

Literally I mean [i.e. we are now literally in the present of poetry]: our own proper immediacies are positive incidents in the good existence which is poetry. To live in, by, for the reasons of, poems is to habituate oneself to the good existence. When we are so continuously habituated that there is no temporal interruption between one poetic incident (poem) and another, then we have not merely poems — we have poetry; we have not merely immediacies — we have finality. Literally.[7]

This moral equation of truth with the good existence replaced the Keatsian equation of beauty with truth, and set the tone for her future quest and for her evangel, *The Telling*. It also begs questions that are beyond the scope of this work on her poetry.

The final sentence of the blurb raises further questions:

They [the poems] are, moreover, very consciously the work of a woman, introducing into poetry energies without which it is no more than 'a tradition of male monologue', not a living communication.[8]

To take the latter point first, at the surface level the idea seems to be that for her poetry was in principle a dialogue, perhaps in the way *The World and Ourselves* engaged with others in correspondence. This may be a reason why she included 'Midsummer Duet', a dialogue with Graves, in her *Collected Poems*, although it is not one of her (or Graves's) stronger poems. As we saw in 'Poet: A Lying Word' she includes the reader, and the readers, directly and from the outset in that poem: 'You have now come with me, I have now come with you'. It can be more subtle, as we saw at the end of 'Come, Words, Away' where the poet apparently pulls up the trapdoor – the words go with her into the silence – but the reader can choose to include his or her self in the 'us' of the poem's final word, and accompany her and the words.[9]

At a deeper level, for her, poems are people, living things as in 'The Troubles of a Book', the final trouble of which is: 'To breathe live words, yet with the breath | Of letters; to address liveliness | In reading eyes, be answered with | Letters and bookishness.' In other words, the book, or the poem, fails to elicit a living response. If our reading is correct then she viewed her poems, at the time of writing them, as not just living but eternal, a view she later renounced along with the practice of poetry.[10]

Her abandonment of the poet-position was in part an attempt to avoid the pitfalls of 'a tradition of male monologue', and its association with the wrong kind of authority, as she describes in her 'Preface for a Second Reading' of *The Telling*:

Poems can seem to the silent laity to fill the void of their non-speaking, to be their speaking on the Subject. [...] When I abandoned the poet-position, I took up place in the lay-position. Authority, then, required transposition from the poetic to the lay region: it had to be looked for wherever personhood, from which comes the ability to say 'I', is. It is to be found, in that region, in all the crossing pathways in which mutual assurance in the authenticity of 'I' courses to and fro from one to another. Such avowing of our being by each of us in truth's unity of interlaced responsibleness, *The Telling* suggests.[11]

The final point from the blurb is the apparently very simple one that the poems are 'very consciously the work of a woman', introducing energies without which (etcetera). Again, there are several levels at which this is true of her poems. At its most straightforward it is part of the 'subject' of the poems beginning with life as a girl ('Forgotten Girlhood') and as a woman in the world of men ('Chloe Or...', 'The Tiger', etc.). Love in all its aspects, including sexual love, longing and lust, is unashamedly present, pervades the poems, even up to the last poems, such as 'Wishing More Dear' and 'Eventual Love' in 'Poems Continual' . But from the start the destiny of woman goes beyond the love of man, as in 'The Virgin', as in 'Druida', where 'she' passes beyond the man 'like a blind bird | Seeing all heaven ahead', and as in 'Helen's Faces', where 'she' wards off the men bitterly contesting for her, giving each a replica of love:

> But the original woman is mythical,
> Lies lonely against no heart.
> Her eyes are cold, see love far off,
> Read no desertion when love removes,
> The images out of fashion.
>
> Undreamed of in her many faces
> That each kept off the plunderer:
> Contest and bitterness never raged round her.

The inadequacy of man as lover and as poet is most eloquently described in the last three stanzas of 'The Dilemmist', in which we read:

> When's man a poet then?
> And was he ever one? [...]
> The man's away after the man.
> She understood his wooing wrong.
> He never meant her more than paper,
> Nor does his heart one icy line remember.

At a deeper level she progressively explores both the difference between woman and man and the sense of unity through which woman operates. As she put it in an essay written when a practising poet, but published only in 1993:

> We can get truth — how things are as a whole — only from woman: man operates through the sense of difference, woman through the sense of unity.[12]

In the final section of the essay on 'The Flowering Urn' we paused to examine how, while on the one hand the poet produces peculiarly unsentimental 'unpoetic' unravellings of mysteries as in 'Signs of Knowledge', 'Poet: A Lying Word' and the first part of 'Disclaimer of the Person', on the other, by contrast, she is capable of an equally peculiar complexity and compactness, a ravelling up and interfusing of words and images into a unitary density that is genuinely difficult, so that the reader has to slow down to a halt to absorb what is being said.[13]

NOTES

[1] Laura (Riding) Jackson, *The Telling* (London: Athlone Press, 1972), passage 22, 25.

[2] Laura Riding, 'Poetry and the Literary Universe' in *Contemporaries and Snobs* (London: Cape, 1928), 9-121.

[3] Noted in the chapters on 'The Rugged Black of Anger' and 'Earth'.

[4] *Collected Poems*, (London: Cassell, 1938), xxii-xxiii.

[5] This quote is taken from William Gaunt, *The Aesthetic Adventure* (London: Cape, 1945), 15.

[6] 'Good' is used a few times in 'The Last Covenant', *Collected Poems*, 270.

[7] *Collected Poems*, xxvii. This helps clarify, incidentally, what she means by 'Poems of Immediate Occasion', and 'Poems of Final Occasion' and 'Poems Continual'.

[8] I have been unable to identify a source for the possible quote given here 'a tradition of male monologue', although it sounds like something the author herself might have said, possibly elsewhere.

[9] Another poem, 'Letter to Any Friend' comes to mind.

[10] This view is not so strange: the immortality of poetry, 'more enduring than bronze' has been about since antiquity.

[11] *The Telling*, 67.

[12] Laura (Riding) Jackson, *The Word "Woman"* (New York: Persea, 1993), 40-41; from the title essay originally written around 1933-35.

[13] Two examples, given there and repeated here:

> *Earth is your heart*
> *Which has become your mind*
> *But still beats ignorance of all it knows—*
> As miles deny the compact present
> Whose self-mistrusting past they are […] (*from* 'Earth', italics added)

> And she [the moon], illusion and not illusion,
> *A sapphire being fell to earth, time-struck.*
> *In colour live and liquid and earth-pale*,
> Never so near she, never so distant.
> Never had time been futured so,
> All reckoning on one fast page.
> Time was a place where earth had been.
> The whole past met there, she with it.
> *Truth seemed love grown cool as a brow,*
> *And young as the moon, grown girl to self.*
> (*from* 'Tale of Modernity', italics added)

A Journey To Wabasso, Fl.32970
Laura (Riding) Jackson
Mark Jacobs

Box 35
Wabasso
Florida 32970
July 31 78

O Mark!

May all be clear for you, now, from my letters - & the aerogramme letters (become in large part multiplied by Susan's inability to meet you). But, be sure to bring your <u>driver's licence</u>, just in case there comes a need. I am hurrying this letter to you because of feeling you should be apprised of the necessity of your being <u>on watch</u> against <u>possibilities of assault, theft, danger</u>, in your time at the airport – all your time in Miami, and on the bus. <u>Avoid free-and-easy walking about</u> in <u>Miami streets</u> in the time you will have after getting clear of customs, etc., formalities and your getting on the bus for Vero Beach. There is constant <u>danger</u> of attack there, in what might seem a harmless, open innocent environment. Make no trusting associations with strangers, at airport, anywhere in your Miami time, or on the bus. Give no detail of information in any chance conversation about yourself, or where you are going. I am referring just to possibilities – do not be scared, just be <u>very</u> careful. Behave reservedly, be at ease, but observant, watchful. Do not expose any possession, matter or other, to theft-possibility.

Laura

I arrived at the motel at two in the morning. The Caudills, old friends of Schuyler and Laura from their New Hope days in 1940, picked me up from the bus drop-off point and it was a short drive. The flight had been uneventful and not unpleasant although strange in the shift from the cool temperature of England into the sudden clamping heat of Miami. The people seemed different: the loose-and-easy white Americans, the Spanish extrovert and loud, the American black on the whole quiet. The races at a glance kept to themselves for the most part. I wandered around the cool reception area, had a club sandwich and a cold drink at a bar, and waited for two hours to move to the depot to catch the Greyhound bus. It had been a long journey full of painful thoughts of leaving my family behind and a divorce waiting for me when I got back. When I left the airport to walk across the street to the bus depot the heat hit me again for a minute and then suddenly rain fell from the sky and folk were running out laughing and dancing to stand with their arms up to the sky to welcome the cool relief. I smiled and relaxed.

Betty Owle, Darleen's daughter, drove the open-top 1963 Oldsmobile up the lane to the small porch at the side of the wooden-frame house with its red corrugated tin roof. Laura had heard the engine and was standing at the top of the steps. As I walked towards her and up the steps she held out her arms, rocking from one leg to the other, grinning. 'Welcome!' she said, hugging me close for a moment, smiling even more widely, eyes dancing, and turning to Betty, 'And thank you so much for bringing him!' hugging her in turn, and then, 'Oh, that's the first time I ever kissed you, isn't it!' laughing. 'Come in, come in.'

She must have been around five-foot six, a cloud of white hair mixed with some grey, banded with a blue ribbon, light eyes somewhere between blue and grey, blue eye-liner, light powdered face make-up and a touch of lipstick, blue cotton short-sleeved shirt and pants. I had seen a few photographs of her, mainly in books, and two rather odd ones she had sent, one of them double-exposed, making it look as though she was standing in the middle of a bush and rather ghostly, hands gripped behind her back which I later knew was because she had to force herself to stand straight because of her leg, but I had not expected her to look quite this way, quite so bright, vibrant. Her actual appearance belied her photographs, except, I thought later, for the two odd ones she had sent me which conveyed a sense of bright cheerfulness, double-exposed or not. My lasting impression of Laura was her cheerfulness, her sense of fun, and her considerable physical energy.

After seven years of exchanging letters, she was not what I expected.

The letters began simply enough, sparse in number for the first year and then increasing both in intensity, quantity and length as we grew to know each other better. For several years they arrived with the salutation 'Mr. Jacobs!' with no 'Dear' in front, while I addressed her as 'Dear Mrs. Jackson', and on the envelope the full name she requested to be known by, 'Mrs. Schuyler B. Jackson'. The 'Mr. Jacobs!' with the exclamation mark was always somewhat a shock, as though she were shouting, but as I learned, in fact attested to the scrupulousness of her attention to words in every detail, whether personal or public, in all her dealings with others outside the privacy of her home. Every letter delivered to her post-box was carefully read and responded to, sometimes even the circulars, a lifetime habit Robert Graves remembers about her while they were together, and equally anything – and there was a great deal – published about her in books, journals or reviews. She allowed nothing, as he said then, to slip by her. The reason for this was intricately bound up in the rationale of her work and life.

Laura, Betty and I all looked pleased with each other, Betty said goodbye, and Laura and I entered the house through the kitchen. The shade was a welcome relief from the Florida sun. I don't recall what Laura said as we walked in other than generally welcoming me and asking if I wanted a drink. The living area was roomy, a wood table to my right with bench-seats, a rug, a bookcase on the far wall, a desk with an old, upright Adler typewriter, a chair and another bookcase to my left under a window with, notably, the two bottom shelves filled with the Oxford English Dictionary. I think it was the 1932 edition. I noticed there were not, oddly, that many books – coming as I did directly from my bookshop in England and accustomed to being surrounded by thousands of books, and also aware of academic friends who hoarded walls full of books. The number of books here were especially few, the bookcases a mere two or three shelves high. I spotted an edition of Ezra Pound and one or two others, but notably there was *The Wizard Of Oz* and *Charlotte's Web*, of which I was particularly fond. These seemed to stand out for me, I don't know why. A year or so before she had sent me a book for my son's birthday – his fifth, I think – an illustrated edition of *Jack and the Beanstalk*. I still have it. She had written a message of birthday wishes all around the first two pages of the inside cover. The story was quite different from the *Jack and the Beanstalk* books I had read in the past, much longer and detailed, and my son and I both loved it when I read it to him. When I remarked how few books she possessed, she referred, laughing, to a mutual academic friend, and said, 'Oh, academics – yes, they have lots of books. When they can't think of anything to write they crawl across their books to give them ideas.'

Our first words seemed to be about words. I had been lucky enough the year before to have found sufficient money to buy the new OED dictionary set plus supplements. I asked her about her set – something about which edition it was – mentioning that I had the new one, and then I asked her whether she had completed her plan of writing a new kind of thesaurus. She looked at me in surprise. 'Say that again,' she asked. I repeated it. 'When you say 'thesaurus' I see you place the accent on the first syllable,' she said. 'Why do you do that?' 'Oh,' I said. 'That's because when I lived in London with friends, one of them, Billy, who was much older than me and ex-public school and Cambridge, said the correct pronunciation was 'thes-aurus' and I took him at his word. Is that incorrect?' 'I think it's wrong. I've never heard it said like that. Let's check,' she said, and picked up the OED volume of 'T' and began leafing through it. 'There!' she said. 'I thought that was wrong. You can see here the diacritics give the accent as on the second syllable, as I always thought.' 'Oops! Sorry,' I said. 'Oh no, not at all – I've never checked it before and now we know. That's important.' It was important, as I later knew. She was to insist, especially in *Rational Meaning*, published after she died, that one of the essential but much over-looked features of a word is its enunciation – which draws on the pronunciation of a word, of course, but is far more accurate in registering the word clear in the mind. In fact, she was not much bothered by pronunciation as such. A regional accent, such as Yorkshire or Cockney, or Floridian or Brooklyn, might affect pronunciation, but as long as the enunciation was clear, that didn't matter. Her own speech was always fluid and clear and quite distinct – a bit like a 1930s English Chelsea accent, as Michael Kirkham, the Graves scholar, once said, although never in the English sense of 'posh', that imitation-of-the-Queen kind of 'posh' practiced in our public schools. Laura's tonal voice-pitch was varied, almost melodic.

We sat on the bench-seats in the dining-room and talked across the table for a while, about my trip, my wife and the trouble we were having, and various incidental matters. I noticed how her hands seemed quite large. She wore a red lipstick, lightly applied, the blue ribbon tied in a small bow framing her face. Her skin was pale but not white, slightly made up with foundation, her eyes – well, her eyes surprised me, glancing at me when I spoke, and then away when she spoke, looking up backwards and forwards, seeming to dance around while she put her thoughts together. Somehow she made talk seem easy, interspersing it with a wry joke or two, briefly touching my hand or wrist, laughing – when truth be known I was exhausted both from the flight and from the emotional turmoil I had left behind. She obviously sensed this. 'How are you feeling?' she asked. 'Totally confused!' I said. 'I bet you are!' she responded, and we both laughed. We talked about what I might or might not do, about which I had no idea, until conversation settled into talk about this friend and that friend and various projects and plans. After an hour or so she stood up, smiling, and said we must eat, disappearing into the kitchen while telling me to 'be at ease', a phrase she repeated from time to time, and to 'look around.'

The living-room was all wood, floors and walls both, a large rug across the floor. There were the bones of a dead spider in one corner but everywhere looked clean otherwise. There was no electricity, no light-fittings. 'Why don't you have electricity?' I asked later. 'Where would I run the wires?' she replied, nodding at the walls. I immediately saw what she meant. It would look ugly. At the end of the living-room was a hallway with a small rug leading into what looked like another room but was in fact a closed veranda with wide glass doors that opened inwards, typical, as I later learned, of a Cracker house, the open distance between kitchen and rear veranda called a 'dog-run' to allow air to circulate. Down the hallway to the left were a bathroom and a spare bedroom which contained a large safe, brimful, I discovered, with Laura's manuscripts, notes and papers, spilling out when we opened the door, and kept in there for fear of fire, a real risk with the lightning-strikes dancing across the land every so often. One evening, expecting a telephone call from Jim Mathias, the president of the Guggenheim Foundation who was handling Laura's fund application, I was sitting reading in the rocker chair when the 'phone rang. Laura was in the bedroom and I glanced up to see her running across the hallway when she tripped on the rug and fell flat on her face and hands. Jumping to my feet I went toward her but she raised her face and nodded 'no', smiled, and agilely sprang back up to continue running. Not bad for a woman of seventy-seven, I marvelled.

Jim Mathias was to fly down from New York the following weekend to stay for the week, putting up at the motel Laura had arranged for us both, about three miles down the road. The Guggenheim Foundation, partly through Jim if not wholly, had given Laura a $6000 grant to finish her and Schuyler's book, *Rational Meaning: A New Foundation for the Definition of Words*, which they had worked on since first meeting in 1939 and which she had planned from the early 1930s. It was a hugely ambitious work intended, among other things, to rectify the errors of the major dictionaries, such as the *OED*, which define words according to their literary history rather than by their actual meanings. There were thousands of notes in the safe and bedroom each with a word listed and a definition given, first intended to be put in the form of a dictionary, but later set aside in favour of a more concise account of how a word comes to have a specific meaning. The book was published in 1996, a few years after her death, largely through money left when her estate was wound up, as her Will specified.

On that first day, Laura rang Betty to ask if she would drive me back to the motel around 5.00 pm. When Betty arrived she and Laura had a brief conversation in the kitchen and I noticed Laura handing her a few dollars, this for the gasoline. She was scrupulous in her dealings with others. She had rented a bike for me to get backwards and forwards from the motel and this was waiting when Betty took me back, so the first thing I did was to cycle to the store about a mile down the road to stock up on food, coffee, drinks and cigarettes – my first real expedition in the U.S.A., my other being my arrival at Miami. When I got back to the motel I unpacked my things, wary of the bureau drawer across which something large had scuttled when I tried to open it the previous night and which I quickly slammed shut. Probably just a cockroach, but I wasn't about to take a chance in a hot and foreign land. Then Mrs. Cordell came across to welcome me and show me around. She asked me to keep the air conditioning off or low when I wasn't there during the day to save expense. She spoke warmly of 'Mrs. Jackson' for several minutes and how she always put up her guests. Everyone referred to Laura as 'Mrs. Jackson.' I discovered Laura had paid for the motel room for the first week. It was forty-nine dollars which seemed ridiculously cheap even then. When I queried Laura about paying bills she brushed it aside and said we'd settle up at the end, adding that she'd recently sold an early edition of Camden's *Britannia* for six hundred dollars. It surprised me she had a copy of that. In fact in the end I paid for very few expenses, which was a relief since I was more or less broke. I fell into bed, aware for a few moments of the scratching sound in the drawer.

When I was up next morning Mrs. Cordell hurried across to me to tell me Mrs. Jackson had rung to apologise that she had to go out for a funeral of an old Negro friend, that she was sending Betty over to see if I needed anything, and would I mind waiting until lunch-time to visit. As it turned out, Betty was busy so her friend Mary came instead who kindly offered to drive me to the coast a couple of miles away to look around. Police cars were coming and going as we went and Mary stopped one, which one of her cousins was driving, to ask what was happening. Apparently two men were on the run after murdering a woman the previous night and the police had chased them to an off-shore island where they were surrounded. 'They aither come out,' the cousin said laconically, 'or they get et by the alligators – their choice.' We drove across an isthmus onto a beach parking-area where Mary pointed out the densely shrubbed island in question, noticing at the same time two unmarked police cars to the side of us. Were they keeping an eye on the island, she asked? No, they said, they were expecting a drug-boat to pull in from Cuba any minute and were there to arrest them. After a few moments Mary asked me if I'd like to see any more or walk on the beach. 'I think we'd better go somewhere else', I said – 'Mrs. Jackson would not be pleased if I got shot in the crossfire', at which Mary laughed, but we drove off. Mary, as I later found out, was a bit of an adventurer, blonde, rangy, tough, blue-eyed and tall. She was, I told her when I said goodbye at the end of my stay, my idea of America.

When I got back to the motel, Laura had left a message telling me to come over. I was used to cycling in England and it took less than half an hour to get across to the house. Laura had sandwiches and coffee or a choice of lemon tea waiting when I got there. We sat at her bench table while we caught up on news and other matters. She told me about Tom, the friend who had died, and how she hadn't wanted to go to the funeral because they had fallen out some years back, but that he had been a local pastor and his friends had insisted she went, saying how highly he always spoke of her. I asked how they had fallen out and she looked down for a moment frowning. 'You'll think it strange,' she said, 'but it was about giving driving directions for someone coming to visit me from Miami. We sat down over a map to write down the route but got into an argument over the details. Tom insisted he was excellent at giving directions to folk travelling and never made a mistake and to leave it to him, but I pointed out that giving directions were far more complicated than that allowed for, given changes to routes and signs, and I tried to put alternatives to the details, but he got angry and said he knew better than I. I let him do it, but I never spoke to him after that except to explain why I wouldn't speak to or see him.' She paused for a moment. 'It wasn't just that, of course. It was something I had suspected was in him over a long time. He wanted to be *right*. No one, I told him, could be that *right*.' I learned later that the word 'right' and the sense of being 'right', was a signal of danger to Laura. People who want to feel 'right', she later explained, just want to feel good about themselves, they don't want to listen nor do they want to learn.

We talked about Robert Graves for a while. She told me how she deeded the house in Deya to him shortly after they split up in 1940, sending him $8000 she owed him, but gradually she realized things were somehow wrong. First, his and Hodge's book *The Reader Over Your Shoulder* came to her notice in 1943 which was based squarely on an essay she published in the 1930s in her large twice-a-year magazine, *Epilogue*, Graves and Hodge simply lifting her thesis and extending it to a book-length. *The Long Weekend*, published in 1941, was loosely based on her *The World And Ourselves* which appeared in 1938. She let it go at the time because she and Graves had worked so closely together for fifteen years. But then Graves' *The Golden Asphodel* was published in 1949 in which he reproduced a substantial quantity of their joint books published not long after they first met, *A Survey of Modernist Poetry* (1927) and *A Pamphlet Against Anthologies* (1928), editing them as he thought fit without her permission, even though she was lead author of both books and, indeed, most of the content of them, and the important content, derived from her own work, *Contemporaries And Snobs*. He presents the essays taken from both books as seemingly by him, reducing her role in them to a parenthetically described '(with Laura Riding)', as though she is a mere second-author, whereas in fact she was the principal author. She objected at the time both directly to him and to the publisher but it was to no avail. Readers, not to mention scholars, have consistently quoted both *A Survey of Modernist Poetry* and *A Pamphlet Against Anthologies* as being written by Robert Graves, describing Laura Riding as a kind of secretary or amanuensis merely involved with the research. In fact, the direct opposite is true.

From that point on it was war. When we touched on *The White Goddess* I asked: 'Wasn't there a good deal of truth in that book?' She smacked her hand on the table. 'Of course there is,' she said. 'He learned it all from me!' It wasn't until some years later I realized how true that was and just how much Graves took from Riding's work in his white goddess invention, not just the white goddess herself but what he presented as the scholarly investigations of all the key words and etymologies essential to his thesis, although he made a complete mess of it. Her eyes twinkled for a moment. 'He was always interested in sex, of course.' She paused and smiled. 'I soon put a stop to that! And now he's gaga.' She trilled her lips with her fingers. 'Blup, blup, blup, blup.' I looked up astonished. 'Oh, Laura!' I gasped. We looked at each for a second and then both burst out laughing.

The next morning Laura was reading a book which I saw was Susan

Sontag's *On Photography*. 'Sontag?' I queried. She nodded. 'Yes. I'm trying to find whether she took anything from my own essays on photography.' She pushed a sheaf of papers towards me. 'Here,' she said, 'I thought you might be interested in reading this while I finish up for this morning.' It was a chapter from her planned *Praeterita* (published after her death as *The Person I Am*). I took it to the window bench and watched Laura as she read. She was on the second page, tracing each word with her finger and enunciating it under her breath, and then she might repeat the sentence once or twice. I remember thinking it could take her months to get through the whole book, but it was a lesson in taking great care with reading. In fact, as I saw after I returned home, there are certain similarities in Sontag's work with Laura's which are otherwise unaccountable.

Laura finished after an hour or so and began typing some notes she had made. Then she bustled around in the kitchen making coffee while I sat at the bench-table looking out of the window at the palmettos and brightly covered birds flitting in and out of trees. We chatted throughout, and then she said she had an urgent letter to write to Alan and suggested I continue to read for a while. She brought me a further batch of typescript of her memoirs which had been typed by her friend Susan Morris on her portable typewriter, and we settled down, me on the rocking chair near the porch facing the distant sea, Laura at her desk on the other side of the room facing out the window that looked on the orange and grapefruit grove, with her old upright Adler typewriter with the eccentric typeface I had come to know so well during our long correspondence. At one point, after reading a long sentence two or three times and not understanding it, I took the typescript over to Laura and said: 'I think the verb and the subject don't agree in this sentence, do they?' I felt a little apprehensive, but she read through it carefully, grinned and finally said, 'You're absolutely right! Let's correct that!' Phew!

I concentrated on Laura's prose with its intricacies of long sentences and paragraphic structure, one subordinate clause leading to another, each carefully balanced and chain-linked to the next, here or there embedded with surprising flashes of humour, and then on to the next, trying to hold it all in my mind so as not to lose track, which was easily done because of the Florida heat even though the house was cool. I was much later to realize Laura wrote prose in a way not dissimilar to her writing of poems, her focus always being the coaxing of difficult thought into existence. Years later she would be notorious as a writer of 'impossible prose', unreadable to many an academic, just too damned 'difficult' to bother with. Recently a well-known critic and colleague of mine, devoted to poets and poetry, insisted that she never could write prose and that it was only Robert Graves who saved her by re-writing her earlier prose into a plainer form. He was, he said, thinking of *A Survey Of Modernist Poetry* and *A Pamphlet Against Anthologies*, published in the 'twenties. He wouldn't give me time to demonstrate that the actual reverse was true, that both books stemmed principally from her work, rather than from anything Graves ever wrote, but then, it's a complicated story. As a matter of fact, her prose isn't 'difficult' but exceptionally scrupulous, each word and phrase meant, literally meant. While I was reading that morning I recalled her saying that Churchill had been a bad influence on English writers and general readers by his insistence on never using two words where one will do and keep sentences plain and short. Churchill was a politician, she snorted, not a thinker.

After a brief while I became aware of a kind of low buzz-saw sound in the room which I couldn't locate. Perhaps it was a fly or something, I thought, but after a slight lapse it began again, this time a little louder above the clatter of the typewriter. I sat and looked around wondering what it was, and then it became a deep rasping and hissing, a grunting, and I realized it was coming from Laura as she typed. Almost it was unearthly. Laura's voice was very modulated, pitched high, normally, with that 1930s Chelsea accent, but this sound seemed uttered by someone very different. Gradually I made out a word or two: 'Alan! You have not paid heed...' followed by something indistinguishable, then, 'I have said to you... but our long friendship is in danger because... You should know that... I am who I am... My determinations should not be questioned... I must...' Each word was punched into the typewriter, the utterance rasping deep in her throat, voiced but almost impenetrable. I could make out only bits of it but the hair stood up on the back of my neck for a moment. Enemies of Laura in books and the press have sometimes named her as a witch having inexplicable power and influence over others. They have been quite serious. How else could they explain this bundle of force that broke upon the twentieth century, making such an impact in literary areas while seemingly unreadable? How could they explain Graves' adulation of her or the very close fondness, love and affection of her various friends, many of whom would not hear a word against her (until later, after 1940, when a few turned sour after her renouncing poetry, fed by Graves manipulative dripping of poison into the literary by-ways of gossip – but that, also, is a complicated story)? This, combined with the legendary gossip of her leap from the Hammersmith flat window in 1929, breaking her spine, after undergoing the unbearable strains of a complex confusion of betrayals, her allegedly writing 'God is a Woman' on her bedroom wall (which is untrue – a complete misreading of an essay of hers at the time, 'The Idea Of God', in *Epilogue I*), her public denunciations of critics such as Empson, Richards, Ogden and the poet Auden. All this and a number of other factors, such as Graves' distinctly strange 'Epilogue' in *Goodbye To All That*, gave credence to the fact that, of course, she must be a 'witch'. She was, after all, a woman....

For just a moment, hearing the deep rasp issuing from Laura's throat, I admit I thought 'witch'. It was incantatory. I remembered her poem 'The Unthronged Oracle' –

> Your coming, asking, seeing, knowing,
> Was a fleeing from and stumbling
> Into only mirrors, and behind which,
> Behind all mirrors, dazzling pretences,
> The general light of fortune
> Keeps wrapt in sleeping unsleep,
> All mute of time, self-muttering like mute:
> Fatality like lone wise-woman
> Her unbought secrets counting over
> That stink of hell, from fuming in her lap.

I could imagine her writing that poem and a number of others in precisely the same rasping way, each word 'ligatured in the embracing words', as she elsewhere says in a poem.

After she broke from typing she stood to make coffee. 'Alan?' I asked. I knew roughly what this was about. When she learned some months previously that Tom Matthews' book, *Jacks Or Better*, had been published by Harper and Row, full of malice, lies and bitterness about Laura and Schuyler, who had been a fellow student and his friend at Princeton, and Harper and Row astonishingly were simultaneously negotiating with her to bring out *The Telling*, both her and Matthews' editor sitting in the same building almost next door to each other, she first thought she would have to murder Matthews with a knife, but then she decided she would set fire to herself outside the Harper and Row building in New York. She had struggled with this idea for several weeks, fully determined she would do one or the other. She couldn't shoot him, she said, because although Schuyler made her keep a revolver in her bed-side table she had forgotten how to fire it. We, her friends, were left in no doubt of her seriousness. She had been winding up her affairs and making plans to travel to New York. Even her editor didn't know that Matthews' book was underway, a book that was to be the poisoned seed-bed for later Graves biographers and scholars who wanted her sucked out of his life in order for him to be seen as a unique eccentric poet who owed nothing to anybody. Little did they, do they, know! In our various ways we, her friends, tried to think of reasons she shouldn't kill herself. Personally, I was floundering. I was so close to her at that point in our correspondence I couldn't find an answer, short of travelling to New York and shooting Tom Matthews myself. It was a dreadful time. The letter she was writing to Alan was to demand that he try not to deter her from her actions – he believed in all conscience she would be failing the principle of her life and work if she killed herself – that he must take her seriously, that he should cease from arguing against it. He had a particularly difficult time of it which rumbled on for one or two years. I was to have a similarly difficult time some years later over an unrelated matter but my own fault.

It was Jim Mathias who saved the day. He had given her, as I said, the

$6000 Guggenheim grant to finish working on *Rational Meaning*, but more importantly he was in love with her. She meant everything to him at this point, as I learned the following week when he flew down, although he stayed loyal to his wife, Barbara. But more of that later. Meanwhile, he began implementing plans, contacting publishers and editors, writing to various literary quarters and telephoning people. As director of the Guggenheim Foundation he carried a lot of weight in New York and around the world generally, and Laura gradually, bit by bit, backed down, from extreme action, much to everyone's relief.

That week, in fact, Jim was in Europe. It might have been Wednesday, after I returned from the local store with some cokes and salad stuff for hamburgers, and I could hear Laura stomping round the kitchen calling out, 'What a man!' and then a thump, and again, 'What a man! What a man!', thump, thump. She didn't notice me at first as she came into the study area and I saw her bring her fist down on the table: 'What a man!' Thump. She paused when she saw me. 'Jim?' I queried. She nodded and smiled. Over coffee she told me Jim had taken *Rational Meaning* to every major publisher in England to see if they would publish it. Laura had stayed up at night following his progress, from city to city to town to town, on a map, needing to do this because of the six hour time difference, and at that moment he was at Oxford University Press doing battle royal with the chief editor. No one would take it on because, as OUP and others said, she was not a known linguist, had no academic reputation as such. The stupidity of this struck me forcefully, as I said to Jim later: Laura gave her life to words, practiced them, studied them, and knew and had written more about words and language than any other author I could find in that century or the preceding ones, as is evident in her work. Her nearest predecessor was, depending how you look at it, Samuel Johnson and his dictionary.

Later that day she and I walked out to the driveway to inspect the path and the fencing. Children, she explained, used it as a short-cut and a play-area and both path and fence need frequent mending. It brought to mind Robert Frost's poem so I jokingly quoted, 'Something there is that doesn't like a fence...' She turned to face me. 'Don't you think that's a bad poem, that Frost used the occasion of someone's cliché to make a grandiose flourish of a poem instead of turning directly to the cliché and examining *that* for its implications, for its seriousness or its not-seriousness, that he made a sentimental mockery of another person just so that he might show off poetically? And that's exactly where he and poems are wrong,' she said. 'Fences do make good neighbours. They keep us apart to live neighbourly and not mix each other up in our lives too much so that we don't know where we stand. They keep us civilized.' Laura, of course, had renounced the writing of poems after her *Collected* Poems was published in 1938 precisely because of this sort of thing, where the craft or technique of composing a poem undermines the sense, or what she called the 'creed' of poetry. However reluctant I was to let go my good feelings toward Frost I had to agree with her on reflection. Frost's poem is seductive but it is purposely misleading. I also remembered that both Laura and Schuyler had each separately known Frost in the early days.

We went back to the house where Laura continued with her letter to Alan, which ran to several pages, while I made some notes and read. Betty came to take me back to the motel around 5.00 pm to save my having to ride the bike back. We stopped first at her place to have coffee with Mary and then out again to meet her estranged husband at the store they owned. She chatted first about the grocery store and how difficult it was now they were divorcing. She said it was wonderful to talk to a man from England with a wife and child, contrasting her own present misery with my supposed happiness, at which point I had to tell her I was on the point of splitting up with my wife, that being one reason I was visiting Mrs. Jackson. She looked almost chagrined. 'In that case,' she said, 'you, me and Mary must go out for a drink at the club this week and commiserate,' which we did, with an assortment of strange cocktails and a hang-over. When I told Laura the next day she thought for a moment and then said 'Good! It's better than hiding things. There are no secrets left these days, or very few.'

Susan Morris, who typed for Laura and to whom *The Telling* is dedicated, 'the good Susan,' as Laura referred to her, which became a good-natured joke between the three of us, came later in the morning and we were introduced. Susan was divorced and putting herself through college to learn accountancy. She quickly busied herself on her portable typewriter, working remarkably quickly through Laura's hand-written scripts which contained any number of sentences crossed out and re-written above, lengthy marginal notes, revisions on small pieces of paper. 'Isn't she good!' Laura exclaimed as she watched her working. 'I don't know how she can read my scribbles!' Susan's reply was strange. 'It's because you're a perfect angel,' she said. Laura clapped her hands in delight and grinned.

'And what do you think of Mark? Don't you think he's handsome?'

'He certainly is,' replied Susan.

'What do you think of that then?' Laura said, looking at me. 'I am the perfect angel and you're handsome.'

'Modesty overcomes me,' I said and we all burst out laughing. Later I asked Susan what she meant when she said Laura was the perfect angel. Looking at me extremely seriously she said, 'Because it's true – she is the perfect angel.' I had an odd sense of what she meant but I couldn't bring it into focus. Somehow Laura made everyone feel alive. People would call it 'presence' now but it wasn't exactly that. It had something to do with natural grace.

Laura made ham and salad sandwiches and we took an early break. It was hot as usual but not uncomfortably. Susan walked in the garden - that's a misnomer: it was three-quarters of an acre of land of lemon and grapefruit trees surrounded by cabbage palms, palmettos and a variety of other trees. Laura employed a neighbour's son once a month or so to cut the grass. The first time I walked out in it I asked Laura if there was anything I should watch out for that might be dangerous, not that I was especially anxious about such things but just had a natural wariness in such a foreign climate. 'Oh,' she said, 'well, there's talk of an old alligator got loose locally - he's about twelve foot long and weighs a couple of tons - so if you hear any thrashing or noise in the hedge keep away from it. He's around here somewhere.' She paused. 'Then there's rattle-snakes. Schuyler called them nature's gentlemen because they rattle when you get too close.' She laughed at the memory. 'Just walk noisily when you walk through the grass. And then there are the little red spiders in the trees over there. Stay away from them.' I was glad my natural rural country-boy childhood background made me ask!

As we talked after lunch she said she had just been told that Michael Kirkham, the Robert Graves scholar who had visited her the previous year, had described her to someone as 'living in Florida below the poverty-line.' Laura had an uncanny way of getting information from the unlikeliest places. When I asked her who told her she waved it away. 'Oh, just someone I know,' she said. 'What do you think he means?' I looked around. 'Well, I suppose he means you have no electricity, no washing machine, no air-conditioning.' I paused. 'I wouldn't call it below the poverty-line but city people expect these things. Why don't you have electricity installed?' This was when she looked around and asked, 'Oh, but where would I run the wiring?' I said, 'I guess it would run through the roof and under the floor.' 'But then,' she went on, 'the wires will have to come down the walls and along the ceilings for light. It would look ugly.' She was right, of course, it would. The house was beautifully proportioned as it was. She had Calor gas outside the kitchen door kept under wooden housing for her refrigerator and for cooking, and bright storm lamps for light in the evenings. There was a simple wood-burning stove for hot water for baths and laundry. Meanwhile there were no extra bills to worry about. It seemed a life of simple perfection to me when I thought about the complications of my own life back home of bills, mortgages, cars, business to run, and never quite enough money. I thought for a moment. 'I think I envy you,' I told her. And then: 'But what do you do about money?' She smiled. 'Oh, it seems to come in here and there, from various places, through the post and so on.' I guessed she meant royalties or publisher advances but she probably also meant well-meaning friends. I once suggested to all our friends that we contribute a small sum every month to help her out, but it came to nothing and I could see not much later it was largely unnecessary. We all tried to help, though, in whatever little way we could. She didn't live below the poverty-line but she wasn't rich either.

Susan packed her typewriter and left late in the afternoon, she and Laura talking and laughing, Laura thanking her for all her work. 'You're the perfect angel, not me!' Laura exclaimed. 'You have worked so hard!' Then

Susan, looking directly into Laura's eyes, grasped her hands, said something strange: 'Laura, that is because you are so pure, so innocent.' It was for me a perfectly odd moment as I watched them together, they obviously being so comfortable with each other – a perfectly naïve thing to say, old hat, in a different situation, but perfectly natural at that precise moment. I couldn't say why. They laughed again and then we said our goodbyes, waving Susan off from the kitchen stoop as she drove away. We had some ham, scrambled eggs and salad with a thick slice of bread and butter a little later, then Laura returned to writing her letter to Alan, *sotto voce* to start with and then husky again. Her voice normally high – 'Trill-like', Sonia Raiziss called it in a letter once – but certainly hoarse and rasping when she concentrated on typing, especially when the word she wanted was important. 'Pay attention,' I heard her mutter as her fingers rose up and pushed down on the keys. 'No, pay *heed* – *heed* me, give *heed* to what I am saying.' She turned towards me. 'He must give *heed*,' she said. 'Yes, that's the word – *heed*.'

She worked at the letter for several hours. That night, Thursday, was the first time I stayed late enough to watch her light her storm lights. It was slightly magical in the Floridian dusk as she pumped them up, applied a match to the mantle, and adjusted the glow. They gave out a bright warm glow as good as an electric bulb but not so harshly chromatic. She placed three lamps in different places while we settled down to wait for Betty to fetch me and take me back to the motel. It reminded me of the final story in her book *Progress Of Stories* in which a woman carries light into each of thirty-two rooms, in each of which lived a man:

> And the lady of the house was seen only as she appeared in each room, according to the nature of the lord of the room. None saw the whole of her, none but herself. For the light which she was was both her mirror and her body. None could tell the whole of her, none but herself. For the house which she was was both her story and her mind. And its walls were what had once been the earth; the inner surfaces of this house was what had once been an outer surface.

Laura's lamps gave off a bright light to read by but were by no means as bright as electric light. 'You don't wear glasses?' I asked one day. 'No, I have reading glasses just for very close reading but I don't use them much. These eyes have served me well.' 'And,' I said, 'you're in pretty good health, too.' She smiled and thought for a moment. 'Generally speaking, yes,' she said. 'I had to go for an x-ray years ago and they told me my heart is nearly twice the size of a normal heart. Maybe that helps!' she laughed. She was certainly vigorous given her age. I never saw her pause for long, her movement always quick. One day she jumped to her feet and clapped her hands: 'Oh! I've forgotten to water the flowers!' and ran for her watering can to tend the plants round the front of the house.

***

Jim came the following Saturday. Jim – James F. Mathias – had come to visit for the second week to meet me. He would arrive late by car, Laura told me, and would pick me up and go straight to the motel. Laura had listened carefully the previous day to a small fizzing transistor radio to pick up news of a pending hurricane in order to 'phone Jim and warn him about it that evening, but luckily it had swerved away and she was, she told him, relieved.

He arrived at around nine o'clock in the dusk. We were introduced, he and Laura obviously delighted to see each other, while I sat to one side listening while she caught up with his trip. It was small-talk but animated. Then she said he must be tired and he and I ought to go. Back at the motel we crossed the lawn to his room, on the opposite side to mine, where he began unpacking. He was a tall man, slightly taller than me, around six-foot two I guessed, slightly over-weight around the girth but he carried himself upright, probably a remnant of his military service as an officer in the Far East. He was dressed fairly casually in a brown jacket, cream shirt and grey slacks, polished brown leather shoes. He spoke easily and we carried on a conversation about Laura and my stay while he finished unpacking, finally pulling out a bottle of, as I realized later, very good seven-year old malt whisky and a box of equally good Cuban cigars, and we settled down to talk.

He quizzed me about my week with Laura, what she had said, what we had done, and talked about one or two people we knew in common. Then he began telling me about himself, his wife, Barbara, and two sons, his work, and how he had met Laura.

She had applied for a Guggenheim grant to finish her and Schuyler's book, *Rational Meaning*, and to pay for its typing (by Susan Morris), and was awarded $6,000 – quite a handsome amount of money then. She finished work on the book some time before I arrived, Jim told me, and wrote to him asking how she might return the money she hadn't used, which was around $2,000. He replied immediately to say it wasn't necessary to return the money and he was sure she would find some good use for it in her work. A few days later his secretary came into his office looking nervous to say there was a very strange-looking package just delivered by courier and explaining that she didn't want to open it in case it was dangerous. Jim went out to look at it, agreed that, yes, it did look very strange, and decided to carry it tentatively to his desk to examine it further before calling emergency services, telling all the secretaries to go out and have coffee while he looked at it. He knew a little about explosives from his time as a soldier. As there was no return address on it, he gently pried open a corner of the brown wrapping and saw tinfoil underneath. The parcel itself was very light in weight. He slowly tore off a little more brown paper until he could see it was a tinfoil parcel underneath with a blue ribbon holding it all together. As nothing alarming had happened so far, he went ahead, untied the blue ribbon, pulled back a corner of the foil and, he said, astonishingly, suddenly the whole room filled with the perfume of orange blossom. He realized the parcel was packed with orange petals. On top was a handwritten note from Laura thanking him and explaining how grateful she was to him for the generosity in allowing her to keep the remainder of the money. She hoped he wouldn't mind, she said, this small gesture. Thus began a long friendship of visits and correspondence.

We laughed long and loud over his story. By this time we had finished the first bottle of whisky and Jim brought out a second which we were a third of the way through. The cigars were very fine, almost mellow. I was pretty unused to drinking and must have been drunk but felt oddly awake – normally

I would fall asleep – and we continued to talk. Jim was telling me about his correspondence with Laura and what passed between them on this or that serious or not serious subject, and the more he told me the more warmly he spoke of her, until finally I stared at him and said: 'You're in love with her!' He stopped in mid-sentence, staring back at me for a moment, then grinned ear-to-ear, got out of his chair, walked round to mine and kissed me on the mouth. 'I would never kiss anyone except one of my sons,' he said, 'but I make an exception for you – you seem like a sort of son. You've seen right through me.' He walked unsteadily back to his chair. I was, I must say, very slightly astonished, but then it all seemed sort of natural in a way I couldn't fathom. We smiled at each other for a moment or two and then just continued talking – and drinking and smoking. We were both kind of pleased with ourselves, I suppose.

It was getting towards two in the morning and we were both tired. 'Before we finish up,' he said, 'Laura told me you had to sell your collection of her books to pay for the flight here, which I'm sorry to hear. I'm going to pay for your flight with a cheque.' He leaned across to hand it to me. 'No, no…' I began. 'It's fine,' he cut me off. 'As it happens, I bought my son a car some time ago which he sold recently and returned me the money, so in a way it costs me nothing. And anyway, I can afford it.' He pushed a cheque for $300 into my hand. 'And now goodnight!'

As I walked across the lawn in the heat of the Florida night, I paused to sit in the little pagoda in the middle to collect my thoughts, emotions pouring through my mind. I could have burst into tears if truth be told.

Later that year when my wife and I separated and I rented a cottage, Jim unbidden sent me an envelope every month with $100 in it to help pay my bills. I had gotten a job as a part-time lecturer at a college but nothing was guaranteed and I had no income from the book-shop which my wife was running. I still had previous major bills to meet such as the mortgage on the house, central-heating I had on credit, plus child maintenance and all the additional expenses. Jim's gift was most welcome and continued for the best part of a year. I was and, looking back, still am more than grateful to him. He was a generous man.

The next morning I was woken by a knock on the door. It was Jim. 'Come on,' he said, 'time to get going to Laura.' What time is it?' I asked groggily. 'Six o'clock,' he said. I groaned out loud and went back to my bed, a hangover crowding behind my eyes. He sat on the edge of the bed laughing. 'How the hell can you get up so early?' I asked. 'I'm heliotropic,' he replied. 'What?' I said, looking through one eye. 'Purple?' He laughed again. 'No, I have a metal plate in my head, right across here,' pointing, 'I'll tell you about it while you get dressed.'

'Whenever the sun's up I have to get up, can't sleep any longer. It happened in the Far East in the war. We were in a village to flush out some Japanese. My colonel ordered six recruits to run across the middle of the square to some huts on the other side to either kill or capture them, and I told him it was a stupid idea and he had no right to ask recruits to do that. They would assuredly be blown up before they could get half-way across. He threatened me with a court-martial if I got in his way and we shouted at each other for a while. Then I said okay, if someone has to do it, I'll do it, so I picked up my rifle and started to run across. Sure enough I ran straight into a grenade and was blown across the square. When I became half-conscious again, I was being carried on a stretcher through the field-hospital and I heard a doctor say, 'Put him outside with the dead ones – he won't last. Half his head is missing.' The next thing I knew they turned around and were carrying me outside. Then I heard someone say, 'Jim? Jim Matthias? Is that you?' It was a surgeon I had joined up with and a drinking buddy. As luck would have it, he was a head and brain surgeon. He had them take me back inside and began work immediately. He saved my life, God knows how. When I shipped back to the States, he had someone waiting for me to take me to the hospital immediately to fit a metal plate in my skull. And here I am! And the sun is up! So come on, let's go.'

Jim spent most of the day going through some letters of Laura's from the 1950s. He burst out laughing at one point. 'What?' said Laura. 'This letter,' he said, 'about your trying to give up smoking! You really had a struggle! And you're nagging me and Mark to stop!' We had walked outside once or twice to enjoy a cigar while we drank coffee and Laura wagged a finger in admonishment, warning us about the damage to our health. We had coffee at the bench-table by the window and chatted about Michael Kirkham who had visited Jim at his home in New York for a couple of weeks, plus George Fraser, my tutor, and Harry Kemp, an old associate of Laura's who had turned nasty towards her and whom I had met and stayed with a couple of times before we realized there was a conflict. Michael and Jim had got on well but Jim couldn't resist thinking of Ogden Nash and Laura, remembering the poem, fetched Nash's collected poems, and read:

There is something about the English

That makes them when they talk about themselves very nervous and tinglish.

We all laughed. This was as much about me, I'm sure, as Michael, but also Alan, from whom Laura had received a letter that morning which had upset her.

That evening Jim had arranged we go to a local restaurant for dinner. We enjoyed an excellent meal, as one does in Florida, and not too expensive compared to English restaurants. Laura and Jim fell to talking politics while I fell to relishing a shrimp dish. I suddenly realized they were arguing. Jim had been cursing Nixon for being a crook over the Watergate scandal, but Laura said, quite emphatically, that Kennedy had done far worse in his day, was just as foul-mouthed, and came from a family of criminals. L. B. Johnson was equally bad, she added. Jim obviously disagreed – Kennedy still had a high rating with the general public, largely because of his handling of the Cuban crisis one suspects – the scandals with various mistresses, largely unproven, including Marilyn Monroe and her suicide, would follow later. But Jim was objecting at how Nixon handled the New York Vietnam protests. His son, he found out, had joined several of the protest marches. At first he argued with him but later he was persuaded his son was right, so he decided to march with him. The police were brutal at Nixon's behest, he told Laura, beating everyone they could lay hands on, and he and his son, after being hit over the head with batons, spent an uncomfortable night in jail. Laura pointed out that at least Nixon came to office with the vowed intention of an honourable withdrawal from Vietnam, which is more than Kennedy or

Johnson did. And so the argument went back and forth. I wondered how it might end, sensing myself slightly worried at this turn of events, and said something like, 'You're not going to fall out over politics are you?' At which they smiled at each other, then at me, and the conversation turned to other matters. I was relieved, but looking back it pointed to a locking of wills that a few years later would come to a head over Robert Graves and the BBC when, as Jim said, he simply burned out.

'You know, I won't last. I'll burn out,' Jim said that first night we met. 'She's way beyond my ability to understand her. It's up to people like you and Alan to keep up with her and take care of her. The most I'll be is a burned out satellite circling the moon. I'll do my best for as long as I can, but you're the important ones.' It was a candid admission and I felt sympathy. I was not sure myself how long I'd last out. I could not forget an experience I had driving to work five years previously. I had been re-reading her collected poems the night before, trying to make sense of them yet again, and they were much on my mind. I couldn't understand them. Oh, I could see all the brilliant intelligence, the flashes of wit, the beauty of certain poems and lines, to that extent I memorized a few of them, but I came back again and again to the fact I was failing to understand them. 'The Rugged Black Of Anger', for example, I could almost (never quite!) quote verbatim. It is full of verve and meaning but quite what that meaning is I didn't know, couldn't make out, although assuredly it has meaning. That was wholly frustrating. It would take me a few more years before I could grasp it. Meanwhile, that morning driving along the long narrow road across country to get to work at my college – about twenty miles – I was still thinking of that poem and others and not paying much attention to driving. The concentration of trying to understand steadily built up in my brain until finally my mind seized up. I shoved my foot on the brake and swerved into the side of the verge, stopped just short of a hedge, and put my head on the steering wheel. I simply couldn't drive for a moment. I must have stayed like that for five minutes or longer, perhaps ten or more, until I came round and remembered work and being late for a class. That sense of brain-seizure happened to me a number of times in those years, whether sitting in my study, walking in the garden or along the road.

Thankfully it didn't happen again while I was driving. So I knew what Jim meant when he said he would burn out. I had come close myself. I don't know what it was that kept me determined to continue my study except the recognition that here at last was something worth all the time one has. That applies to the prose as well as the poems. Anyone who might like to know further what I mean should look up her poem 'Poet: A Lying Word' as an example, or indeed 'The Rugged Black Of Anger'. As well as that, there is the prose in such books as *Progress Of Stories*, which has the most exciting stories I know, such as the stunning 'A Last Lesson In Geography', or her essays in *Epilogue* which are equally confounding at first but make excellent sense. Or of course there are other books, such as *Contemporaries and Snobs* or the much later *The Telling*. There is thinking here for a lifetime.

The following day we all went in Betty's car along with her twin teenagers to Vero Beach to shop a little for things to take home. I bought my wife some mother-of-pearl earrings set in gold and an electronic game for my son, while Jim bought his wife a chiffon scarf. We had lunch and sat on the beach for two hours or so. Laura and Jim were deep in conversation about something while I talked to Betty and swam with her children. As we were leaving, Laura beckoned to me to come over. 'I should have mentioned to you,' she said, 'never to tell anyone I'm a writer. If folk ask, I just tell them I do a little academic work for the university and leave it at that. I prefer to be just part of the community, nothing more.' Unfortunately it was too late. Betty had her suspicions about Laura and her writing and had just asked me about her, so I outlined her past in Majorca, her work with Graves, her friendship with Gertrude Stein and one or two other things. I didn't have the heart to mention this to Laura.

Betty dropped us back at the house and left. Jim and I sat for awhile on the lawn outside under a maple tree while Laura prepared some tea. That evening they asked if I would read a passage from Laura's book about Troy, *A Trojan Ending*, published in 1937. Laura suggested I read the chapter on the battle outside the walls of Troy between Achilles and Hector when Hector is killed. I was a little uncertain about possible mispronunciation of some names and words but she pooh-poohed it as not important. 'Let's eat first, though,' she said. 'I think real American-style hamburgers for Mark, but perhaps you'll make a little salad to go with it, Mark?' So I made potato mayonnaise with onion and salad while Laura busied herself in the kitchen. She was a good cook.

After coffee we settled down in the dusk and Laura pumped and lit the lamps. It was slightly eerie sitting below the lamp in a low chair with the two of them mostly in shadow sitting opposite, but I gave it my best, even though it is a long description, very intricate, violent, although after an hour or so I felt myself flagging, but they listened intently. Only then I noticed they were holding hands. Laura clapped her hands and sprang to her feet when I finished. 'Thank you!' she exclaimed. 'And now we need more coffee!'

We took Jim back to Jacksonville airport on the Friday. Darleen Caudill, Betty's mother and one of the Cherokee Owle family who helped Laura and Schuyler in their citrus shipping business and also long-time friend, drove. She said not more than three or four words the whole trip, me sitting at the front with her, Laura and Jim in the back chatting. Later at the airport drinking coffee, Laura put her hand on her knee, looked at her and said, 'You *feel* so much, don't you?' Then, looking at me: 'Darleen feels all the time.' I wondered at the time whether it was because she was part Cherokee.

We were still sitting outside in the sun when Jim's flight was called. The two faced each other, hands grasped, staring in each other's eyes. They seemed to stand there for minutes, perhaps as many as four or five, in silence, smiling, Laura shifting very slightly from foot to foot, while Darleen and I sat watching, then they hugged slightly and Jim walked away with a casual 'Bye' to us all.

A few days later I, too, would be flying home. Meanwhile there was a trip in Betty's open-top to the local supermarket the next day. 'Try not to drive too fast, Betty, please. The wind hurts my neuralgia pain,' pointing to her cheek. 'Okay Mrs. Jackson, don't you worry,' replied Betty. We drove down 85th Street at a steady 45mph when Betty spotted a friend on the other side and instantly did a U-turn without slowing down. Just at that moment a flock of pelicans were wheeling just overhead and I was suddenly aware of

Laura standing up next to me, waving her hand towards the sky, tilting rather dangerously to the side of the car, and crying, 'O look! Aren't they beautiful!' with a big smile on her face. Betty, apologizing, continued to our shopping and then dropped us at a small restaurant serving very good crab. Then dancing that night with Betty and Mary at a bar and breakfast at three in the morning. The following day we went to Schuyler's grave on a sandy hillside, Laura kneeling setting flowers and tidying while I fetched water in the hot sun, and after we got back a neighbour with apple-pie and cheese ('Apple-pie without cheese is like a hug with no squeeze,' said Laura) to visit and check on Laura. 'I wish,' said Laura later, 'they wouldn't just come calling like that. They think they need to keep an eye on me and it often disturbs my working.' But she was grateful. And then I was packing to leave, Darleen and her husband driving me to Miami, a quick photograph of Laura outside the house, and I was gone.

Appendix

Cover text on rear dust jacket of Cassell's 1938 edition

COLLECTED POEMS

This impressive compilation of Laura Riding's Poems, drawn from nine previous volumes, and containing much hitherto unpublished material, reveals at full length a poet for whom it has long been difficult to find a label. We can now understand why her poems have defied conventional classification. We must read them in relation to one another to appreciate the large coherence of thought behind them. Then, instead of assuming a mysterious personality at work in intellectual isolation, we recognise that here is a complete range of poetic experience controlled with sensitive wisdom.

We cannot, in fact, describe Laura Riding's poems as of such or such a type or tendency: rather, they set a new standard of poetic originality. They are undiluted: no politics or psychology, no religion or philosophical sentiment, no scholastic irrelevancies, no mystical or musical wantonness. This does not mean that they lack any of the graces that it is proper to expect in poetry: they have memorable beauty of phrase, serene humour, and a rich intricacy of movement that redeems the notion of 'pure poetry' from the curse put upon it by the aestheticians. They are, moreover, very consciously the work of a woman, introducing into poetry energies without which it is no more than 'a tradition of male monologue', not a living communication.

Select bibliography

For the period with which this book is mainly concerned, when Laura Riding was a practising poet and devout advocate of poetry, Joyce Piell Wexler's *Laura Riding: A Bibliography* (New York and London: Garland Publishing, 1981) provides a far more comprehensive and detailed resource. It includes an account of poems in periodicals, anthologies and published individually. There is also a section on 'Writings about Laura Riding' (117-154) with some fascinating brief quotations from critics of the day in response to Riding's work.

A. Main editions of the poems

The Close Chaplet (London: Hogarth, 1926) under the name Laura Riding Gottschalk.

Voltaire: A Biographical Fantasy (London: Hogarth, 1927).

Love as Love, Death as Death (London: Seizin Press, 1928).

Poems, A Joking Word (London: Jonathan Cape, 1930), with a preface by the author.

Though Gently (Majorca: Seizin Press, 1930).

Twenty Poems Less (Paris: Hours Press, 1930).

Laura and Francisca (Majorca: Seizin Press, 1931).

The Life of the Dead (London: Arthur Barker, 1933).

Poet: A Lying Word (London: Arthur Barker, 1933).

Collected Poems (London: Cassell, 1938), with a preface 'To the Reader'.

Selected Poems: In Five Sets (London: Faber and Faber, 1970), with a preface explaining the author's renunciation of her faith in poetry.

The Poems of Laura Riding (Manchester: Carcanet, 1980), a reissue of the 1938 *Collected Poems* with a new 'Author's Introduction'.

First Awakenings: The Early Poems (Manchester: Carcanet, 1992): early poems not published previously in book form.

A Selection of the Poems of Laura Riding, edited with a valuable introduction by Robert Nye (Manchester: Carcanet, 1994).

The Poems of Laura Riding: A newly revised edition of the 1938/1980 collection with a substantial centennial preface by Mark Jacobs (New York: Persea Books, 2001). Appendix V gives fascinating 'Excerpts from a Recording (1972) Explaining the Poems' by Laura (Riding) Jackson.

B. Other writings by the author on poetry when a practising poet

What follows are additional to the author's prefaces and introductions to editions of her own poems, already noted above.

'A Prophecy or a Plea', *The Reviewer*, 5(2), April 1925, 1-7 (reprinted in Appendix C of *First Awakenings*, 1992, 275-280).

A Survey of Modernist Poetry by Laura Riding and Robert Graves (London: Heinemann, 1927).

A Pamphlet Against Anthologies, by Laura Riding and Robert Graves (London: Garden City, 1928).

[Both the above reprinted in *A Survey of Modernist Poetry* and *A Pamphlet Against Anthologies* by Laura Riding and Robert Graves edited by Charles Mundye and Patrick McGuinness (Manchester: Carcanet, 2002)].

Anarchism Is Not Enough (London: Cape, 1928); reprinted and edited by Lisa Samuels (University of California Press: 2001).

Contemporaries and Snobs (London: Cape, 1928); reprinted and edited by Laura Heffernan and Jane Malcolm (University of Alabama Press, 2014).

Several essays in *Epilogue* I, II and III (Majorca and London: The Seizin Press and Constable & Co, 1935, 1936, 1937), in particular: 'The Cult of Failure' by Laura Riding (Volume I, 60-86); 'Poems and Poets' by Riding with questions by Graves (Volume I, 141-156); 'The Exercise of English' by Riding and Graves (Volume II, 110-136). The second and third of these essays are reprinted in *Essays from Epilogue 1935-1937*, edited with an introduction by Mark Jacobs (Manchester: Carcanet, 2001).

C. Other selected writings on poetry by Laura (Riding) Jackson (after the author's renunciation)

The Telling (London: Athlone Press, 1972), in particular in the 'Preface for a Second Reading' (59-80) and in an 'Addendum' (177-185).

The Failure of Poetry, the Promise of Language, edited by John Nolan (University of Michigan Press, 2007).

The Person I Am: The Literary Memoirs of Laura (Riding) Jackson Volumes One and Two, edited by John Nolan and Carroll Anne Friedmann (Nottingham: Trent Editions, 2011).

D. Other significant criticism of Riding's poetry

As noted above Joyce Wexler's bibliography of 1981 has brief accounts of reviews, essays and comments in letters on Riding's work, including many by literary heavyweights of the day. The comments range from the bewildered or tentative to the frankly hostile and occasionally adulatory.

The authorized biography of Laura (Riding) Jackson by Elizabeth Friedmann (New York: Persea Books, 2005) contains valuable biographical context to, and commentary on, many of the poems.

There are also the introductions to editions of her poems by Nye (1991) and Jacobs (2001) noted in A. above.

Robert Fitzgerald, 'Laura Riding', *Kenyon Review*, 1 (Summer, 1939), 341-345.

Roy Fuller, 'The White Goddess', *the Review*, 23 (1970), 3-9.

Michael Kirkham, 'Laura Riding's Poems', *The Cambridge Quarterly*, 5 (Spring, 1971), 302-308.

Michael Kirkham, 'Robert Graves's Debt to Laura Riding', *Focus on Robert Graves*, 3 (December 1973), 33-44.

Joyce Piell Wexler, *Laura Riding's Pursuit of Truth*, (Ohio University Press, 1979).

Alan J. Clark, 'Where Poetry Ends', *PN Review*, 22 (1981) 26-28.

Mark Jacobs, 'Rewriting History, Literally: Laura Riding's *The Close Chaplet*', *Gravesiana*, Volume 3, Number 3 (Summer 2012).

Acknowledgements

The essays on the poems of Laura Riding were developed in close correspondence with Mark Jacobs, whose vivid memoir of Mrs Jackson in later life is included in the book. The essays benefited throughout from his critical reflections and deep knowledge but most particularly from his generosity in sharing some of his own as yet unpublished and original work on the poems.

The book has also been improved by the scrupulous critical attention and reflection of Alan J. Clark, another long term advocate of the poems. Critical comments from Elizabeth Friedmann, Mrs Jackson's biographer, and from John Lucas and Jim Tyler have also helped me to strengthen the text.

I have valued the encouragement of Joyce Wexler, who wrote the first book about Laura Riding. I was especially grateful for the encouragement and support of the poet Robert Nye in response to my submission to him of early versions of several chapters. Sadly Robert died on 2nd July 2016 before the book was published.